Temples in India

Perspective in Indian Art & Archaeology
ISSN 0971-4723

1. **The Splendour of Mathurā Art and Museum**; by R.C. Sharma; ISBN 978-81-246-0015-3
2. **Proto-Historic Pottery of Indus Valley Civilisation**; by Sudha Satyawadi; ISBN 978-81-246-0030-6
3. **Saptamātṛkā Worship and Sculptures**: An Iconological Interpretation of Conflicts and Resolutions in the Storied Brāhmanical Icons; by Shivaji K. Pannikar; ISBN 978-81-246-0074-0
4. **Elements of Indian Art** — Including Temple Architecture, Iconography & Iconometry; by S.P. Gupta; Shashi Prabha Asthana; ISBN 978-81-246-0213-3 (Hb); ISBN 978-81-246-0214-0 (Pb)
5. **Bull in Early Indian Art** (up to sixth century); by Bhogendra Jha; ISBN 978-81-246-0255-3
6. **Bibliography on Indian Buddhist Art and Archaeology**; by Utpal Chakraborty; ISBN 978-81-246-0361-1
7. **Prehistory and Protohistory of India** : An Appraisal : Palaeolithic, Non-Harappan, Chalcolithic Cultures; by V.K.Jain; ISBN 978-81-246-0372-7 (Hb); ISBN 978-81-246-0373-4 (Pb)

8-9. **Śiva-Pārvatī and Allied Images:** Their Iconography and Body Language; by Thomas E. Donaldson (2 vols.); ISBN 978-81-246-0359-8 (set)

Perspectives in Indian Art and Archaeology, no. 10

Temples in India

– Origin and Developmental Stages –

S.P. Gupta
S.Vijayakumar

Centre for Research and Training in History, Archaeology and Paleo-Environment
New Delhi

PRINTWORLD
Publishers of Indian Traditions

Cataloging in Publication Data — DK
[Courtesy: D.K. Agencies (P) Ltd. <docinfo@dkagencies.com>]
Gupta, S. P. (Swarajya Prakash), 1931-2007.
Temples in India : origin and developmental stages / S.P. Gupta, S. Vijayakumar.
p. cm.
Includes bibliographical references (p.)
Includes index.
ISBN 13: 978 8124604953 (HB)

1. Temples, Hindu — India — History. 2. Temples, Hindu — India — Designs and plans. 3. Temples, Buddhist — India. 4. Temples, Jaina — India. 5. Architecture, Hindu. 6. Architecture — India — Details. I. Vijayakumar, S., 1977– , joint author. II. Title.

DDC 726.145 095 4 22

ISBN 13: 978 81-246-0495-3 (HB)
ISBN 13: 978 81-246-0496-0 (PB)

First published in India in 2010
Second impression, 2016

Published by:
Centre for Research and Training in History, Archaeology and Paleo-Environment
B-17, Qutab Institutional Area, New Delhi - 16

and

D.K. Printworld (P) Ltd.
Regd. Office: "Vedaśrī", F-395, Sudarshan Park
(Metro Station: Ramesh Nagar), New Delhi – 110 015
Phones: (011) 2545 3975, 2546 6019; *Fax*: (011) 2546 5926
e-mail: indology@dkprintworld.com
Website: www.dkprintworld.com

Printed by: D.K. Printworld (P) Ltd., New Delhi

Preface

THIS book is meant for all those who want to know something which every intelligent man should know about the temples of India existing in all her major regions and States. Normally, all regions have not been covered in one small manageable book. This book, in fact, is the outcome of the demands of my students who had liked my earlier book, now in its second enlarged edition, *The Elements of Indian Art.* They wanted something written exclusively on temples as well. It was, therefore, to be written in a straightforward manner, explaining with adequate illustrations every part of a temple. Their enquiry also concentrated on knowing the basic differences in the Nāgara (north Indian), Draviḍa (south Indian) and Vesara (Andhra–Karnataka) styles of temples generally mentioned as three ancient temple-styles in India.

They also wanted an analysis of the factual data in time and space so that they could understand the directional changes in temple architecture over 2000 years. And, of course, they also wanted to know the stages of changes from an all-India perspective. They always started by asking simple questions about the concepts which had given birth to temple architecture as we see them in actuality in every part of the country, and how these concepts differed from the concepts of Islam developed for its mosque and Christianity for its church.

They were always curious to know as to why most of the architectural terms used in the context of a temple are the same used for the human body, such as *pāda* (पाद), *jaṅghā* (जंघा), *grīvā* (ग्रीवा), *mastaka* (मस्तक), *śīrṣa* (शीर्ष), etc. Did our ancestors see the temple as the replica of a human body? Also, then why do we say in the same breath that "temple is universe in the miniature"? Even, in what way did *saguṇa bhakti* (सगुण भक्ति) become responsible for architectural changes and elaborations and additions in temple architecture and complexes? We have tried to answer these and many other related questions in this book.

The credit for preparing the first draft of the chapters goes to my young Research Associate in the Indian Archaeological Society Shri S. Vijayakumar (presently at University of Ferrara, Italy) to whom I shall always remain grateful. I thank Dr P.K. Trivedi, Superintendent Archaeologist, ASI, for sending us photographs of Bhubaneswar temples. Thanks are also due to Shri Kulbhushan Misra, Mohit Srivastava, Bharat Singh, M.S. Mani and Kumari Raj Rani of the Society for their devoted services without which this volume would never have been completed. I owe special thanks to Shri Susheel Mittal and Shri Rajendra Agarwal of the D.K. Printworld, New Delhi, who took great pains in seeing the book through the press.

S.P. Gupta

Contents

List of Plates and Figures

Plates

Figures

The photographs and the line-drawings reproduced in this book are by the courtesy of the following authors and institutions:

Agrawala, P.K., 1968, *Gupta Temple Architecture*, Varanasi: Prithivi Prakashan.

Brown, Percy, 1965, *Indian Architecture: Buddhist and Hindu Period*, Bombay: D.B. Taraporevala and Sons.

Chandra, Promod, 1975, *Studies in Indian Temples of Architecture*, New Delhi: American Institute of Indian Studies.

Datta, Bimal Kumar, 1975, *Bengal Temples*, New Delhi: Munshiram Manoharlal.

Dayalan, D., 1992, *Early Temples of Tamil Nadu*. New Delhi: Harman Publishing House.

Deva, Krishna, 1990, *Temples of Khajuraho*, vol. 2, New Delhi: Archaeological Survey of India.

Dhavalikar, M.K., 1984, *Late Hinayana Caves of Western India*, Poona: Deccan College.

Encyclopaedia of Indian Temple Architecture—North India: Foundation of North Indian Style, vol. II, part 1, Texts, American Institute of Indian Studies

Encyclopaedia of Indian Temple Architecture—North India: Foundation of North Indian Style, vol. II, part 1: Plates

Encyclopaedia of Indian Temple Architecture, North India: Period of Maturity, vol. II, part 2: Text

Encyclopaedia of Indian Temple Architecture, South India: Later Phase, vol. 1, part 4-A: Text

Encyclopaedia of Indian Temple Architecture, South India: Later Phase, vol. 1, part 4-A: Plates

Encyclopaedia of Indian Temple Architecture, South India: vol. 1, part 1: Plates

Gangoly, O.C., 1957, *The Art of the Pallavas*, Calcutta: Rupa and Company.

James Fergusson and James Burgess, 2000 (rpt.), *The Caves Temples of India*. New Delhi: Munshiram Manoharlal.

Jayashanker, S. 1997, *Temples of Kerala*, Directorate of Census Operations, Kerala.

Kamesvara Rao, V., 1976, *Select Vijayanagara Temples of Rayalseema*, The Govermment. of Andhra Pradesh.

Nagaraju, S., 1981, *Buddhist Architecture of Western India*, Delhi: Agam Kala Prakashan.

Patil, Channabasappa S., 1992, *Temples of Raichur and Bellary Districts*, Directorate of Archaeology and Museums.

Sarkar, H., 1978, *An Architectural Survey of Temple of Kerala*, New Delhi: Archaeological Survey of India.

Sharma, P.C., 1988, *Architecture of Assam*, Delhi: Agam Kala Prakashan.

Singh, Amarendra Kumar, 2002, *Temples of the Kalachuri Period*, Delhi: Pratibha Prakashan.

Soundararajan, K.V., 1981, *Cave Temples of the Deccan*, New Delhi: Archaeological Survey of India.

Soundararajan, K.V., 1978, *The Art of South India: Tamil Nadu and Kerala*, Delhi: Sundeep Prakashan.

Stierlin, Henri, 2002, *Hindu India: From Khajurāho to the Temple City of Madurai*, Köln: Taschen.

Subhashini Aryan, 1994, *Himadri Temples (AD 700-1300)*, Shimla: Indian Institute of Advanced Study.

Tadgell, Christopher, 1998, *The History of Architecture in India*. London: Phaidon Press Limited.

Thakur, Laxman S., 1996, *The Architectural Heritage of Himachal Pradesh*, New Delhi: Munshiram Manoharlal.

Trivedi, R.D., 1990, *Temples of the Pratihāra Period in Central India*, New Delhi: Archaeological Survey of India.

Key to Transliteration

VOWELS

अ *a*	आ *ā*	इ *i*	ई *ī*	उ *u*	ऊ *ū*	ऋ *ṛ*	ॠ *ṝ*[1]
(Roman)	(palm)	(it)	(police)	(put)	(rule)	(rig)	
ऌ *ḷ*	ॡ *ḹ*[1]	ए *e*	ऐ *ai*	ओ *o*	औ *au*		
(able)		(there)	(aisle)	(no)	(loud)		

CONSONANTS

Guttural	क *ka* (skate)	ख *kha*[2] (blockhead)	ग *ga* (gate)	घ *gha*[2] (ghost)	ङ *ṅa* (sing)
Palatal	च *ca* (chunk)	छ *cha*[2] (catch him)	ज *ja* (john)	झ *jha*[2] (hedgehog)	ञ *ña* (bunch)
Cerebral	ट *ṭa* (start)	ठ *ṭha*[2] (anthill)	ड *ḍa* (dart)	ढ *ḍha*[2] (godhead)	ण *ṇa* (under)
Dental	त *ta* (path)	थ *tha*[2] (thunder)	द *da* (that)	ध *dha*[2] (this)	न *na* (numb)
Labial	प *pa* (spin)	फ *pha*[2] (philosophy)	ब *ba* (bin)	भ *bha*[2] (abhor)	म *ma* (much)
Semi-vowels	य *ya* (young)	र *ra* (drama)	ल *la*[3] (luck)	व *va*[4] (vile)	
Sibilants	श *śa*[5] (shove)	ष *ṣa*[5] (bushel)	स *sa* (so)	ह *ha* (hum)	
Others	क्ष *kṣa*	त्र *tra*	ज्ञ *jña*		
			(*kṣatriya*)		(*triśūla*)

(*jñā~~nī~~*)

अं (ं) *ṁ anusvāra* is a nasal off-glide that immediately follows the pronunciation of a vowel as in *saṁskṛti.*

अः *visarga* = *ḥ* consists in abrupt release of breath after a vowel as in *prātaḥ.*

ऽ *Avagraha* shows non-pronunciation, that is, deletion of "a" after "e" or "o" as in *ime 'vasthitāḥ*. In Vedic Sanskrit, it can also show word division.

HINDI LETTERS (extras)

ँ = m̐	ं = ṅ	ड़ = *ṛa*	ढ़ = *ṛha*
(*candrabindu*)	(*anusvāra*)		

---

1. Longer form of the preceding vowel.
2. Aspirated forms of the preceding consonants. The compound words given as examples should be pronounced without a syllabic break at the underlined places. *tha* and *pha* should not be pronounced as fricatives.
3. retroflexed and written as "L *la*" in certain phonetic contexts.
4. Pronounced like "w," without aspiration.
5. *śa* is palatal; *ṣa* cerebral or retroflex.

Introduction

Some Basic Facts about the Origin and Developmental Stages of Temples in India

The Formative Stage

THE Temple in India, as an architectural entity, emerged out of certain *concepts* about God and gods *vis-à-vis* human being. They seem to have developed over a long period of time, starting perhaps around 4500 years ago from now, i.e. during the urban or mature phase of the Indus-Sarasvatī (इण्डस्-सरस्वती) or Haṛappan (हड़प्पन) Civilization (2600–2000 BCE) and continuing thereafter, till about the sixth century CE.

However, since the script of the Indus-Sarasvatī Civilization still remains undeciphered, we have no clear-cut idea about the philosophical concepts concerning the relationship of the human beings with God or gods which the people of this civilization may have actually developed. We can make only some guesses on the basis of antiquarian remains discovered in archaeological excavations conducted at the Indus-Sarasvatī sites during the last eight decades, starting from 1922, in the present-day territories of India and Pakistan. One of these guesses is that the tradition of APSIDAL TEMPLE may have started at Banawālī (बनावली) in Haryana where within a large complex of mud-brick structures of around 2500 BCE an apsidal structure made of mud-bricks with the remains of fire-altars was unearthed by R.S. Bisht. However, we are not sure if it was a closed structure with walls, roof, entrance, etc.; it could be only an "open structure" of the Vedic fire altar type.

The Vedic literature is extremely rich in the concepts related to extra-mundane or heavenly entities and their residents, called *devas* (देव) or gods, but in it there is no reference to any "architectural temple" as such. The *Sulba-Sūtras* (सुल्ब-सूत्र) do provide details of ritualistic architecture, including their various shapes and various measurements, but all of them relate to open-air sacrificial (or *yajña,* यज्ञ) platforms or altars only, devoted primarily to fire related rituals and not closed buildings or regular temples as we see them built in the historical period with images of deities housed in an enclosure or room called *garbha-gṛha* (गर्भ-गृह).

The Stage of Early Developments: The Era of Integration — Pan Indian Integration

In the Early Historical Period (Mauryan–Śuṅga–Early Kuṣāṇa (मौर्य–शुंग–कुषाण) period: 400 BCE – CE 100) ***open-air shrines*** or objects of worship kept under sacred trees or near water bodies seem to have predominated since we have several examples of this kind of "places of worship" and "symbols of worship" in sculptural representations of this period of Indian art history. Apparently, it is the continuation of the age-old Indus-Sarasvatī and Vedic tradition.

The traditions of "places of worship" and "symbols of worship" when combined and fused together gave birth to the concept of *House of God* in which lies the origin of "temple" as such. The important element in it was the feature of "house" which, by its very nature, is a "closed structure" with walls and roof. This phenomenon seems to have developed in India only after 700 BCE, the generally accepted date of the beginning of the Mahājanapada (महाजनपद) period.

Hence the "Temple" (Hindu, Buddhist, Jaina, etc.) has not been just "a place to offer prayer" as a Muslim mosque and a Christian church. Temple in fact is the "residence" of the god.

One offers prayers to the deity directly by standing or sitting right in front of the deity. This is the most vital point to be noted and kept in mind all the time since terms like *ālaya* (आलय), *devālaya* (देवालय), *prāsāda* (प्रासाद), *devaprāsāda* (देवप्रासाद), *bāḍī* (बाडी), *Kālībāḍī* (कालीबाडी), *mandira* (मन्दिर), etc. mean one and the same — "house."

Since a temple is primarily a HOUSE, its basic architecture emerged out of the types of houses, including huts, India had from Neolithic Period of the pre-Indus-Sarasvatī times, around 6000 to 5000 BCE from Baluchistan through the Gaṅgā basin.

The thatched huts of ordinary folks in village datable in northern India to the period between 700 and 500 BCE seem to have provided the earliest models to the temple-builders. This supposition is based on the fact that the remains of an apsidal or elliptical temple dated to 500 BCE were unearthed at Vidiśā (विदिशा) by M.D. Khare.

The village-houses were of different types in ground plan: (1) ROUND (2) SQUARE, and (3) RECTANGULAR. However, when "round" is combined with "rectangular" it gave birth to the fourth form, (4) the APSIDAL. It also gave birth to (5) OVAL or ELLIPTICAL ground plan. Take any temple plan; basically it will fall in any one of these categories, irrespective of its religious affiliation. There may be different kinds of offsets, making it "star-shaped" or attachments and additions in a temple, making them "transepted," etc. but these things remained matters of details of innovations, style and choice and did not at all change the basic plans.

The evidence of architectural representations in the Early Historical Art (300 BCE – CE 300) shows that, to begin with, the ELEVATIONS of the huts were also adopted by the architects. However, as time passed, the architects, or *sthapati*s (स्थपति), freed themselves from the inherent limitations of the ground-floor-alone model of the huts. New patrons, emerging out of the elite class, with bags of money, from 200 BCE through CE 200, i.e. Śuṅga–Kuṣāṇa (शुंग–कुषाण) period, demanded from them multi-storeyed, or else high ceiling buildings, with elaborately carved entrances or gateways. The emphasis laid was on height of the built temple structure. Imposing proportions were conceived even in the late Kuṣāṇa period (second–third century CE). Now foreigners were also there in the ruling and business classes at places like Mathurā (मथुरा) from where the Kuṣāṇas (कुषाण) ruled and also made the city prosperous with the help of foreign traders. They too contributed to the changing scenario of not only the society and its tastes but also in artistic and decorative elements. The architectural remains unearthed at Mathurā do throw a flood of light on this aspect of early temple-buildings.

The Mature Phase (CE 400–600): The Stage of National Integration

The fourth century CE was a turning point in the history of India. In CE 320 one Śrīgupta (श्रीगुप्त) laid the foundation of the Gupta empire and Gupta culture. His successors followed not only the "cultural ideology" of Śrīgupta but also greatly elaborated and enhanced it. This was the ideology of SAGUṆA BHAKTI (सगुण भक्ति), *bhakti* in which the *bhakta* (भक्त) or devotee perceives his god in some FORM, image or symbol, particularly Vaiṣṇava (वैष्णव), since they called themselves *parama-bhāgavatas* (परम-भागवत). Of course, it was not the negation of Śaiva (शैव), Śākta (शाक्त), Buddhist and Jaina religions. During the Gupta period (गुप्त-काल) (CE 400–600) temples of all the religions flourished side by side. There was no clash amongst them. Their distinctiveness was based only upon intellectual debates and following of *gurus* (गुरु). Their co-existence in a single space and time is the eloquent testimony of this fact.

Bhakti (भक्ति) or "devotion" stands for two entities — one the Supernatural, who is considered to be "the ultimate controller of our destiny," and second, ourselves, "the human beings," who, through the golden road of unflinching "personal-devotion," called "FAITH," can make the Supernatural yield to help them in all their mundane (worldly) and extra-mundane (other-worldly) needs, desires and aspirations, from "earning money" to *mokṣa* (मोक्ष). Thus, the element of *personal devotion to a personal god* became the cornerstone of the *bhakti* movement in the fourth to sixth centuries CE, although the roots of *bhakti* as a devotional concept went deep down in Indian history to as early as the second century BCE, if not still earlier, as Ms Sushmita Pande has convincingly shown in one of her books on this subject.

The important point to note is the DUALITY IN BHAKTI — the God and the devotee, the former being the most sacred entity. *It is in this concept that now two separate spaces had to be provided in the temple, one for the God and the other for the devotee, though juxtaposed*. The physical space for the God, represented by his image, was called *garbha-gṛha* (गर्भ-गृह), while the physical space for the devotees, located in front of the *garbha-gṛha* was called *maṇḍapa* (मण्डप). The room for the god was called *garbha-gṛha* simply because the mother's womb is the only place which is untouched by atmospheric pollution, hence purest. Hence sacred. As a human being emerges after remaining for nine months in the womb or *garbha* (गर्भ) of his mother so also the god emerges everyday from the *garbha-sthāna* (गर्भ-स्थान), the sanctum for his devotees. This is called "God in the image of man."

The earliest example of this arrangement of a temple comes from Sāñcī (साँची). It is Temple No. 17, a Buddhist temple with a flat-roofed sanctum enclosed by walls around and one entrance and the flat roofed porch raised on pillars but with open sides. The Kaṅkālī Devī (कंकाली देवी) temple of Tigawā (तिगवा), the Viṣṇu (विष्णु) and Varāha (वराह) temples found at Eraṇ (एरण),

and Pārvatī (पार्वती) temple located in the villages of Nacanā (नचना) and Kuṭhāra (कुठार), all in Madhya Pradesh, are also largely similar in form and plan. Undoubtedly, there must have been temples of similar kind dedicated to Viṣṇu and Śiva both in Vidiśā (विदिशा) and elsewhere where Buddhism was not so dominant though they may have existed side by side as at Ellorā (एल्लोरा) at a later date; we should never forget that archaeological discovery is also a matter of chance.

It may be noted that although the vital step of separation of the "room" or *kakṣa* (कक्ष) for the deity, the *garbha-gṛha,* and the "hall" or *maṇḍapa* (मण्डप) for the devotee was achieved in the fourth-fifth centuries CE, the limitation of single-storey structure of this fourth century did not allow these early temples to grow in height and provide it vertical monumentality. This limitation was broken both in the north and the south around the late fifth and early sixth century, still within the Gupta–Vākāṭaka (गुप्त-वाकाटक) and Early Pallava (पल्लव) period. The Daśāvatāra (दशावतार) temple of Deogaṛh (देवगढ़) in district Jhansi has given us the evidence of a second storey as well as *śikhara* (शिखर) or spire or *vimāna* (विमान) raised over the main temple.

This was also a great breakthrough in architectural engineering since the building was raised without the use of mortar. It is reflected in the rock-cut temples of Mahābalipuram (महाबलिपुरम्) carved out by the Pallavas also.

There was yet another breakthrough in this innovation of the Gupta period — *combining art with architecture in the fully integrated fashion*. Creating a new aesthetics in architecture became the most important feature of this phase of development in "temple architecture." Bringing images of the heavenly world and integrating them in the fabric of the architecture became yet another significant point of development. Translating mythologies in stone and making them not only talk eloquently to the faithful but also to win converts now became easy. It greatly helped in winning patronage from the common man to the king. It also helped the sculptors and painters to develop their skill to the superb level for which the Gupta (गुप्त) art is so well known. No doubt it was the period of the "Indian Classical Art." Its excellence has been unparalleled.

The Stage of Regionalization:
The Era of All Round Development

The Gupta temples of central India thus laid the firm foundation to the temple art and architecture of a new genus. Now onwards there was no looking backward — every period in history and every region in the country produced *sthapati*s (स्थपति) who experimented new, or else hybrid, forms in temple architecture suited to the climatic conditions of their regions. In the south, the element of *GOPURAM* (गोपुरम्) as a several storeyed gateway in the *prākāra* (प्राकार) or boundary wall was one such innovation. Highly sloping but hat-like roof for temples in Kerala was an imitation of the Megalithic *ṭopī-kal*s (टोपीकल). The stepped pyramidal roof, used for the subsidiary structures erected in front of the main temple, in several regions create an overall hybrid picture with the curvilinear *śikhara* (शिखर) on the *maṇḍovara* (मण्डोवर) in the background.

Up to the fifth-sixth century we find a kind of UNILINEAR development in temple architecture which was applicable more or less to the entire country but from the seventh century MULTILINEAR development became the rule. We now enter into the Period of Regionalization. While the north Indian or Nāgara (नागर) style developed curvilinear *śikhara* (शिखर) ending in a pointed finial at the top, the south Indian or Drāviḍa (द्राविड) style developed stepped *vimāna* (विमान) ending in a round *stūpī* (स्तूपी). The curvilinear *śikhara* was a solid or hollow or segmental hollow structure, as in the

Jagannātha (जगन्नाथ) Temple in Purī (पुरी), Orissa. The *vimāna* in the Bṛhadīśvara (बृहदीश्वर) temple at Tañjāvūr (तंजावूर) had hollow storeys at each floor. However, later on the floors or storeys became non-functional — no one could come out in the open terrace at each floor any more; it was only notional.

As far as temple architecture is concerned the north Indian style is becoming more and more chaotic in the modern times. This is mainly because of the lack of technical know-how and able *sthāpatis* in this field. Fortunately, the south still retains the classical traditions. And so also Gujarat and Orissa where the new temples are still keeping the old traditions in temple-building alive.

1

Rock-cut Stūpas, Vihāras, Caityas and Temples

THE antiquity of rock-cut and structural monuments in India goes back to third millennium BCE and not to the third century BCE, as is usually mentioned in history textbooks. Recent archaeological discoveries have completely falsified what has been said in this regard so far. In fact, India possesses some of the great traditions in the fields of art and architecture innovations and water management systems from the times of the Haṛappan (हड़प्पन) or the Indus-Sarasvatī (इण्डस्-सरस्वती) Civilization of the third millennium BCE — the Mauryans (मौर्य) only carried forward that tradition in third century BCE.

As far as the Indus-Sarasvatī period is concerned, there is the archaeological evidence of an apsidal sun-dried brick temple at Banawālī (बनावली) in Haryana. It was erected for fire worship. There were some rooms also attached to it but built separately with some space left in between. During the same period, the Haṛappans of Dholāvīra (धोलावीर), located in the Rann of Kacch (कच्छ का रण्ण) in Gujarat, used highly polished stone pillars in their monuments. It also negates the theory that the polished pillars were introduced in India by the Persians during the time of Aśoka (अशोक). Moreover, the Indus-Sarasvatī (इण्डस्-सरस्वती) settlement of

Dholāvīra (धोलावीर) also yields the evidence of first rock-cut architecture in India in the form of an exquisite rock-cut water reservoir. It was created by partly excavating through the alluvium and partly by cutting the underlying rock. Inside this reservoir was found a rock-cut well with a few rock-cut steps and a stone-made enclosure.

It is important to note that all of these elements — the apsidal temple, polished pillars and tank in the temple complex — characterized the Buddhist and Hindu religious complexes during the historical period as well. The tank, of course, serves the cause of non-religious activities as well — the multitude of stepped wells in Gujarat serving the utility of wells as the source of water for everyday use have their origin in them.

A Little History

From 700 BCE, i.e. pre-Buddhist times, we get the references in literature about the sixteen *mahājanapadas* (महाजनपद) or large estates with townships as centres of political entities, kingdoms and republics, in northern India. In one of them there was a great city of Vidiśā (विदिशा) in Madhya Pradesh. We get here the evidence of the construction of a large oval-shaped temple dedicated to Viṣṇu (विष्णु). It is dated to the fifth century BCE.

However, with the establishment of the Mauryan (मौर्य) empire, in the last quarter of the fourth century BCE, we start getting the remains of many more examples of not only the structural temples, oval or apsidal in shape, but also the rock-cut ones, not existing earlier (*figs*. 1a, 1b & 1c). Both flourished side by side. Earlier to the Mauryan (मौर्य) period,

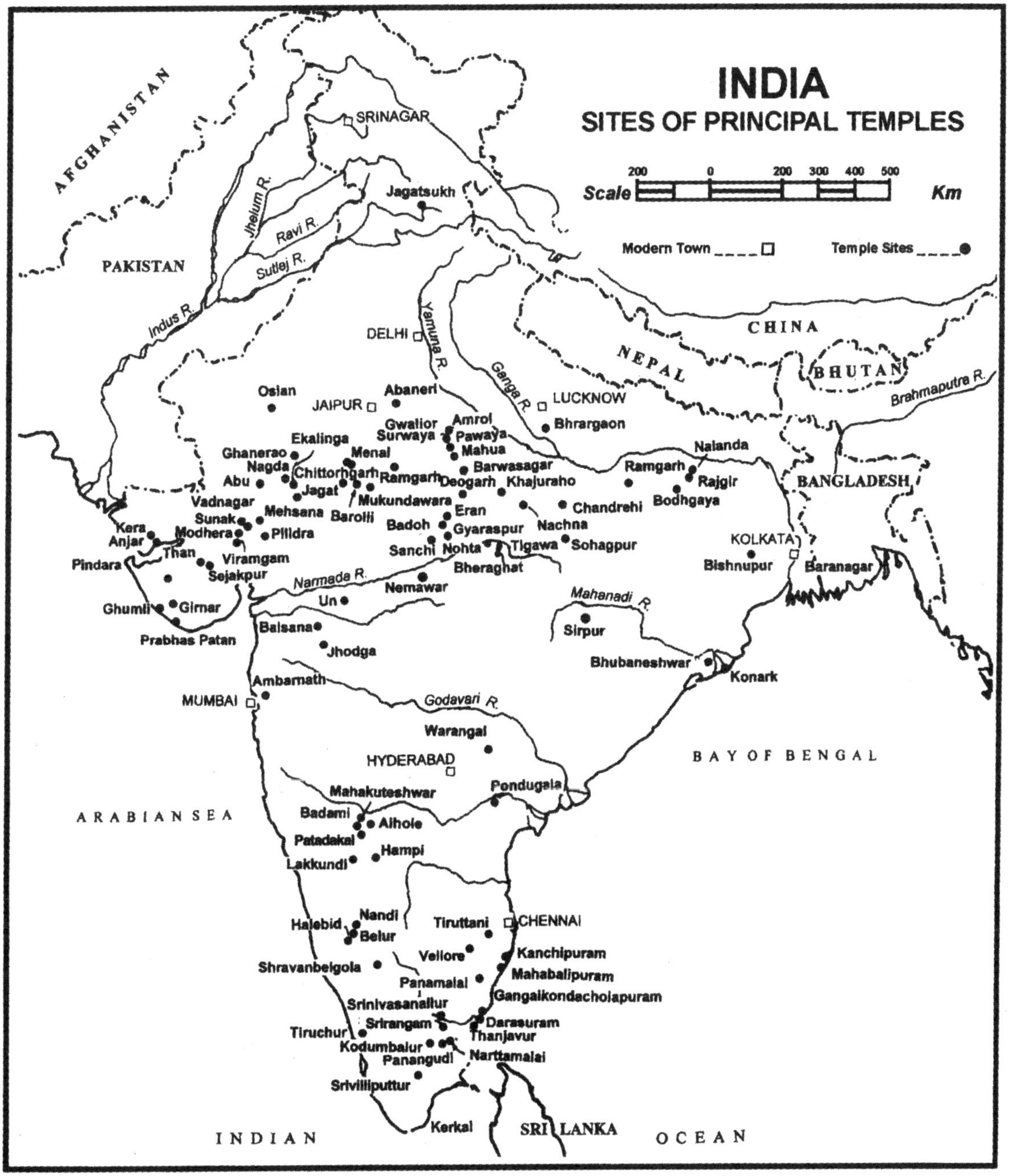

Fig. 1a : Map showing the principal structural temples of India

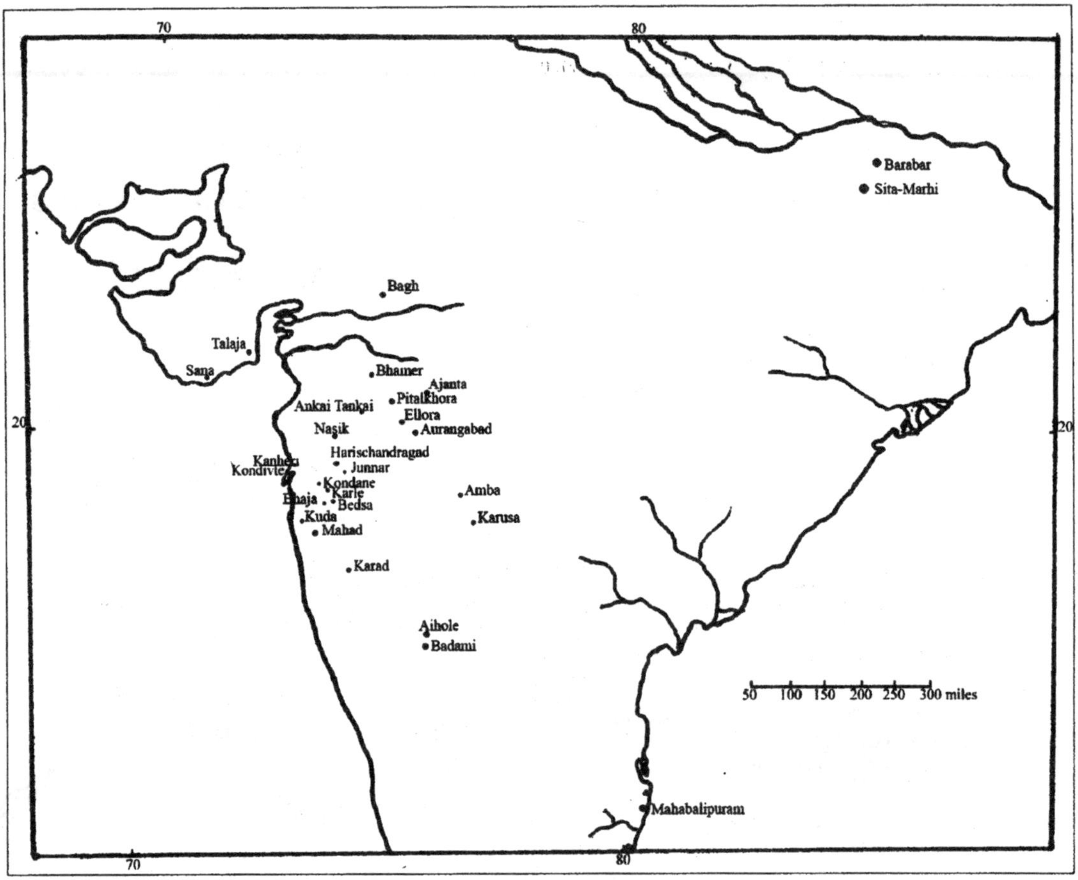

Fig. 1b : Map showing the principal rock-cut caves of India

earth, mud-brick and timber alone were used. There are several examples of mud and mud-brick structural remains excavated at sites like Vaiśālī (वैशाली) in Bihar. The earliest rock-cut caves dedicated to Buddhist as well as non-Buddhist creeds in India have been ascribed to the period of the Mauryas, particularly of Aśoka (अशोक). This is firmly established on the basis of inscriptional evidence recorded on the surface of the caves at Barābar (बराबर) and Nāgārjunī (नागार्जुनी) hills, existing side by side, in Bihar.

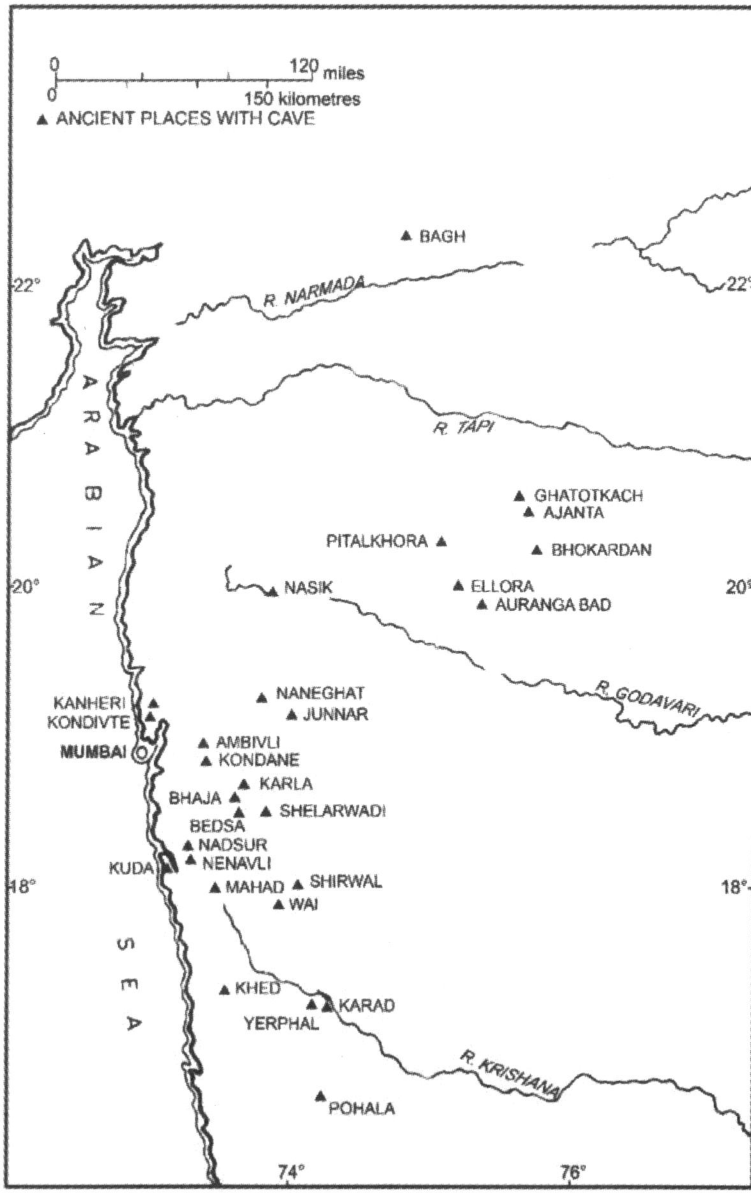

Fig. 1c : Map showing the rock-cut cave sites of western India

The rock-cut caves were meant mainly for ascetics to practise meditation and offer prayers. However, they were also creating spaces for religious structures, whereas rulers and subjects lived in structures built of wood and bricks, and rarely of stones. During the same period they became aware of the importance of town planning for a better civic life. According to Kauṭilya's *Arthaśāstra* (कौटिल्य का अर्थशास्त्र) the settlement area was divided into several zones, religious as well as secular. The travelogues of Megasthenes (मेगस्थनीज़) (third century BCE) and Fa-Hien (फाहियान) (fifth century CE) also speak of well-planned cities like Pāṭaliputra (पाटलिपुत्र) with specific quarters meant for the royalty and for religious activities. Such descriptions are endorsed by archaeological excavations conducted in the twentieth century at

Bulandībāgh (बुलन्दी बाग़) and Kumrahār (कुम्रहार), both located near Patna. At Bulandībāgh huge palisades, made of large planks of wood are still intact, probably the remnants of the Mauryan (मौर्य) palace, buried under huge deposits of the silt brought by the yearly floods in the Gaṅgā (गंगा). These were unearthed nearly a century ago by Bloch. At Kumrahār, however, tall and plain Chunār (चुनार) sandstone pillars were also made use of in erecting an 80–pillared open hall or pavilion along a waterway. Near it monasteries were also built of burnt-bricks in later times. However, the Mauryan period is known for a new genus of architecture — the rock-cut architecture — consisting of highly polished caves and cave temples.

The Buddhists raise two types of sacred structures, viz. *stūpa* (स्तूप) and *caitya-gṛha* (चैत्य-गृह). They also established monasteries for the monks to live in. These are called *vihāra*s (विहार). The word *vihāra* means "walking for pleasure," "garden," etc., but as a technical term it stands for the abode of the monks who were usually spending in it four months of the rainy season since then they could hardly go out from place to place as wandering mendicants which Buddha wanted them to be.

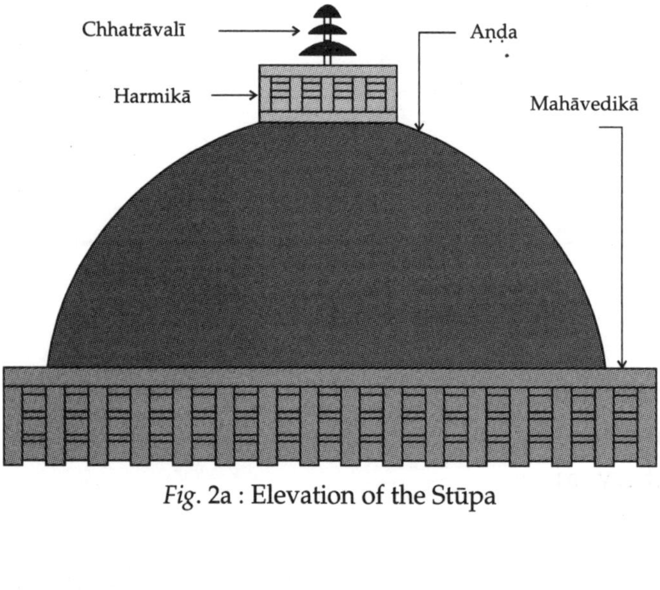

Fig. 2a : Elevation of the Stūpa

Stūpa

The term *stūpa* and *thūpa* or *thuba* in Pāli (थूप या थुब पालि में), used widely by the Buddhists originated from the Sanskrit word *stūpa* meaning "pile-up" or mound. Thus, *stūpa*

(स्तूप) is a simple "earthen mound heaped over the relics of the dead." In that sense, it is a sepulchral monument. However, since the Vedic literature also makes mention of *stūpas* (*Hiraṇya-stūpa*) (हिरण्य-स्तूप) it is believed that the Vedic Āryans (आर्यन्) also had the practice of erecting *stūpa*s, centuries earlier to the birth of Buddha (बुद्ध). In fact, it is said that when death came near to Buddha, his main disciple, Ānanda (आनन्द) by name, asked him "How should we honour the body (relic-bones) of the *tathāgata* (तथागत)?" Buddha replied, "As they do for the remains of a Cakravartī (चक्रवर्ती, king), so, Ānanda, they should do for the remains of the *tathāgata.* At the four cross-roads, similar to the *stūpa* they raise for the *cakravartin* (चक्रवर्तिन्), should they raise a *stūpa* for the *tathāgata.*" It will mean that Buddha asked his disciples to follow this ancient practice in his case also.

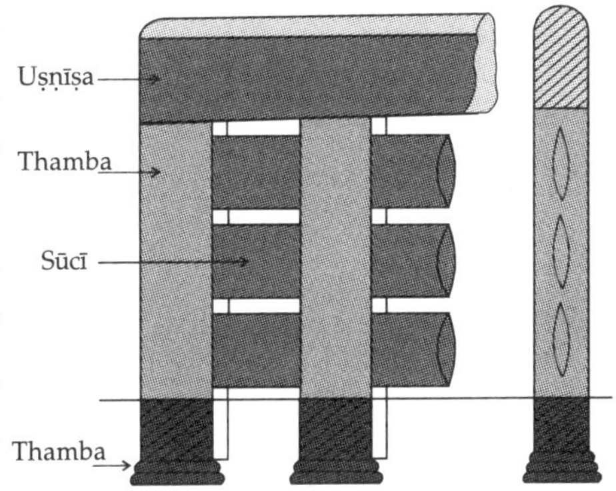

Fig. 2b : Vedikā parts of the Stūpa

As the archaeological evidence shows, at Vaiśālī (वैशाली) in Bihar, for example, the practice started by erecting a *stūpa* with the help of only earth, piled over the relics. Later on, however, permanent materials were used, bricks or else stone, often plastered with lime-paste since the earthen *stūpa*s required yearly maintenance as otherwise it could be washed out. The practice of erecting a *stūpa*, was, however, not confined to the relics of the Buddha; after him his disciples also followed this practice for their colleagues as well as the honoured saints of other faiths also — called *pratyekabuddhas* (प्रत्येकबुद्ध). Initially, *stūpa*s were erected on the site of the funeral pyre (Sanskrit: *citā*, चिता), hence called not only *stūpa* (स्तूप) but also *caitya* (चैत्य). That is

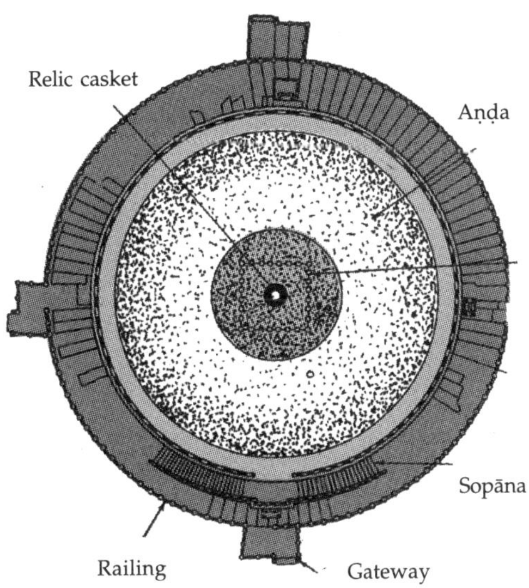

Fig. 2c : Plan of the Stūpa

why in a *caitya-gṛha* (चैत्य-गृह), in place of Buddha image, the *stūpa* could also be worshipped. The *stūpas* are soon found erected also at the sacred places associated with Buddhism in general. They may or may not have in their core even the relic-casket. When devoid of relics, these were called *votive stūpas*, i.e. meant only for symbolic worship. A *stūpa*, however, symbolized Buddha himself even when it did not entomb his relics and remained simply "votive." It enabled the worshipper to epitomize his *bodhi* (बोधि, enlightenment) as well as *nirvāṇa* (निर्वाण, complete liberation).

The *stūpa* structure of the pre-Common Era was composed of a hemispherical or round dome called *aṇḍa* (अण्ड) about which even the *Śatapatha Brāhmaṇa* (शतपथ ब्राह्मण) has spoken by using the term *parimaṇḍala* (परिमण्डल) (*figs*. 2a, 2b & 2c). The bubble-shaped dome was erected on a low circular base or platform of stone. It was then surmounted by a square-shaped box with railing called *harmikā* (हर्मिका) as at Sārnāth (सारनाथ) and Sāñcī (सांची). It was further crowned by three discs *chatras* (छत्र) or parasols, later on seven, of successively diminishing sizes, the smallest being on the top. The three were mounted on a stick called *yaṣṭi* (यष्टि), projecting above the *harmikā*. A circumambulatory path called *pradakṣiṇāpatha* (प्रदक्षिणापथ) encircles the *stūpa*. It was meant to undertake sacred circumambulation on the ground level, though these could be provided at different levels above the ground level as at Sāñcī (सांची) in Madhya Pradesh where the "Mahā-Stūpa" (महा-स्तूप) is double storied (*Pl.* 1) and Kesariā (केसरिया) in Bihar where the *stūpa* was multistoried.

The entire complex was then fenced by a railing called *vedikā* (वेदिका), a Vedic term emerging from the *vedī* (वेदी) of *yajña* (यज्ञ). One important variation in the *stūpa* architecture has been noticed in the case of Andhra Pradesh examples, particularly of Amarāvāti (अमरावती) and Nāgārjuṇikoṇḍa (नागार्जुनकोण्ड), both on River Kṛṣṇā (कृष्णा). In them we see box-like projections on all the four cardinal directions of the *stūpa*. These are called *āyaka* (आयक) platforms, *ayaka* meaning "the altar on which offerings are made." Over this five tall pillars (*stambhas*, स्तम्भ) are erected which are called *āyaka stambhas* (आयक स्तम्भ).

The *vedikā* or railing, in later stages, became elaborate, architecturally as well as decoratively with the images of nymphs (*devakanyās*, देवकन्या), lotus, etc. It was built of massive stone balustrade consisting of octagonal pillars (*stambha*, Pāli: *thaba* थब), and cross-bars (*sūcī*, सूची) of lenticular section. It

Pl. 1 : Māha-Stūpa, Sāñcī

was finally capped by horizontally laid stone rails with rounded top (*uṣṇīṣa*, उष्णीष), pieces of "U" section, joined together so as to run the entire length of the railing, leaving only the vacant spaces of the gateways. On the four sides of the *stūpa* four gateways (*toraṇa*, तोरण), generally of stone, were built that project a little beyond the level of the ground balustrade. However, in many extant examples, only one gateway was erected. Even this was not found necessary in most of the examples which we have at Sāñcī (साँची). The most elaborate gateways, for example, the ones found at Sāñcī and Bharhut (भरहुत्), consist of two upright posts (*stambhas*, स्तम्भ) and three architraves or cross-bars, set one above the other at a great height.

The gateways were often richly carved with sculptures, generally in low relief (bas-relief, in French). The uprights and the cross-bars used in the railing of the *stūpa*-complex (स्तूप) were also decorated though less elaborately; many a time not even that much, they remained plain. The *triratna* (त्रिरत्न) motifs, in which the Buddhists seek refuge, i.e. Buddha (the Founder), *dharma* (his Principles or Law of Piety) and the monastic order (*saṁgha*) — *buddham śaraṇaṁ gacchāmi* (बुद्धम् शरणं गच्छामि), *dhammam śaraṇaṁ gacchāmi* (धम्मम् शरणं गच्छामि), *saṁgham saraṇaṁ gacchāmi* (संघम् शरणं गच्छामि) — are placed at the top of the gateway, though exceptions to this rule are many.

Building a *stūpa* was always a great event for the Buddhists. Besides being a great act of piety it was scientific and ritualistic. The Hīnayāna (हीनयान) of Sri Lanka has the famous book entitled *Dīpavaṁsa* (दीपवंस)

written in Pāli (पालि). It has given detailed accounts of the process — from the selection of the land to the erection of the structure.

The *triratna* symbol was generally combined with the *dharmacakra* (धर्मचक्र) or the "Wheel of Piety" symbol which too had the Vedic origin but adopted, adapted and popularized by the Buddhists. It was often further embellished with lotus, the most sacred flower on which stood or sat all gods and goddesses of Indian origin.

Buddhist Rock-Cut "Architecture"

Rock-cut architecture is a misnomer since the term "architecture" implies the technique of joining together pieces of some material, generally stone, brick and wood. It was not, however, the case in rock-cut monuments which was, in fact, a sculptural art since these were made by scooping out rocks. However, in practice the term is used widely since the early cave temples are seen copying all the important elements of structural buildings made of wood. For example, these caves imitate the skeleton of thatched roof comprising curved ribs, rafters, reepers, lintels, etc. Similarly, unlike the wooden structures, the pillars "supporting" the ceilings of these caves do not have any functional importance. Here we have thus a very interesting situation — the "form" is architectural but the "substance" is not, it is cent per cent sculptural.

The practice of scooping out the rocky hillsides to be used either as shrines or dwelling places or burial chambers has been very old in the world context. The Egyptians had been doing it since at least 1500 BCE and the Persians from the sixth

Pl. 2 : Lomas Ṛṣi Cave, Barabar Hill, Bihar

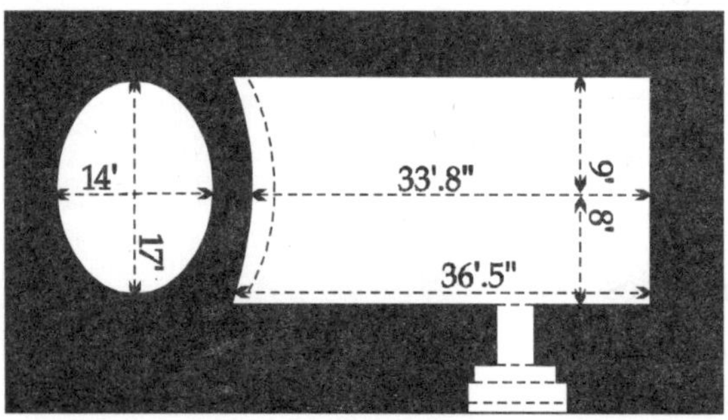

Fig. 3a : Plan of the Lomas Ṛṣi Cave, Barabar Hill

century BCE. Among the earliest rock-cut caves in India, however, eight rock-cut chambers carved in the gneissic or granitic rock are in the Barābar (बराबर) and Nāgārjunī (नागार्जुनी) hills, and one near Rājgīr (राजगीर) in Bihar. These have been dated to the time of Aśoka (अशोक) and his successors although the Swarṇa Bhaṇḍāra (स्वर्ण भण्डार) cave of Rājgīr or Rājgṛha (राजगृह) could be older by two to three decades but still within the Mauryan (मौर्य) period. The caves of Barabar and Nāgārjunī were dedicated to the monks of the Ājīvika (आजीविक) sect founded by the seer-monk named Gopāla (गोपाल) of the sixth century BCE (died *c.* 484 BCE), hence contemporary of Mahāvīra (महावीर) and Buddha. The sect was atheistic and pessimistic in nature, totally opposed to Jainism and Buddhism. But the monks of this sect, clad in saffron clothes, were favourites of some of the queens of Aśoka since they were the soothsayers making the welfare of the sons of the queens.

Some of the rock-cut chambers reflected the forms of the contemporary wooden architecture of the Mauryan era since the stonecutters of the time borrowed many elements from them. The famous caves like the Lomas Ṛṣi (लोमस् ऋषि) (*Pl.* 2, *Fig.* 3a) and the Sudāmā (सुदामा) (*Pl.* 3, *Fig.* 3b) in the Barabar hills and the Sītāmaṛhī (सीतामढ़ी) cave in the Nāgārjunī hill (*Fig.* 3c) close by are among the earliest examples of such architectural adaptations in rock-cut caves. The Lomas Ṛṣi (लोमस् ऋषि) was unique since it alone in this group was adorned with an arched gateway with pointed finial having mouldings, all in rock-cut. The arch was beautifully decorated with floral, faunal (crocodile or *makara* मकर) and geometric motifs (intersecting circles) as well as *stūpa*s (स्तूप), with central rope-like simple mouldings, being worshipped by elephants. All the other caves were, however, plain with no arched gateway or entrance like the Lomas Ṛṣi. The most significant point to note in this case is that this is the earliest example of a rock-cut cave architecture which unmistakably shows a carbon copy of some unknown pre-existing wooden architecture using grooved rafters and curved frames and finials, screens and low-relief sculptural decorations. The 100 years-later example of the Bhājā (भाजा) cave has in fact still a part of one wooden beam in position, fully establishing the fact that the rock-cut architecture of the period bracketed between 300 BCE and CE 100 is the slavish copy of wooden architecture.

Pl. 3 : Sudāmā Cave, Barabar Hill, Bihar

The spread of Buddhism and Jainism in south

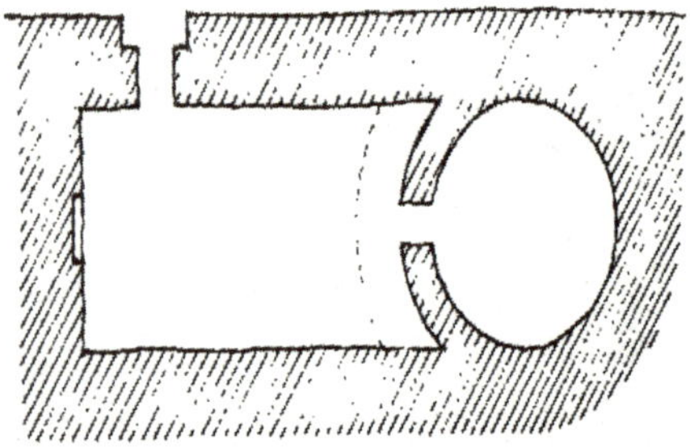

Fig. 3b : Plan of the Sudāmā Cave, Barabar Hill

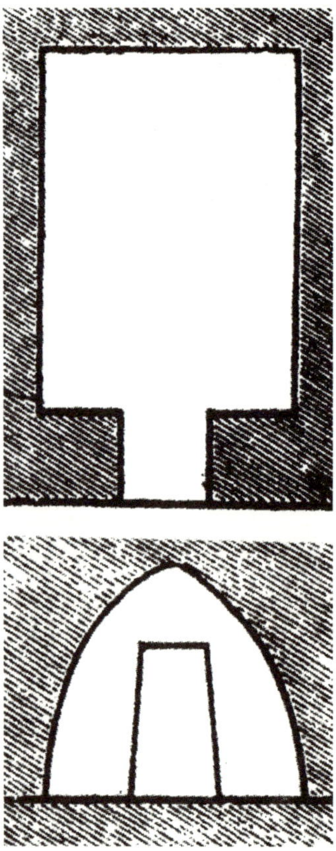

Fig. 3c : Plan and section of the Sītāmaṛhī cave, Nāgārjunī hill

India resulted in the diffusion of rock-cut architecture in Karnataka, Andhra Pradesh, Tamil Nadu and Kerala. Later it paved way for the Hindu rock-cut architecture in these regions.

Caitya-gṛhas and Vihāras

There are two major types of the Buddhist rock-cut architecture, viz. the *caitya-gṛha* (चैत्य-गृह) and the *vihāra* (विहार). However, *stūpa*s were also carved out of the *in situ* rock formations. The rock-cut caves of the Mauryan era influenced the forms, decorations and techniques of scooping rocks in the subsequent periods of times in many regions of the country. Gujarat, Maharashtra, Andhra Pradesh, Karnataka and Tamil Nadu witnessed its extension and growth during the period bracketed between 200 BCE and CE 200 and also beyond.

The technique involved in creating rock-cut architecture is simple, though the process requires much skill and patience. First the irregular rock cliff was chiselled, starting from the top and reaching the bottom, to produce a roughly uniform surface. On this plain surface the entrance of an intended cave was outlined. After this the scooping or cutting the rock started in the marked area. Through this portal further quarrying could begin with iron hammers and chisels from the front to the rear and from top downwards and not the other way round. Thus only after completing the ceiling, the workmen quarried downwards up to the floor. This method helped them carrying out their work without the use of scaffolding and other support systems. This reconstruction is based upon the sculptural representations we see in some of the panels and friezes decorating the railings of Bharhut (भरहुत) *stūpa*-complex of the second century BCE.

CAITYA-GṚHAS

The Buddhist rock-cut architecture is reflected best in their *caitya-gṛha*s. Although, etymologically, the term *caitya* (चैत्य), emerging out of the root *citi* (चिति), means mound raised on the cremated bones of a person, yet for the Buddhists the term is applied to any object deserving their worship, be it a *stūpa* (स्तूप), which was a sepulchral mound, the *bodhi* (बोधि) or *pīpal* (पीपल) tree under which Buddha got Enlightenment, Buddha image, images of *bodhisattva*s (बोधिसत्त्व), the Votive Tablet with pictures from the life of Buddha, etc. The term *gṛha* (गृह) means house. Hence, *caitya-gṛha*s (चैत्य-गृह) are of different types, though fulfilling one and the same purpose — worshipping Buddha mainly through symbols and symbolic associations.

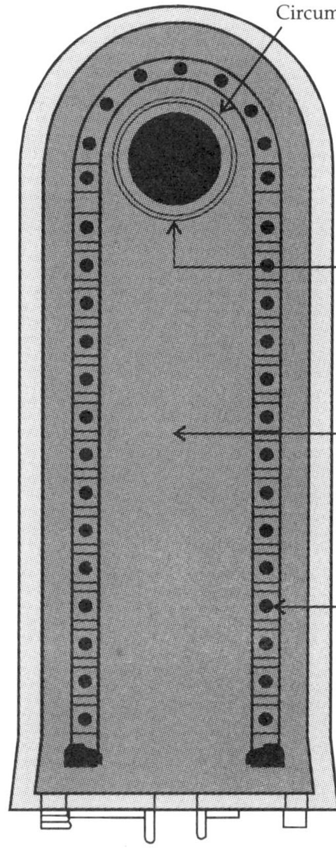

Fig. 4 : General layout of the Hīnayāna Caityagṛha, Kanheri

The architecture of a *caitya-gṛha* is very simple in plan (*fig.* 4). It has generally only a long hall. The hall has the barrel-vaulted roof, lending a semi-cylindrical appearance. Its end is apsidal, like the back or hind part of an elephant, or horse-shoe shaped. The *stūpa*, carved out of the living rock, was located in the apse but leaving enough space all around for circumambulation or *pradakṣiṇā* (प्रदक्षिणा). Some of the important *caitya*s (चैत्य) belonging to the Hīnayāna (हीनयान) sect of Buddhism are at Bhājā (भाजा) (*Pl.* 4, *fig.* 5), Kondāne (कोन्दाने) (*fig.* 6), Pītalkhora (पीतलखोर) *fig.* 7), Bedsā (बेद्सा) *fig.* 8), Kārle (कार्ले) (*fig.* 9a), Paṇḍu-lena (पण्डुलेन) *caitya* at Nāsik (नासिक) (*fig.* 9b) and caves bearing numbers 9, 10 and 12 at Ajantā (अजन्ता) (*Pl.* 5), all in western Maharashtra, some near Pune (पुणे)

Pl. 4 : Facade of the Bhājā cave

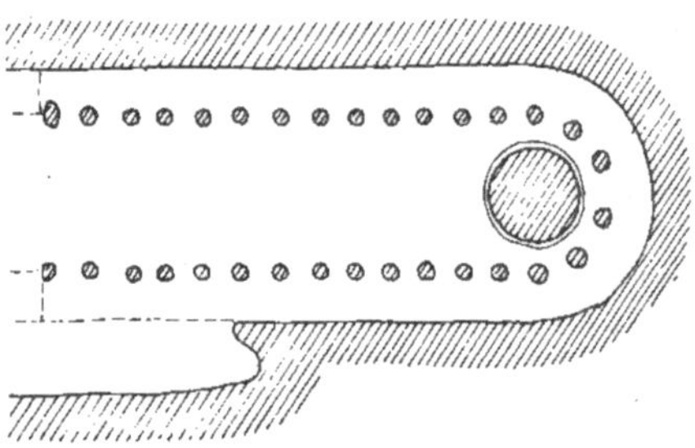

Fig. 5 : Plan of the Hīnayāna Caitya, Bhājā

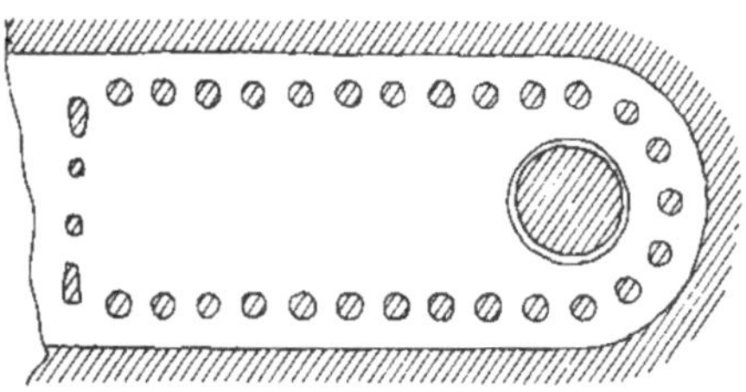

Fig. 6 : Plan of the Hīnayāna Caitya, Kondane

and others near Auraṅgābād (औरंगाबाद).

The *caitya*s belonging to the period from second century BCE to around 50 BCE do no depict Buddha in human form; he was represented by symbols alone, generally associated with the life of the Buddha himself, *stūpa* (स्तूप) in particular, but also his seat-of-meditation, called *vajrāsana* (वज्रासन), *pīpal* (पीपल) tree, called *bodhi-vṛkṣa* (बोधि-वृक्ष), feet, turban, parasol, hair, etc. The other category of symbols included *triratna* (त्रिरत्न), symbolizing Buddha's creed — Buddha, Dharma (धर्म) and Saṁgha (संघ). However, the exterior of these *caitya-gṛha*s (चैत्य-गृह) shows animal and human figures, including semi-divine beings, like the *yakṣa*s (यक्ष) and *yakṣī*s (यक्षी).

The pessimistic Buddhist thoughts could not withstand the refined Vedic philosophy which assumed the world as the manifestation of the

"Supreme God." And, it allowed a person to worship any god of his choice, either in the form of images (*saguṇopāsanā,* सगुणोपासना) or else as formless (*nirguṇopāsanā,* निर्गुणोपासना). It also influenced a section of Buddhist philosophers. Subsequently, the first century CE witnessed the decisive schism in the Buddhist Saṁgha when it got divided into two major sects — the Mahāyāna (महायान) and the Hīnayāna (हीनयान). The roots of this division went down in the First, Second and Third Councils of the Buddhists held after the death or *mahāparinirvāṇa* (महापरिनिर्वाण) of Buddha over a period of 400 years. A group of monks called themselves *mahāsāṁghikas* (महासांघिक). They held the view that the Buddha was in fact a Transcendental Being, beyond his human body. In other words, he was a *divine* person who had descended on the earth from the heaven as the saviour of Humanity. However, this was hardly acceptable to the traditionalists or Hīnayānists since they held the view that the Buddha's stand on this philosophical issue can never be changed. It was, therefore, now very easy for the new group to give birth to the Buddha image. The *avatāra* (अवतार) concept of the Vaiṣṇavas (वैष्णव) appears to have influenced the Mahāyānists. However, those who did not subscribe to this new view kept to the old traditions of not showing the Buddha in the form of a human being. The *mahāsāṁghikas* (महासांघिक) soon came to be known as "Mahāyānists," i.e. those who have chosen a "great (*mahā,* महा) path or vehicle (*yāna,* यान)," while the traditionalists as "Hīnayānists," i.e. those who have chosen a "narrow/lesser (*hīna,* हीन) path or vehicle (*yāna,* यान)." There are, therefore, Hīnayānist *caitya-gṛhas* (चैत्य-गृह) and Mahāyānist

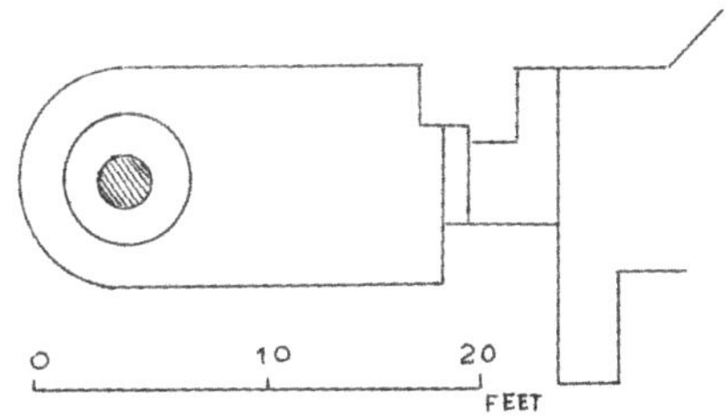

Fig. 7 : Plan of the Hīnayāna Caitya, Pītalkhora No. 10

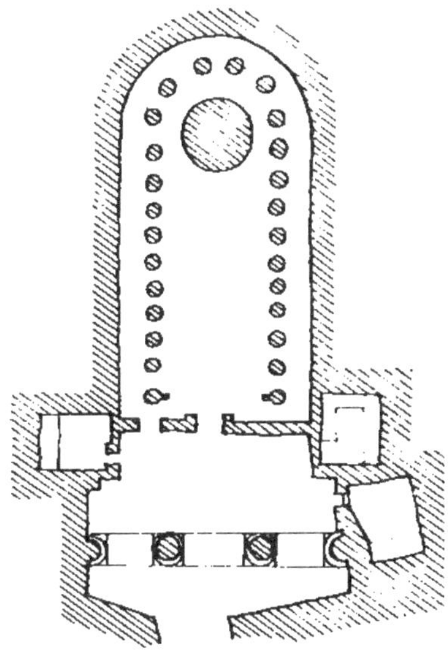

Fig. 8 : Plan of the Hīnayāna Caitya, Bedsā

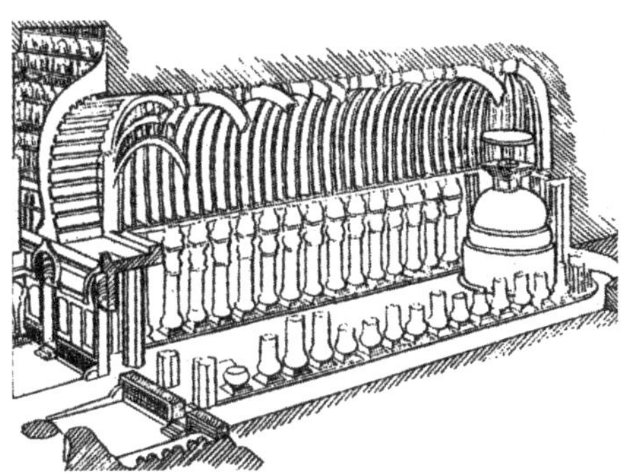

Fig. 9a : Interior of the Caityagṛha at Karle

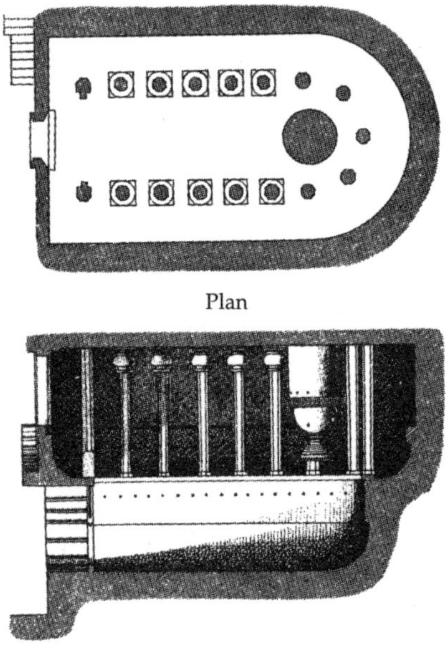

Fig. 9b : Plan and section of the Pāṇḍu-lena Caitya, Nāsik

*caitya-gṛha*s. However, the Mahāyānist *caitya-gṛha*s also followed the apsidal plan. With the spread of Mahāyānism from the First century CE onwards, some of the earlier *caitya-gṛha*s, like Kārle (कार्ले) and Kanheri (कन्हेरि) in Maharashtra, and some of the newly carved ones added the Buddha images for the purpose of the worship of the founder of their religion. While some of the Hīnayānist rock-cut caves are at Bhājā (भाजा), Kondāne (कोन्दाने), etc. some of the main rock-cut caves of the Mahāyānists are Cave nos. 19 (*fig.* 10) and 26 (*fig.* 11) at Ajantā (अजन्ता) (*Pl.* 6), and the Viśvakarmā (विश्वकर्मा) cave (Cave no. 10) at Ellorā (एल्लोरा) (*Pl.* 7, *fig.* 12).

The Mahāyānist *caitya*s (abbreviation of *caitya-gṛha*s) are profusely adorned with sculptures showing themes and representations based upon new mythologies which started emerging in the Mahāyānist literature. More and more ornamental features also appeared in them for decorative purposes. Images of the Buddha and *bodhisattva*s (बोधिसत्त्व), however, cover much of the façade, i.e. entrance and windows, etc. of the frontal surface of these rock-cut temples. The inside was adorned with images and pictures related to Buddhist themes as well as secular subjects as at Ajantā (अजन्ता) in a variety of ways and techniques, including wall-paintings done by the "tempera" method. Buddha in various poses, standing or sitting, with or without a canopy over the head, occupied prominent locations inside and outside the caves. Similarly, figures were also carved or else painted on the pillars, brackets and friezes in the interior. The shafts of the columns in these caves, as can be seen at Ajantā, are many-sided and the ceilings and walls large and plain. All of these bear geometric, floral and faunal motifs in paintings which decorated them. The imitation of wooden architecture comparatively decreased during this period of Mahāyānism (first century to seventh century CE) though not completely given up. Traditions die hard. Also, they provide legitimacy to the new.

VIHĀRAS

Etymologically, *vihāra* means "dwelling-place." In the context of Buddhists and the Jainas, it was meant only for the monks. Prior to the Mauryan (मौर्य) period, i.e. before the third century BCE, there were structural *vihāras* (विहार) made of impermanent materials like wood and sun-dried bricks. The remains of these structures are sometimes found in archaeological excavations. Their unmistakable reflections are present in their slavish copies found in the rock-cut examples where they had absolutely no architectural function to perform. In fact, at Bhājā (भाजा) a wooden rafter is still there *in situ*, as noted earlier also.

Pl. 5 : Façade of Ajantā Cave no. 9

The rock-cut *vihāra* comprises just a central hall for the congregational worship of the monks and a few cells around it for the monks to live in. The hall, square or rectangular, is entered through a rock-cut doorway and a pillared verandah. The rooms, opening either

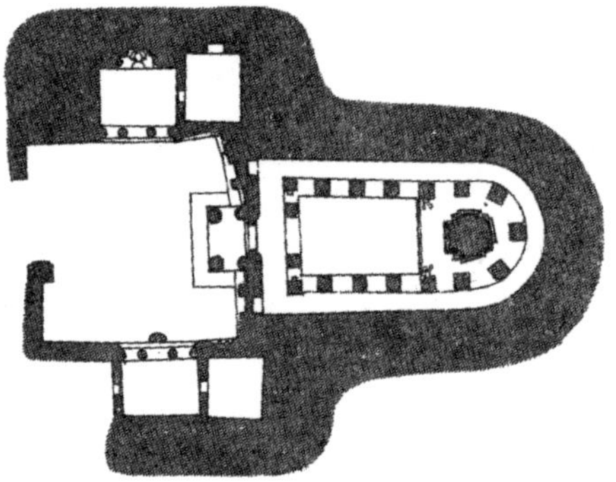

Fig. 10 : Plan of the Mahāyāna Cave No. 19, Ajantā

in the verandahs or the hall, were provided with stone beds shaped out of the existing rock *in situ*. However, these cells were devoid of windows.

Hīnayānist *vihāras* occur in the Western Ghāṭs (घाट), at sites like Ajantā (अजन्ता) and Ellorā (एल्लोरा). At Ajantā, they include Caves no. 8, 12, 13 and 15a (*figs.* 13, 14 & 15). Hīnayāna (हीनयान) *vihāras* in the Western Ghāṭs also include those at Bedsā (बेद्सा), Kondāne (कोन्दाने) and Pītalkhora (पीतलखोर), and Caves no. 3, 8, and 15 at Nāsik (नासिक). These *vihāras* (विहार) are famous for their highly decorated façades, i.e. frontals, as well as sculptural panels and friezes, for example, the one found at Bhājā once taken to be the march of Indra, but now identified by V.S. Agrawala with King Māndhātā's (मान्धाता) visit to Uttara-Kuru (उत्तर-कुरु) country.

The Mahāyānism also had an impact on the architecture and concept of the *vihāras*. The Mahāyānists sometimes converted the purely residential *vihāra* of the Hīnayānists into a place of worship as well as residence, i.e. *caitya-gṛha* (चैत्य-गृह)-cum-*vihāra*. That is why sometimes they converted the central cell of the back wall into a shrine enclosing the image of the Buddha, often flanked by attendants or by Avalokiteśvara (अवलोकितेश्वर) and Maitreya (मैत्रेय), two of the most important *bodhisattvas* (बोधिसत्त्व). Instead of a *stūpa* (स्तूप), the image of the Buddha, or the image of Buddha carved on the body of the *stūpa*, became the object of worship. Sometimes shrines flanked the sides of the verandah. However, the basic plan of the *vihāra* remained unchanged, consisting of a pillared central hall with cells leading out of it. The façade and porch were profusely decorated with

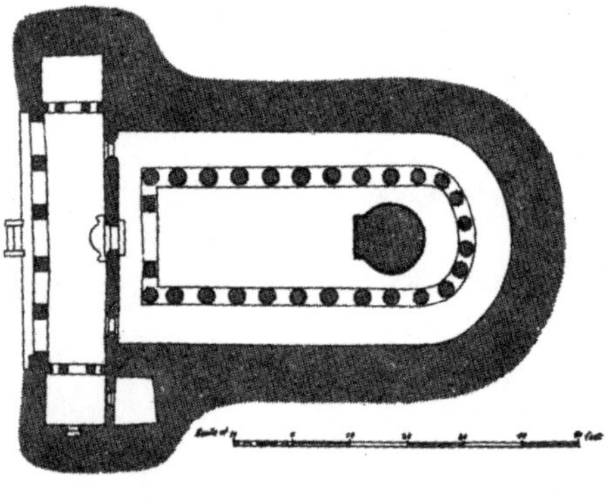

Fig. 11 : Plan of the Mahāyāna Cave No. 26, Ajantā

sacred motifs and symbols common to all religions, such as the lotus, wheel and *svastika* (स्वस्तिक), and geometric designs of triangles, rectangles and intersecting circles. Some double-storeyed *vihāra*s also exist, such as Cave no. 6 at Ajantā (अजन्ता) and Caves no. 11 and 12 at Ellorā (एल्लोरा). It may be noted that Ellorā is a unique example since the rock-cut temples and shrines and also *vihāra*s did not belong to a single religion exclusively some belonged to Buddhism while others belonged to Jainism and Hinduism.

Pl. 6 : Façade of Ajantā Cave no. 19

Hindu Rock-Cut Architecture

The history of the rock-cut Buddhist architecture starts in the third century BCE and ends in the seventh century CE when the "Mahāyāna Phase" as such comes to its near-end, and Tāntric (तान्त्रिक) Phase starts with emphasis on different kinds of esoteric rituals. By the end of the twelfth century CE Buddhism almost ends its life-history in India, which got revived only in the beginning of the twentieth century by a Sri Lankan monk, Bhikku Anāgārika (भिक्कु अनागारिक).

From the fifth century CE onwards, the brāhmaṇas (ब्राह्मण) also started making rock-cut shrines in the Deccan and south India, especially at Bādāmī (बादामी), Aihoḷe (ऐहोळ), Ellorā (एल्लोरा), Elephaṇṭā (एलिफेन्टा), Auraṅgābād (औरंगाबाद) and Mamallapuram (ममल्लपुरम्).

Pl. 7 : Façade of Viśvakarmā Caitya (cave no. 10), Ellorā

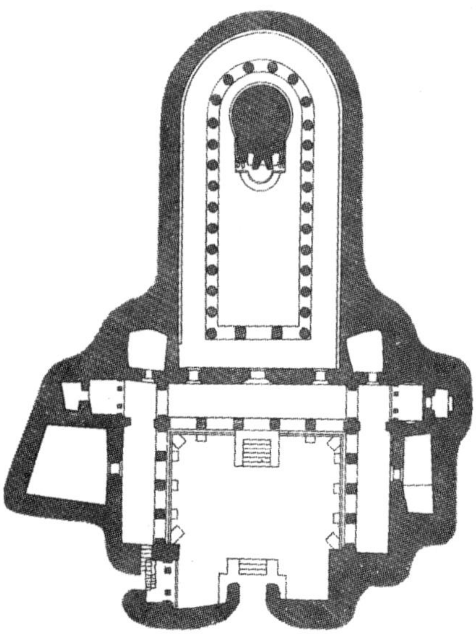

Fig. 12 : Plan of the Viśvakarmā Caitya (Cave No. 10), Ellorā

These shrines flourished under the patronage of the Cāḷukyas (चाळुक्य), the Rāṣṭrakūṭas (राष्ट्रकूट) and the Pallavas (पल्लव). These rock-cut temples yield the story of gradual evolution of the rock-cut architecture in India.

The question as to why the Hindus did not follow the Buddhist and Jaina traditions from the third century or the second century BCE is often asked. It is no great mystery since it can easily be explained from the fact that Hinduism had not encouraged the system of "Monastic Order" or *saṁghārāmas* (संघाराम); it was a temple-based Order of the householders even though wandering mendicants, the *tapasvīs* (तपस्वी) and *munis* (मुनि) were there from the Ṛgvedic (ऋग्वेदिक) times, even Buddha was a *muni*, and he was called so, Śākya-muni (शाक्यमुनि). There were *gurukulas* (गुरुकुल); i.e. households of individual teachers having their own families, but not monasteries for *munis* and *tapasvīs*.

It may be noted that the Buddhists adopted the *vihāra* (विहार) system only when monks said to Buddha that during the four months of rainy season they could not leave the place of temporary stay, they were expected to, and cross the flooded rivers to reach the next village the next day. Buddha, it is said, saw the point and allowed them to live at one place during this period. It was called *varṣāvāsa* (वर्षावास). The *vihāra* was thus meant to be only a temporary abode, strictly for four months in a year belonging to the rainy season. However, with the passage of time this kind of *vihāra*-living became permanent, on round the year basis, particularly for those monks who became old and infirm, to begin with, at least. In fact, a time came when some of these *vihāras* became *mahāvihāras* (महाविहार) where the religious as well as secular teachings were provided on long-term basis.

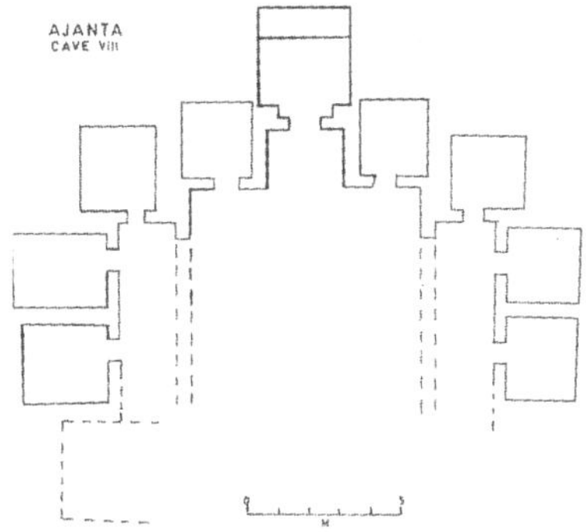

Fig. 13 : Plan of the Hīnayāna Vihāra, Cave no. 8, Ajantā

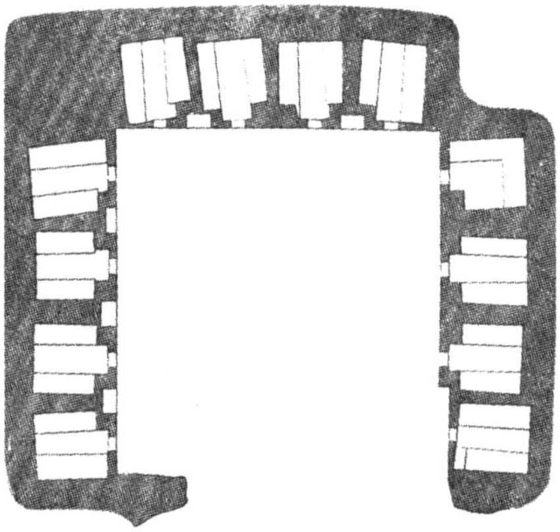

Fig. 14 : Plan of the Hīnayāna Vihāra, Cave no. 12, Ajantā

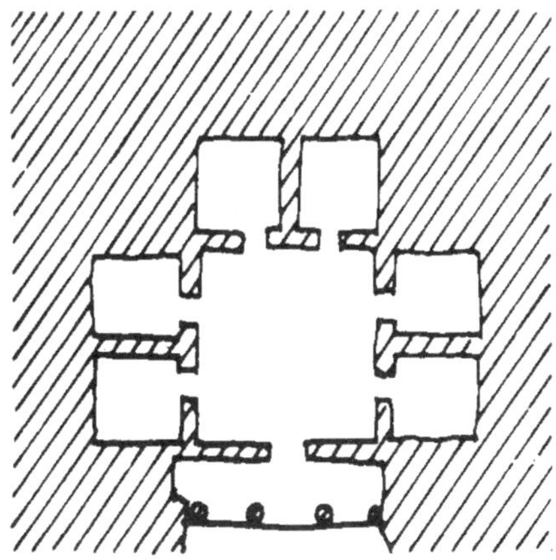

Fig. 15 : Plan of the Hīnayāna Vihāra, Cave no. 13, Ajantā

Cāḷukyan Rock-cut Architecture

The Cāḷukyan (चाळुक्य) architecture generally falls into two main groups: (i) the rock-cut shrines, and (ii) the structural temples belonging to Hinduism, except one. The rock-cut caves are found in the sandstone outcrops of Bādāmī (बादामी) (*Pls.* 8, 9 & 10, *figs.* 16, 17 & 18) and Aihoḷe (ऐहोळ) (*figs.* 19a & 19b). These shrines influenced the later developments in the structural temples in and around Bījāpur (बीजापुर) in Karnataka.

The main components of the Cāḷukyan (चाळुक्य) cave temples were, however, one and the same, i.e. which characterized a structural temple: *mukha-*

maṇḍapa (मुख-मण्डप) (front porch), *mahāmaṇḍapa* (महामण्डप) (main or central hall) and a small, square *garbha-gṛha* (गर्भ-गृह) (sanctum cella) cut deep into the rock. At Bādāmī (बादामी), four such cave shrines are found amongst which Cave no. 4 is a Jaina shrine and the rest are Brāhmanical. Cave no. 3, dedicated to Viṣṇu (विष्णु), was the earliest and largest shrine carved during the reign of the Cāḷukya king Maṅgaleśa (मंगलेश) (CE 578). This cave consists of the *mukha-maṇḍapa*, the *mahāmaṇḍapa*, and the *garbha-gṛha* cut deep into the rear wall. The sanctum contains a *liṅgam* (लिंगम्). This north-facing shrine stands on a

Pl. 8 : Frontal view of Cave 1, Bādāmī

high, well-decorated *adhiṣṭhāna* (अधिष्ठान, base or plinth below the wall). A flight of steps leads to the *mukha-maṇḍapa.* Six pillars and two pilasters adorn the façade. These pillars and pilasters have highly decorated brackets with celestial, human and animal figures. The *poṭikā* (पोटिका, corbel) above them has a massive overhanging *kapota* (कपोत, cornice or eave). Panels of Trivikrama (त्रिविक्रम), Narasiṁha (नरसिंह), Śaṅkaranārāyaṇa (शंकरनारायण), Bhūvarāha (भूवराह), Anantaśayana (अनन्तशयन) and Harihara (हरिहर) are sculpted in a lively style on the walls of the *maṇḍapas* (मण्डप).

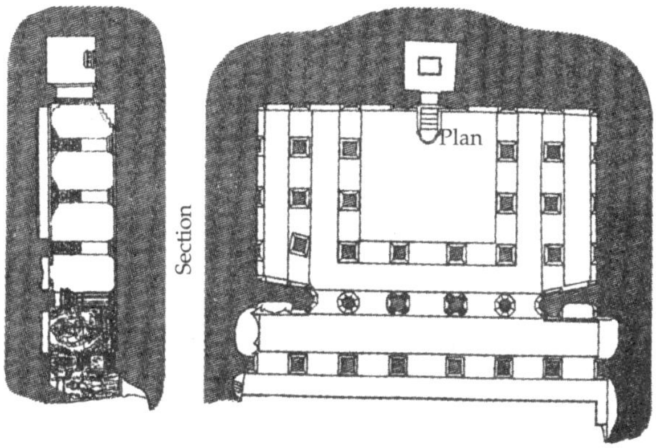

Fig. 16 : Plan and section of the Bādāmī Cave no. 1

The plan of Cave no. 1, dedicated to Śiva (शिव),

Pl. 9 : Frontal view of Cave 2, Bādāmī

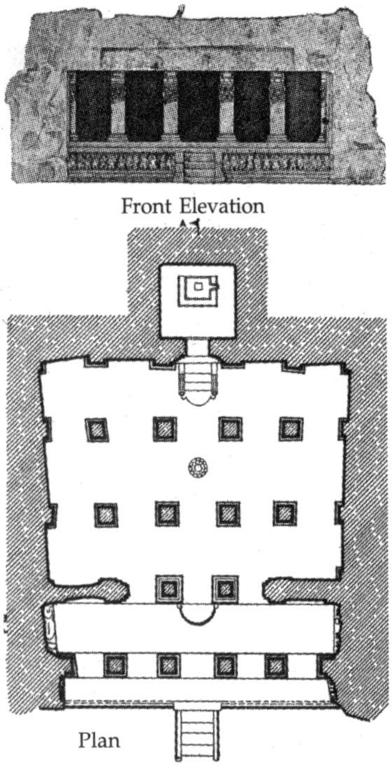

Fig. 17 : Plan and front elevation of the Bādāmī Cave no. 2

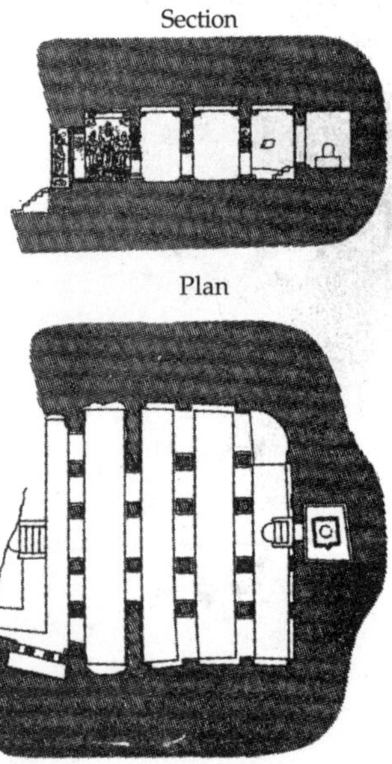

Fig. 18 : Plan and section of the Bādāmī Cave no. 3

is slightly different from that of Cave no. 3. Two rows of four pillars divide the floor into central nave and side aisles. The important carvings in this cave are an 18-armed dancing Śiva (*Pl.* 11), a two-handed Gaṇeśa (गणेश), Mahiṣāsuramardinī (महिषासुरमर्दिनी), Ardhanārīśvara (अर्धनारीश्वर) and Śaṅkaranārāyaṇa (शंकरनारायण). The ceiling is decorated with a serpent motif and other carved figures. Caves no. 2 (Viṣṇu विष्णु) and 4 (Tīrthaṁkara तीर्थंकर) resemble Cave no. 1. Cave no. 2 displays carvings of Anantaśayana (अनन्तशयन), Brahmā (ब्रह्मा), Viṣṇu (विष्णु), Śiva (शिव) and Aṣṭadikpālas अष्टदिक्पाल) on its ceilings. Cave no. 4 portrays an image of Mahāvīra (महावीर) adorning the sanctum. Other carvings here are of Padmāvatī (पद्मावती) and the Tīrthaṁkaras.

There are, however, two rock-cut temples at Aihoḷe (ऐहोळ), one Śaiva (शैव) and the other Jaina. Rāvaṇa (रावण) Phaḍi (फड़ी), the Śiva shrine, is dated to sixth century CE. The temple is approached by a flight of steps, called *sopāna* (सोपान). The façade has two square pillars "supporting" the roof. The temple contains the main *maṇḍapa* (मण्डप), an antechamber and the *garbha-gṛha* (गर्भ-गृह). The sanctum contains a rock-cut Śivaliṅga (शिवलिंग). The side walls are carved with various Hindu deities, including dancing Śiva with his son Gaṇeśa (गणेश), the Seven Divine Mothers (Saptamātṛkās सप्तमातृका), Ardhanārīśvara (अर्धनारीश्वर), Varāha (वराह) form of Viṣṇu, the goddess Durgā (दुर्गा) in the form of Mahiṣāsuramardinī (महिषासुरमर्दिनी), Śiva (शिव) and Pārvatī (पार्वती). There are two chambers on either side of the main *maṇḍapa*. The ceiling of the antechamber depicts Viṣṇu-on-Garuḍa, a central lotus and Indra on his mount, the white elephant named Airāvata (एरावत).

Rock-cut Caves of the Kaḷacuris and the Rāṣṭrakūṭas

Pl. 10 : Frontal view of Cave 3, Bādāmī

The stupendous workmanship of the Ellorā (एल्लोरा) caves with some of the breath-holding huge free-standing rock-cut religious entities of the Kailāsa (कैलास) temple represents the final and yet the most elaborate and mature phase of the rock-cut architecture in India. The caves are cut in the high solid hills of the Charnadarī (छर्नदरी) formation in the Western Ghāṭs (घाट) of the Deccan. The site is about 30 km north-west of Auraṅgābād (औरंगाबाद) town and 80 km south-west of Ajantā (अजन्ता) Caves in Maharashtra. It is significant to note that the Ellorā (एल्लोरा) caves house shrines and temples of Hinduism and Buddhism as well as Jainism and not belonging exclusively to a single religion. This, therefore, presents the best example of Indian spirit of co-existence of different forms of worship and belief systems which originated in the Indian soil. It also breaks the myth created by the Westerners that there was as much rivalry amongst ancient religions in India as between Christianity and Islam. The caves, however, are tentatively datable from the sixth-seventh century to eleventh-twelfth century CE. In total, there are nearly 100 caves in the hill range, out of which 34 caves are known for their exceptional workmanship and artistic creations. Caves 1 to 12 are Buddhist; Caves 13 to 29 are Brāhmanical, and Caves 30 to 34 are Jaina.

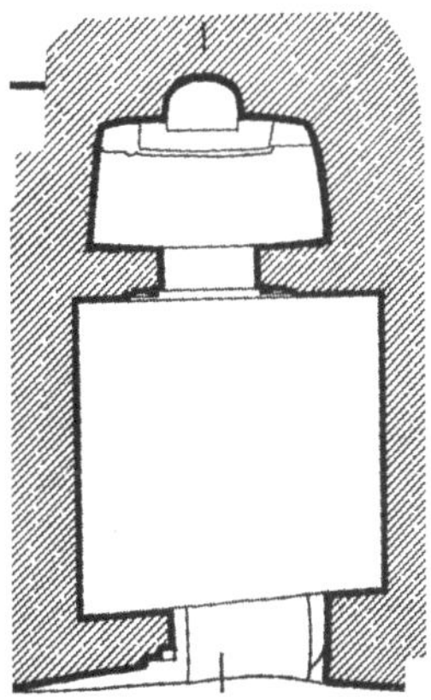

Fig. 19a : Jaina Caves at Aihoḷe

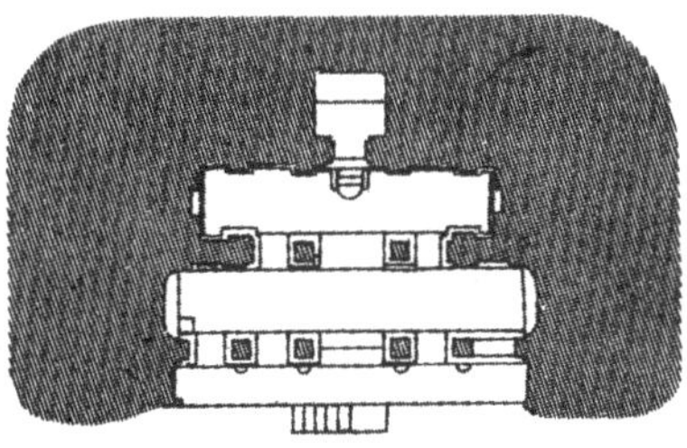

Fig. 19b : Jaina Caves at Aihoḷe

Pl. 11 : Naṭarāja Śiva, Cave 1, Bādāmī

Among the Ellorā caves only one Cave no. 15, has yielded an inscriptional evidence of their date of excavation. Thus, it is securely ascribed to the period of Rāṣṭrakūṭa (राष्ट्रकूट) Dantidurga (दन्तिदुर्ग) (*c.* CE 753-57). According to a copper-plate grant from Barodā (बड़ोदा) (fifth century), the Great Kailāsa temple (Cave 16) at Ellorā was carved under the direction of Kṛṣṇa (कृष्ण) I (*c.* CE 757-83), the successor and uncle of Dantidurga (दन्तिदुर्ग). Apart from the above two inscriptions, all the cave-complexes lack inscriptions of the nature found at other cave-sites in India like that of Ajantā (अजन्ता), Nāsik (नासिक), Kārle (कार्ले), Kanheri (कन्हेरि), etc. Notwithstanding this, the rock-cut architecture at Ellorā (एल्लोरा) had already started prior to the arrival of the Rāṣṭrakūṭas (राष्ट्रकूट). For example, Caves 1 to 10 and Cave 21 have been ascribed on stylistic and sculptural grounds to the period of the Kaḷacuris (कळचुरि) of Mahiṣmatī (महिष्मती). Yādavas (यादव) of Deogiri (देवगिरि) (Daulatābād दौलताबाद) might have influenced the execution of the Jaina rock-cut caves since they were great patrons of Jainism during this period.

KAILĀSA TEMPLE

The west-facing Kailāsa (कैलास) temple (Cave 16) at Ellorā (एल्लोरा) is a huge monolithic temple complex with walled compound (*Pls.* 12 & 13, *fig.* 20). Its axial alignment consists of the entrance gateway, the *mukha-maṇḍapa* (मुख-मण्डप), the oblong *gopuram* (गोपुरम्) with barrel-vault *śikhara* (शिखर), the Nandī Maṇḍapa (नन्दी मण्डप) flanked by pillars, the main pillared hall with porch (*mukha-maṇḍapa*) and balconies and the *garbha-gṛha* (गर्भ-गृह), all of them are resting on a raised rectangular platform in east-west orientation.

The sanctum is surrounded by subsidiary shrines on the main high platform, the *adhiṣṭhāna* (अधिष्ठान). The four-storey central *vimāna* (विमान) with the statues of bulls on the top platform has an octagonal "cupola" type bulbous (*stūpī* स्तूपी) *śikhara* end. The *śālā* (शाला) elements in these *vimāna*s form the characteristic element of Draviḍian temple architecture during later periods, particularly in the Pallava (पल्लव) temples.

Pl. 12 : Kailāsa temple, Ellorā

Pallava Rock-Cut Architecture

The true Draviḍian style of temple architecture starts with the emergence of the Pallavas of Kāñcī (कांची) as a powerful royal house during the second half of the sixth century. It ruled over the Telugu (तेलुगु) and northern parts of Tamil (तमिल) region till the end of ninth century. Unlike the Cāḷukyas (चाळुक्य), the Pallavas used hills of hard rock formations such as granite, gneiss and basalt for carving out their rock-cut as well as structural temples since the soft sandstone outcrops were not available in the Pallava kingdom.

Pl. 13 : Main *śikhara* of the Kailāsa temple, Ellorā

Though the Pallava dynasty has been traced back to third century, its architectural tradition started much later, only from the times of Mahendravarman I (महेन्द्रवर्मन् I) (*c.* CE 580-630), who initiated rock-cut architecture in Tamil Nadu. The first rock-cut cave of Mahendravarman I was the Lakṣitāyatana (लक्षितायतन) Tridevamūrti (त्रिदेवमूर्ति) cave temple at Maṇḍagappaṭṭu (मण्डगपट्टु), hewn out of a granite outcrop (*Pl.* 14). The inscription states that "it was brickless, timberless, metal-less and mortarless abode of Lord Lakṣita (लक्षित), caused to be made by King Vicitracitta

(विचित्रचित्त) for Brahmā (ब्रह्मा), Īśvara (ईश्वर, for Śiva शिव) and Viṣṇu (विष्णु)."

The Pallava rock-cut temples are known as *maṇḍapa* (मण्डप) since these are free-standing small pavilion type pillared halls though embellished with exquisitely carved sculptures. The *maṇḍapa* (मण्डप) is divided into the *mukha-maṇḍapa* (मुख-मण्डप) leading to the *mahāmaṇḍapa* (महामण्डप). However, unlike the rock-cut caves of the Cāḷukyas (चाळुक्य), there is no specially hewn out *garbha-gṛha* (गर्भ-गृह) in the early Pallava cave shrines to house the image of the deity. A shallow niche in the rear wall might have supported painting on stucco for worship since there is no rock-cut image here.

The façade of the *mukha-maṇḍapa* of these temples contains equal-spaced pillars, four, six or

Pl. 14 : Lakṣitāyatana cave temple, Mahendra style, Mandagapaṭṭu, South Arcot District

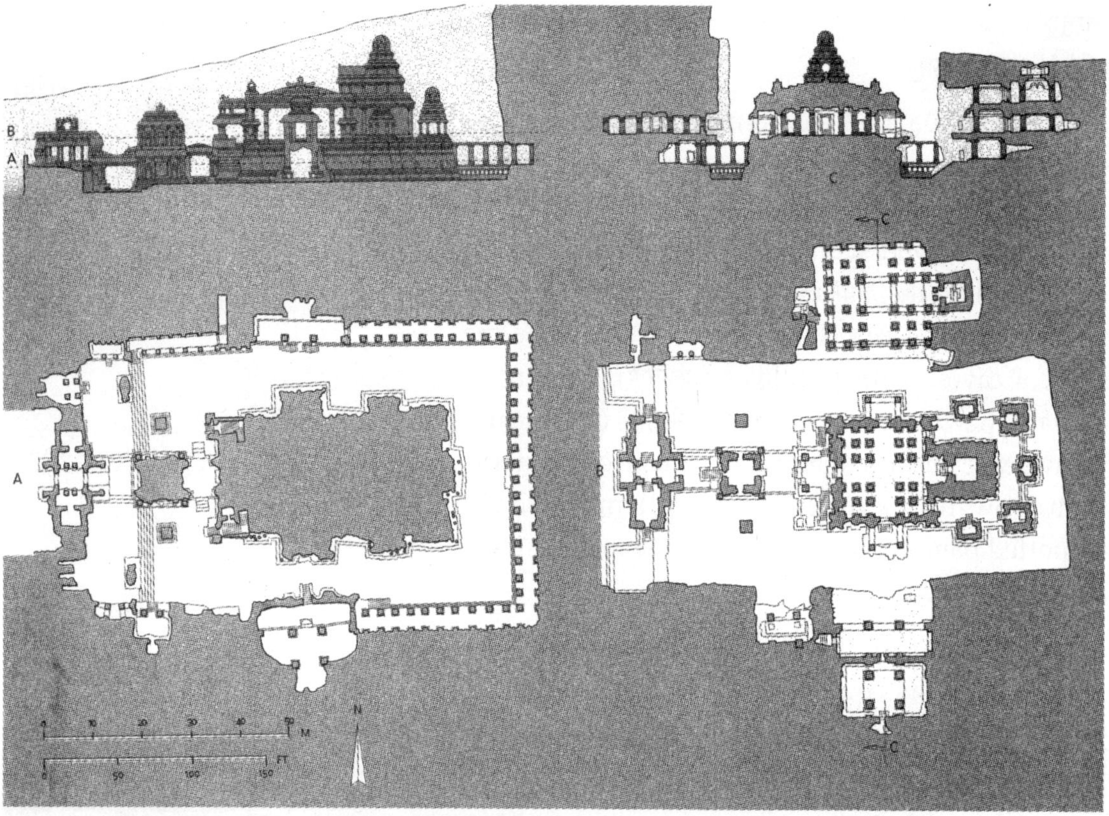

Fig. 20 : Plan of the Kailāsa temple, Ellorā

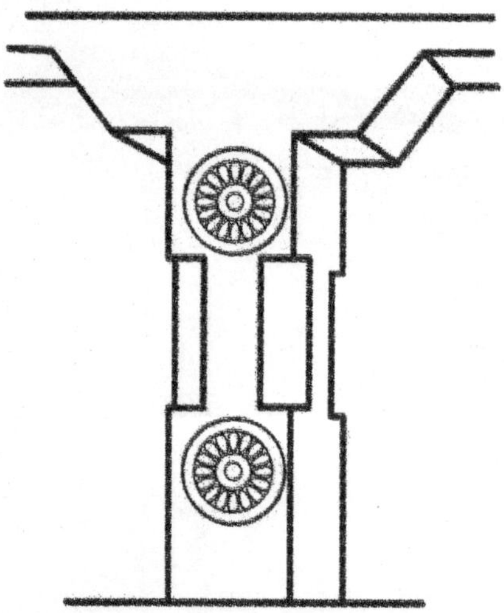

Fig. 21a : Mahendra-style pillars

eight in number, and terminating with pilasters at both ends. The *mukha–maṇḍapa* and *mahāmaṇḍapa* are delineated by a row of pillars. If there are no pillars marking the separation between the *mukha-maṇḍapa* and the *mahāmaṇḍapa,* their varying floor levels or differences in the heights of roofs mark their identity.

Unlike the pillars of the Cāḷukyan caves, the *maṇḍapa* pillars of the Pallavas are divided into three parts: square *sadūrams* (सदूरम्) at the top and bottom, with an octagonal (eight-sided) section, called *kaṭṭu* (कट्टु), in the middle (*fig.* 21a). The *sadūrams* are generally decorated with lotus medallions. However, in the Lalitāṅkura Pallaveśvara Maṇḍapa (ललितांकुर पल्लेश्वर मण्डप) at Tiruchirappalli (तिरुचिरापल्लि), various other motifs such as *gaja* (गज), *makara* (मकर), *kinnara* (किन्नर) and creepers are also seen in the medallions. In many examples the massive *poṭikā* (पोटिका) (corbel) above the pillars are no longer angular, they are curved and carved with a central *paṭṭa* (पट्ट) (flat median band) flanked by a series of wavy (*taraṅga* तरंग) ornamentation with multiple folds (*fig.* 21b). These early caves do not exhibit a developed *prastara* (प्रस्तर) (entablature or parapet wall) and the *kapota* (कपोत) (cornice or eave). To indicate the presence of *kapota* in the parapet, the architects just cut a straight line deep into the rock. Incidentally, in structural temples, the projecting *kapota* is an integral part of the entablature because it prevents the seepage of water during the rainy seasons.

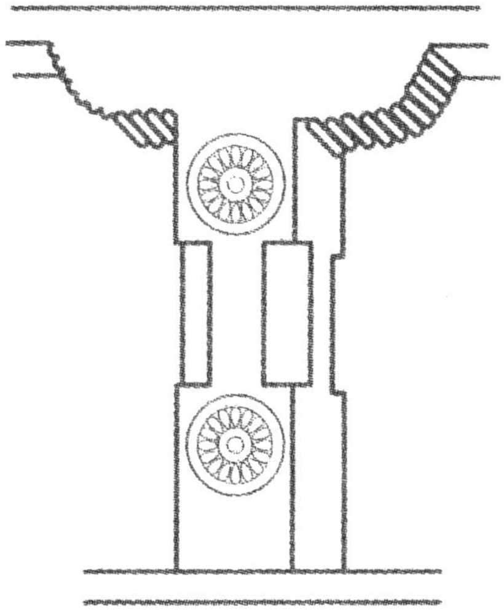

Fig. 21b : Mahendra-style pillars

The early Mahendra (महेन्द्र) style caves were simple and sculptural representations were very few. For example, generally two *dvārapāla*s (द्वारपाल) or door-guards stood at either end of the façade, while in the later ones they also flanked the sanctum, as in the Viṣṇu (विष्णु) cave temple at Mamandur (ममन्दुर). However, none of the cave-temples of the Mahendra style yields sculptures of deities consecrated in the supposed-to-be *garbha-gṛha* (गर्भ-गृह) area.

Post-Mahendra Style Rock-Cut Temples

The post-Mahendra period also witnessed rock-cut activities, but with a slightly modified form, though the general plan and lay-out remained the same as before. During this period the sanctum is more elaborately carved out. Unlike the Mahendra style pillars, the pillars of this period are rectangular, tall and more slender (*fig.* 21c). The façade was provided with two pillars with wider spaces between them

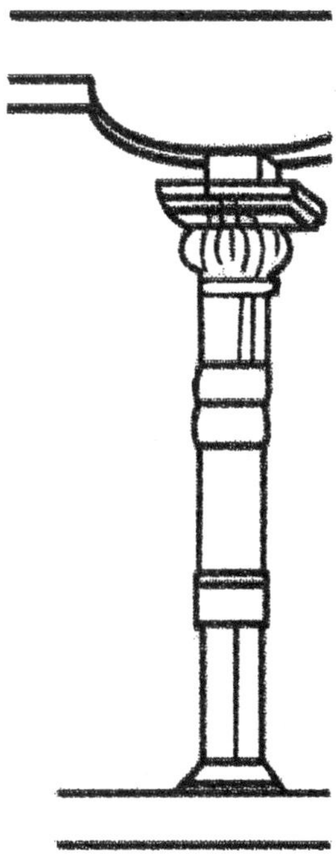

Fig. 21c : Rājasiṁha-style pillar

Pl. 15 : Varāha Maṇḍapam, Mamalla style, Mamallapuram

which allowed better visibility of the interior from outside (*Pl.* 15). The representation of Somaskanda (सोमस्कन्द = Śiva शिव along with Skanda स्कन्द) began to appear for the first time during this period. In addition to these, the cave-temples of this period were profusely decorated with relief sculptures and other ornamental elements.

Post-Mahendra period also witnessed the emergence of free-standing monolithic shrines known as *rathas* (रथ). It was initiated by Mahendra's successor Narasiṁhavarman (नरसिंहवर्मन) I Mamalla (ममल्ल) (CE 630-68) in his newly built capital of Mamallapuram (ममल्लपुरम्).

ELEVATION OF CAVE-TEMPLES

The *maṇḍapa* (मण्डप) of Mamalla style has three *aṅgas* (अंग, parts): (1) *adhiṣṭhāna* (अधिष्ठान, in this context, the bottom-most base of the monolithic structure which was carved out from the same rock) with or without mouldings, (2) *kuḍya-stambha* (कुड्य-स्तम्भ, pilasters) with their capitals, and (3) *prastara* (प्रस्तर, entablature or parapet encompassing the cornice which is protective and decorative). The *prastara* contains a developed *kapota* (कपोत, cornice/eave/sun-shade) decorated with *kuḍu* (कुडु, horseshoe-shaped arches) motifs. Above it runs a line of miniature decorative *śālās* (शाला), oblong in plan with a barrel-vaulted (half-cylindrical shaped) roof. In later temples, this row of *śālās* terminates at either end with decorative miniature *kūṭas* (कूट), square in plan with a domical roof. All these elements, in the round, together called *hāra* (हार), i.e. garland since *kūṭas* (कूट), *śālās* (शाला) and *kūṭas* form a long chain decorating the parapet. The *garbha-gṛha* (गार्भ-गृह) tends to be more centrally placed. The cave shrine was provided with the *sopāna* (सोपान, staircase) in front, starting from the ground level and reaching the top of the *adhiṣṭhāna* (अधिष्ठान) or plinth on which stood the temple proper. The well-planned elevation of a temple of this style and elaborate decorations made the structure extremely pleasing to behold.

PILLARS

The pillars are taller and more slender than those of

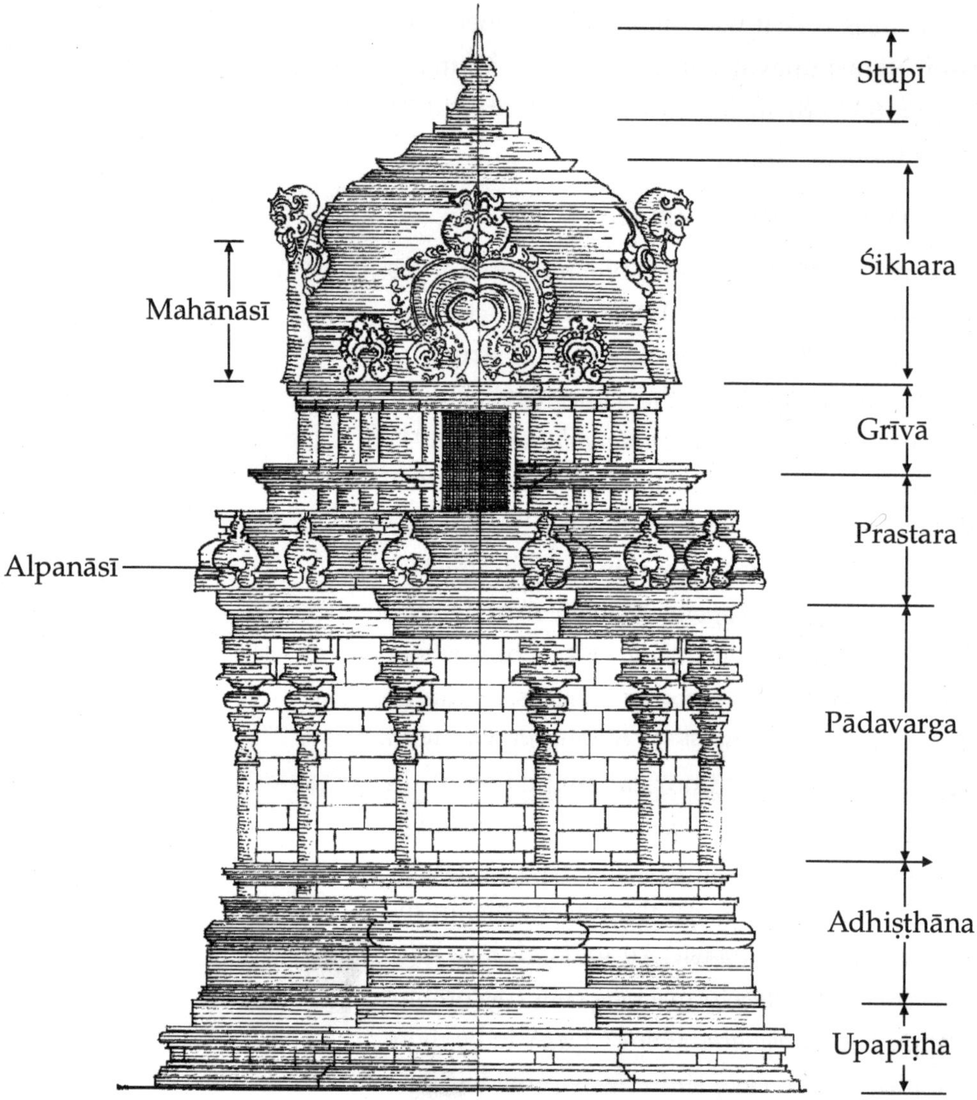

Fig. 22 : Elevation of the monolithic Ratha
Pallava style

the earlier times. In section they are circular, octagonal or fluted. Their bases resemble crouching *vyāli*s (व्यालि, stylized mythical lions) which is a characteristic feature of the Mamalla (ममल्ल) style temples. There are various elements decorating the pillar. These are *mālāsthāna* (मालास्थान, loops of garlands), *padmabandha* (पद्मबन्ध, lotus petals band), *kalaśa* (कलश, vase), *tadi* (तदि, saucer-shaped moulding), *kumbha* (कुम्भ, bulbous member representing water-pitcher), *pali* (पलि, resembling a lotus but without any scalloped petals) and the *phalaka* (फलक, abacus or basal stone-tablet). On the *phalaka* rests *poṭikā* (पोटिका, boat-shaped bracket) with *taraṅga* (तंरग, wavy or corrugated) ornamentation, and a *paṭṭa* (पट्ट, flat median band). The *paṭṭa* was decorated with creepers. Undoubtedly, architectural elaboration resulted in the better creation of artistic elements also.

Monolithic Rathas

The Pallava *rathas* (पल्लव रथ) are free-standing monolithic (single stone) rock-cut temples (*fig.* 22). These were chiselled out of the large hard granite and gneiss outcrops at the coastal site of Mamallapuram (ममल्लपुरम्), also known as Mahābalipuram (महाबलिपुरम्) (*Pls.* 16, 17, 18, 19, 20, & 21). They consist of a small *mukha-maṇḍapa* (मुखा-मण्डप) in front of the sanctum. The *ratha* (रथ) may be either single-

Pl. 16 : Dharmarāja Ratha, Kuṭina-śikhara, Mamallapuram

Pl. 17 : Bhīma Ratha, Sala-śikhara, Mamallapuram

storeyed or multi-storeyed *vimāna* (विमान). The single-storeyed (*ekatala vimāna,* एकतल विमान) (also called *alpavimāna* (अल्पविमान), *alp* = small, and *vimāna* = temple-tower; or *ṣaḍaṅgavimāna,* षडंगविमान) has six parts (*ṣadaṅga* (षडंग), *ṣaḍa* = six and *aṅga* = parts) from base to top, namely the *adhiṣṭhāna* (अधिष्ठान, bottom-most base/plinth), *bhitti* (भित्ति, wall), *prastara* (प्रस्तर, entablature), *grīvā* (ग्रीवा, neck), *śikhara* (शिखर, rising spire), and the *stūpī* (स्तूपी, finial) crowning the top of the *śikhara*.

The second form of *vimāna* is *dvitala* (द्वितल) (two-storeyed: *dvi* = two; *tala* = floor or storey) each one with *hāra* (हार) elements decorating the parapet wall or the *prastara,* such as *śālā* (शाला), *kūṭa* (कूट) and *pañjara* (पञ्जर) (*fig.* 23). Like *śālā* and *kūṭa,* the *pañjara* or *nīḍa* (नीड, literally cage) is also a miniature parapet shrine which is apsidal in plan. The *kūṭas*, placed at the corners, are square in plan with a domical roof,

Pl. 18 : Arjuna Ratha, Mamallapuram

round but faceted, and crowned by a single *stūpī* (finial of lotus bud-like form). Such *śikhara* with domical roof is known as *kuṭina-śikhara* (कुटिन-शिखर). The *śālā* is elongated in form with barrel-vaulted roof surmounted by a row of *stūpīs*. This type of wagon-vaulted *śikhara* is known as *śālā-śikhara*. The apsidal-ended *pañjara* appears between *śālās*, or *kūṭas* and *śālās*. The different elements of *hara* are interconnected by *hārāntara* (हारान्तर) (the recession between *kūṭa* कूट and *śālā* शाला). A *kṣudranāsikā* (क्षुद्रनासिका) (or a small nose like element or arched *kuḍu* (कुडु) motif projects from the middle of the *hārāntara*.

Pl. 19 : Nakula Ratha, Mamallapuram

Besides the *ekatala* (एकतल, single storeyed) and *dvitala* (द्वितल, two storeyed) *vimānas* (विमान), there are also *tritala* (त्रितल) and *catuṣtala* (चतुष्तल) (three- and four-storeyed) *vimānas*. These are known as *jāti* (जाति) *vimānas*. The *vimānas* with five or more *talas* (तल) are known as *mukhya* (मुख्य, main) *vimānas*. Every additional storey will have a *hāra* (हार) inserted between the *prastara* (प्रस्तर, entablature/parapet wall) and the *grīvā* (ग्रीवा, clerestory neck), which is the most characteristic feature of the Draviḍian order of temples.

Pl. 20 : Sahadeva Ratha, Mamallapuram

The size of each superimposed storey is smaller than the lower one. This arrangement provides more stability and durability to the rising as well as tapering superstructure. Thus, the *vimāna* or *śikhara* (शिखर) of the south Indian temple is a single- or multi-storeyed structure of successively diminishing sizes meant not only to provide height of a tapering mountain to the temple but also strength to the structure as a whole.

Rock-cut Temples of the Pāṇḍyas

Following the tradition of the Pallavas (पल्लव), the Pāṇḍyas of Madurai (मदुरै) started rock-cut architecture towards the end of the seventh century. On the basis of an inscription found on the outer rock wall, one of the earliest rock-cut shrines of the Pāṇḍyas, the Śrī Karpaga Vināyakar temple (श्री कर्पग विनायकर्) at Pillaiyarpaṭṭi (पिल्लेयर्पट्टी) in Śivagaṅgai (शिवगंगइ) district near

Karaikuḍī (करैकुडी) is assignable to the first quarter of the seventh century CE. Since then, the cave has been modified by different rulers. Other Pāṇḍya (पाण्ड्य) caves, datable to seventh-eighth century, are the Śiva

Pl. 21 : Draupadī Ratha, Mamallapuram

(शिव) cave shrine at Malaiyadikurichi (मलैयदिकुरिचि) (*Pl.* 22); the Narasiṁha (नरसिंह) cave at Anāmalai (अनामलइ) and the Subrahmaṇya (सुब्रह्मण्य) cave at Tirupparankunram (तिरुप्परंकुंरम्). The Pāṇḍya cave

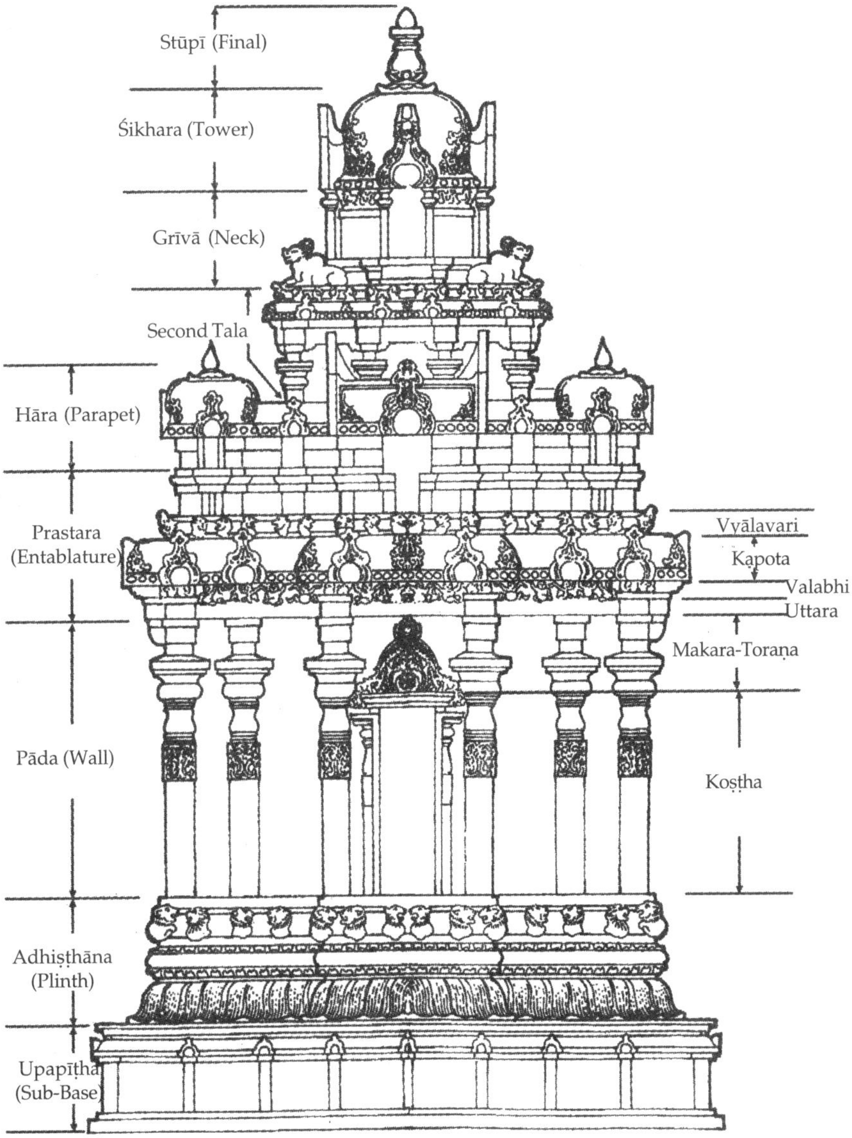

Fig. 23 : Architectural components of the Dvī-tala Vimāna, Pallava style

Pl. 22 : Śiva rock-cut temple, Pāṇḍya style, Malayadikkurichi, Tirunelveli

Pl. 23 : Unfinished Veṭṭuvankoil cave, Pāṇḍya style, Kalugumalai, Tirunelveli

shrines are also found at Tiruttaṅgal (तिरुतंगल), Piranmalai (पिरन्मलइ), Kuḍumiyamalai (कुडुमियमलइ) and Sittannavasal (सित्तन्नवसल).

The unfinished rock-cut shrine of Vettuvankoil (वेत्तुवंकोइल) at Kalugumalai (कलुगुमलइ), datable to the eighth century, provides some glimpses of the Pāṇḍya rock-cutting technique (*Pl.* 23). The quarrying was started from top to bottom shaping initially the *kuṭina-śikhara* (कुटिन-शिखर) with its ornamentation. However, the bottom of this shrine is left unfinished because of some unknown reasons. The dome-shaped *śikhara* has six faces and each face is carved with a *kuḍu* (कुडु) arch.

The Pāṇḍya caves followed the Pallava (पल्लव) scheme, i.e. the *garbha-gṛha* (गर्भ-गृह) fronted by the pillared *maṇḍapa*s (मण्डप). Unlike the Pallava rock-cut shrines, the stone images of the presiding deities were consecrated in the *garbha-gṛha* of the Pāṇḍya rock-cut caves. Following the Cāḷukyan (चाळुक्य) tradition, the Pāṇḍyas also carved the Śivaliṅga (शिवलिंग) and the Nandī (नन्दी) out of living rock. The *maṇḍapa* in front of the *garbha-gṛha* is provided with pillars topped by the cushion capitals. The *poṭikā* (पोटिका) of the pillars is generally plain while in the Pallava caves it is highly ornate.

2

Gupta Temples

Pl. 24 : Temple no. 17, Sāñcī

The Gupta (गुप्त) Age (c. 350–600 CE) witnessed new experimentations in the construction of structural temples by means of dressed stones in dry stone masonry, i.e. without the use of mortar. In this technique, blocks of stone were joined together by tenon-and-groove method, i.e. the tenon of one block of stone is inserted in the hole created in the other. Some of the famous Gupta structural temples in stone are Temple number 17 (Buddhist) at Sāñcī (सांची) (*Pl.* 24, *fig.* 24), the Kaṅkālī Devī (कंकाली देवी) at Tigawā (तिगवा) (*Pl.* 25, *fig.* 25), the temples of Viṣṇu (विष्णु) and Varāha (वराह) at Eraṇ (एरण्) (*figs.* 26 & 27) and the Pārvatī (पार्वती) temple at Nacanā-Kuṭhāra (नचना-कुठार) (*Pl.* 26, *fig.* 28), all in Madhya Pradesh. The Daśāvatāra (दशावतार) temple at Deogaṛh (देवगढ़) in Distt. Jhansi, Uttar Pradesh (*Pl.* 27, *fig.* 29), the Śiva (शिव) temple at Bhūmarā (भूमरा) in Madhya Pradesh (*Pl.* 28, *fig.* 30) and the brick temples at Bhītargāon (भीतरगांव) (*Pl.* 29, *fig.* 31) and Bhītarī (भीतरी) (U.P.) and the Viṣṇu Temple at Sirpur (सिरपुर) in Chhatisgarh (छत्तीसगढ़) (*Pl.* 30, *fig.* 32) are some of the evolved Gupta temples.

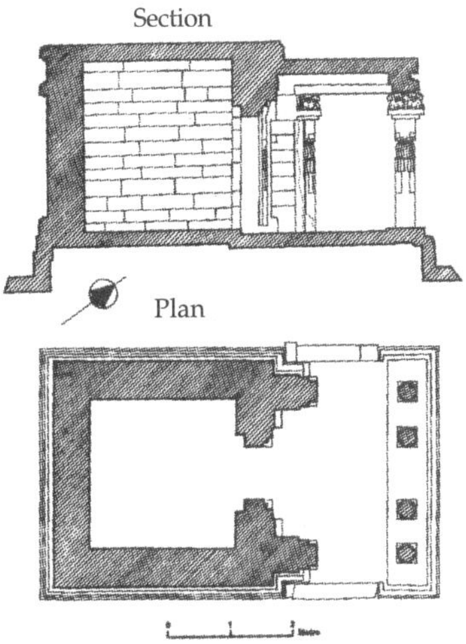

Fig. 24 : Plan of Temple no. 17, Sāñcī

Pl. 25 : Kaṅkālī Devī temple, Tigawa

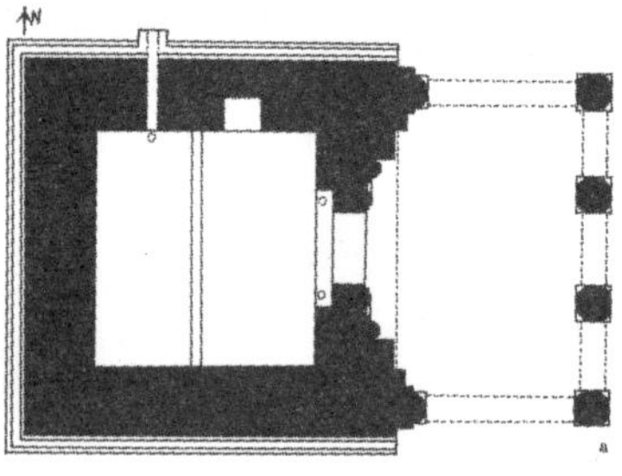

Fig. 25 : Plan of the Kaṅkālī Devī temple, Tigawa

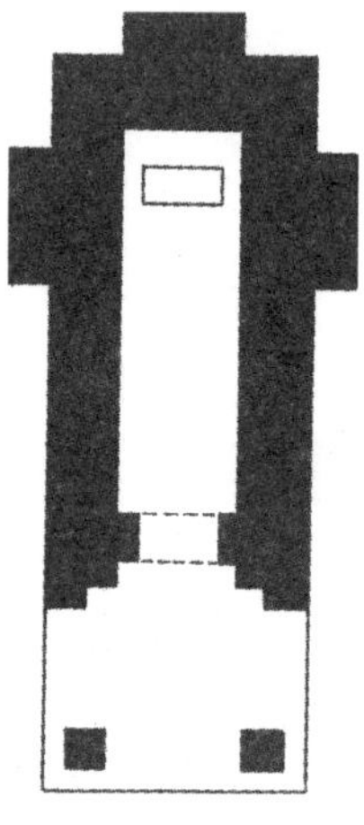

Fig. 26 : Plan of the Viṣṇu temple, Eraṇ

The basic plan of the structural temple, which became the standard for the temples in India for all time to come also emerged during this period. As a result, a simple square cella with flat roof fronted by a low-pillared porch or *maṇḍapa* (मण्डप) (for example, Sāñcī Temple 17), represented the beginning of new structural temple architecture in India. This two-unit plan, it may be noted, was the product of the two basic needs of the devotee, the *bhakta* (भक्त) of all India-born religions — the cella exclusively for the deity, and a porch for the devotees. Further, and this is equally important, both the units — the former called *garbha-gṛha* (गर्भ-गृह) and the latter *maṇḍapa* have necessarily to be located in one and same axis since the devotee should have the *darśana* (दर्शन) or visibility of his god standing right in his front. The sanctum had no ventilation other than a door in the front wall. Later, a covered *pradakṣiṇā-patha* (प्रदक्षिणापथ) was added to the *garbha-gṛha* (गर्भ-गृह) for the devotees to go round it. As time passed, the *śikhara* (शिखर) was raised over the roof. It was a great innovation that added imposing verticality to the otherwise modest house-like structure. Many decorative motifs like goblins, couples, flying angels, door-keepers, nymphs (*apsaras*es अप्सरस्), etc., appeared on the walls, pillars, door-jambs, lintels and ceiling of the *śikhara* as well as the *maṇḍapa* (मण्डप). In other words, attention was now also paid to the embellishment of the structure to create the right type of ambience, religious and spiritual, for the devotees. It also helped in the growth of the number of the devotees visiting the temples. The needs also became important for the architects. They therefore, decided to add a vestibule or *antarāla* (अन्तराल) between the *garbha-gṛha* and the *maṇḍapa*. Later, this *maṇḍapa* became quite large to accommodate more people. It was then called *mahāmaṇḍapa* (महामण्डप). But to enter it directly from the outside was not considered the right thing to do. So they first added a small *maṇḍapa* and called it *ardha-maṇḍapa* (अर्ध-मण्डप). Later, a small porch was also added to it. They called it *mukha-maṇḍapa* (मुख-मण्डप). The outer surface was, however, much more decorated.

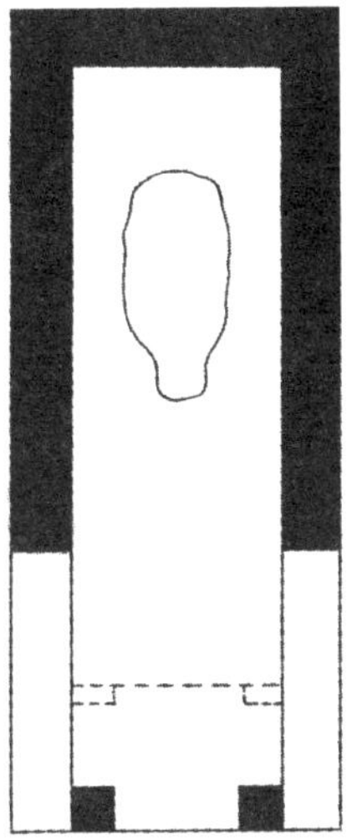

Fig. 27 : Plan of the Varāha temple, Eraṇ

The pillars in front of the porch were fashioned in the shape in which they were wider at the centre and narrow at the sides. The lower part of the pillar is plain and square which is succeeded by octagonal and then sixteen-sided shaft. On top of the pillar appeared a new form of capital known as "vase capital" (*pūrṇa-kalaśa* पूर्ण-कलश) which replaced the so-called "bell-capital," or "inverted lotus" of the Mauryan (मौर्य) tradition although the Mauryas used this form exclusively in their free-standing pillars. The

Pl. 26 : Ruined Pārvatī temple, Nachna-Kuthara

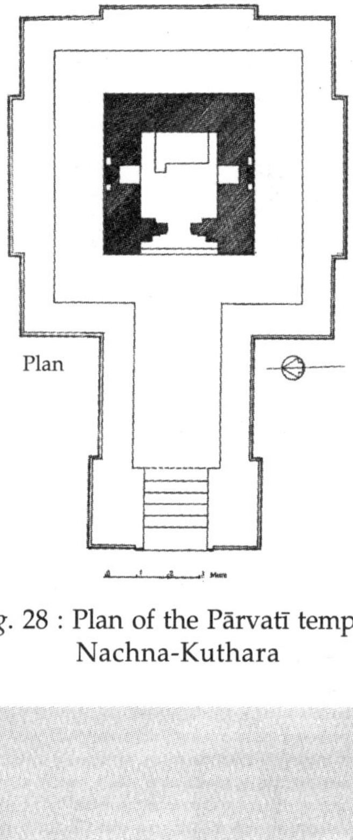

Fig. 28 : Plan of the Pārvatī temple, Nachna-Kuthara

fact that the Guptas (गुप्त) were also fascinated by this motif is attested by the examples of the four structural pillars of the *maṇḍapa* of Temple 17 at Sāñcī. However, at the Kaṅkālī Devī (कंकाली देवी) one can notice the initial form of "vase capital" which is also typical Gupta capital crowning structural pillars. The capital supported a massive block of stone serving the function of the abacus which in turn carried lion finials. The "Vase" or *pūrṇa-kalaśa* (pot of plenty) with foliage also became the basal decoration of the structural pillars of the Gupta (गुप्त) temples as at Khoh (खोह). However, in the free-standing pillars the Guptas kept the Mauryan (मौर्य) tradition and not replaced it by vase capital as is proved from the example located at Bhītarī (भीतरी) in District Gazipur, U.P., erected by King Kumāragupta (कुमारगुप्त).

Among the earliest Gupta shrines Temple 17 at Sāñcī (सांची) shows the beginning of the Gupta tradition of temple building in ashlar or dressed stone masonry. The *garbha-gṛha* (गर्भ-गृह) is square, plain and devoid of any decoration from inside as well as outside. It is fronted by a pillared porch or *maṇḍapa* (मण्डप) raised separately and joined with the cella on a plain low platform or *adhiṣṭhāna* (अधिष्ठान) approached by a couple of steps, or *sopāna* (सोपान). The walls of the cella are

Pl. 27 : Daśāvatāra temple, Deogarh

built of dressed stone without any mortar. Provision of water spouts on top of the flat roof helped prevent water seepage during the monsoons. The elevation of the top portion of the cella is decorated by a plain band or moulding (*bandha* बन्ध) as well as slightly projecting band of the cornice, called *kapota-vallī* (कपोत-वल्ली) or resting-place for the birds.

The *maṇḍapa* in front of the cella is rectangular. It has four pillars with necessarily wider intercolumnation space in the centre than between the side pillars. Such pillar arrangement provided ample space to have a *darśana* (दर्शन) of the enshrined deity without disturbing the visibility of the interior of the sanctum. The pillars are square at the base, followed by octagonal and then sixteen-sided sections, and culminated in an "inverted lotus" capital. It is finally topped by a plain block of stone which served as the abacus or *pīṭha* (पीठ) for the lion finial.

The Kaṅkālī Devī (कंकाली देवी) temple at Tigawā (तिगवा) represents the next stage of Gupta architecture. It presents the earliest known evidence of vase-like

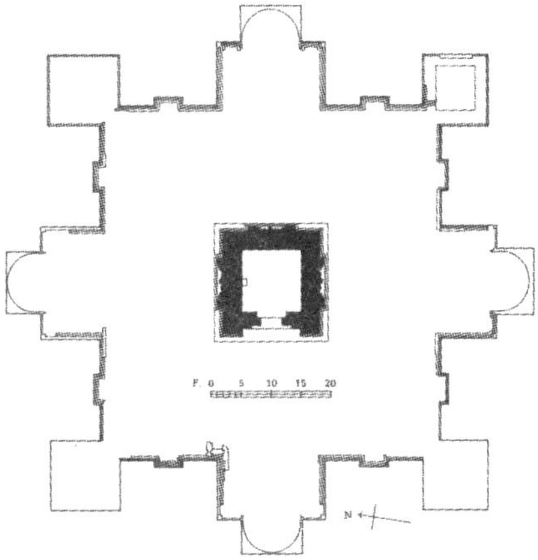

Fig. 29 : Plan of the Daśāvatāra temple, Deogaṛh

Pl. 28 : Ruined Śiva temple, Bhumara

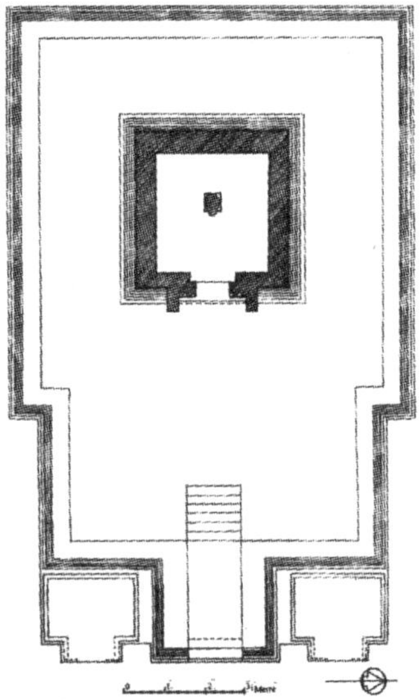

Fig. 30 : Plan of the Śiva temple, Bhumara

capital called *pūrṇa-kalaśa* (पूर्ण-कलश). On top of the capital is a massive abacus with lion as the crowning animal, certainly borrowed from the Mauryan examples at Sāranāth (सारनाथ), Sāñcī (सांची), Vaiśālī (वैशाली), etc. The lintel on top of the doorway of the sanctum is carved with river goddesses — Gaṅgā (गंगा) on *makara* (मकर, crocodile) and Yamunā (यमुना) on *kūrma* (कूर्म, tortoise). As usual, the *maṇḍapa* (मण्डप) in front of the cella which is rectangular, has four pillars spanning wider space at the centre and narrow at the sides. Similar to the pillars of the Temple 17, each pillar base of the Tigawā (तिगवा) temple is square while the shaft is many-sided. Significantly, a simple podium has been provided to the temple for making the circumambulation or *pradakṣiṇā* (प्रदक्षिणा) of the sanctum possible.

Pl. 29 : Brick temple, Bhītargāon

In course of time, more decorative elements in terms of religious motifs and icons began to appear on the entrance, walls, ceilings and pillars of the temples. The river goddesses started appearing at the base of the door (*dvāra*, द्वार). More and more divine and semi-divine figures such as *gaṇas* (गण, dwarfs), *mithunas* (मिथुन, amorous couples), flying *gandharvas* and *vidyādharas* (गंधर्व एवं विद्याधर, celestials), and *dvārapalas* (द्वारपाल, door-keepers) were added to adorn the entrance of the temples. The middle of the lintel above the doorway carried a stone panel called *lalāṭa-bimba* (ललाट-बिम्ब) which depicted the deity consecrated in the sanctum. Sometimes a deity directly related to the main enshrined deity may appear in the *lalāṭa–bimba*. For example, a Śiva (शिव) temple may have Gaṇeśa (गणेश) here.

Some of the fifth-century temples of Udayagiri (उदयगिरि) and neighbouring areas exhibit some new developments in architecture. For example, the Viṣṇu (विष्णु) temple at Eraṇ (एरण्) gives the initial evidence of central projections called *bhadra* (भद्र) one each on the three sides of the *garbha-gṛha* (गर्भ-गृह). A broad podium provides for circumambulation, as in the Kaṅkālī Devī (कंकाली देवी) at Tigawā (तिगवा).

Provision of a podium or open platform large enough for circumambulation has been later on developed into a well defined covered *pradakṣiṇāpatha* (प्रदक्षिणापथ, circumambulatory passage) as in the Pārvatī (पार्वती) temple at Nacanā-Kuṭhāra (नचना-कुठार), two nearby villages, in the Pannā (पन्ना) district of Madhya Pradesh. The temple stands on a platform (*adhiṣṭhāna* अधिष्ठान) and is fronted by a pillared *maṇḍapa* (मण्डप). A flight of steps (*sopāna*, सोपान) leads to the temple. When some of the inherent limitations of the closed temple architecture were realised lattice (*jālī*, जाली) windows were created on each outer wall. They provide enough air and lighting to the interior. The walls of the *garbha-gṛha* (गर्भ-गृह) were also provided such artistic openings. Significantly, in this temple an extra cella over the main *garbha-gṛha* was added. It appears to have influenced the emergence of fully-developed *śikhara*s (शिखर) during later times since this device provided imposing vertically to the upper part of the main shrine. But certainly it was not as simple as observed

Fig. 31 : Elevation of the ruined brick temple, Bhumara

Pl. 30 : Viṣṇu temple, Sirpur

here, it had to pass through some experimentations of different kinds in architectural designing.

The culmination of the early Gupta (गुप्त) temple architecture is witnessed in the Daśāvatāra (दशावतार) temple at Deogaṛh (देवगढ़) in the Jhansi district, Uttar Pradesh, tentatively dated to late fifth or early sixth century CE. This is a *pañcāyatana* (पञ्चायतन) temple complex in which the main central shrine is surrounded by four subsidiary shrines at its four corners. However, in this temple the four subsidiary shrines were not erected on the main platform of the central shrine. The central shrine stands on a high, broad platform called the *piṣṭa* (पिष्ट). The platform can be reached with a flight of steps from each of the four cardinal sides — east, west, north and south. The vertical face of the platform is beautifully decorated with sculptures in relief and arranged in panels, depicting scenes related to the stories from the life of Rāma (राम) and Kṛṣṇa (कृष्ण).

The main central temple is of square plan.

However, this temple is known for some other reason. It is the earliest known example of a Hindu temple which has true *śikhara* (शिखर) over the sanctum, even though much of it is now gone. The flat-roofed porticos projecting from each side of the temple wall, however, give the impression of the advent of a *triratha* (त्रिरथ) or three-storeyed type *śikhara*. The entrance portal or the *dvāra* (द्वार) of the sanctum is profusely decorated with the images of the river goddesses Gaṅgā (गङ्गा) and Yamunā (यमुना), *dvārapāla*s (द्वारपाल, door-guards), *pūrṇa-kalaśa*s (पूर्ण-कलश, full vases) over the pilasters, *caitya* windows, demi-gods, dwarfs, lion heads and floral scrolls. The centre of the lintel has a square stone panel, the *lalāṭa-bimba* (ललाट-बिम्ब), depicting Viṣṇu enthroned on Ananta Nāga (अनन्त नाग), the primordial serpent. This temple is also known for some of the most equisitively carved panels in the recesses framed in pilasters and architraves and created on the plain walls of the sanctum. One panel depicts Śeṣaśāyī Viṣṇu (शेषशायी विष्णु), one *Gajendramokṣa* (गजेन्द्रमोक्ष) theme and the third Penance of Nara (नर) and Nārāyaṇa (नारायण). All the three panels have been hailed in the world of Indian art as the best works of art from the point of view of artistic creations, besides providing the earliest examples of the Rāma (राम) theme — the body-parts are absolutely proportionate, light in visual weight and exhibiting animation. The figures are presented in different postures, the hand-gestures (*mudrā*s, मुद्रा) are iconographically perfect and gaits of images swift and supple. The hands and legs are soft and shining like the inner trunk of the banana plants. The faces are oval, the cheeks and lips full and the eyes are like the lotus-buds — sharply defined and partially closed.

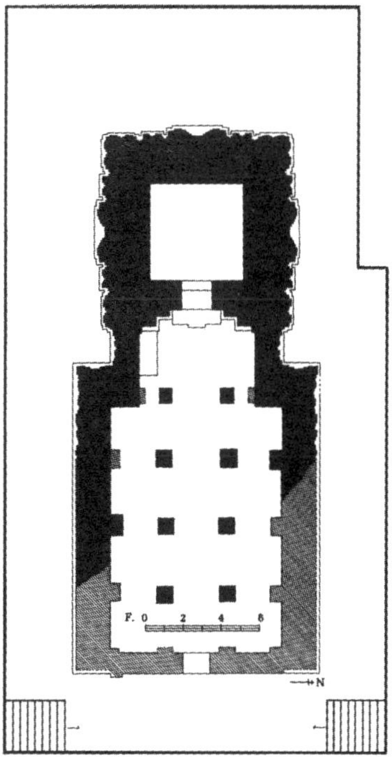

Fig. 32 : Plan of the Lakṣmaṇa/Viṣṇu temple, Sirpur

The Gupta (गुप्त) Age also witnessed the erection of temples made of burnt bricks. The best one is located at Bhītargāon (भीतरगांव) in Kanpur district of Uttar Pradesh. The temple stands on an *adhiṣṭhāna* (अधिष्ठान). It has a *triratha* (त्रिरथ) plan, with large projections on all sides of the *śikhara* (शिखर). The gateway of the temple has a round arch made of bricks placed edge to edge. Such round arches without the use of a central keystone is a marvel of the Hindu architectural achievements. The temple wall is decorated with recessed panels of alternating pilasters with arches and terracotta panels with or without images. One of the terracotta panels depicts a *Rāmāyaṇa* (रामायण) story involving Rāma (राम), Sītā (सीता) and Kākāsura (काकासुर), the son of Indra.

The temple has a double cornice enclosing long recesses decorated with friezes of figurative sculptures over which rises *śikhara* in receding tiers of brickwork. The *śikhara* is decorated with *caitya* (चैत्य) heads, busts of demi-gods and deities. Unfortunately, the *śikhara* is highly damaged which does not give us any idea of the crowning elements. However, the lower part, the *garbha-gṛha* (गर्भ-गृह) has its outer wall full of recessed plain rectangles, the *koṣṭhaka*s (कोष्ठक), with *pilaster*s on either side in the form of typical Gupta pillars.

The brick temple at Bhītarī (भीतरी) near Saidpur (सैदपुर), U.P., for the first time, gives the inscriptional evidence of the consecration of a temple by the Gupta ruler. The inscription, found on the red sandstone *garuḍadhvaja* (गरुडध्वज, the pillar with *garuḍa* (गरुड) emblem on the top) of Skandagupta (स्कन्दगुप्त), states that the king consecrated an image of Lord Sāraṅgī (Viṣṇu, सारंगी विष्णु) in the temple and donated a village for the maintenance of the temple. A bell-shaped capital crowns the pillar. Bhītarī (भीतरी) has also yielded numerous inscriptions related to Kumāragupta (कुमारगुप्त). Among them, the most important one is the silver plate inscription.

The seventh-century Viṣṇu temple at Sirpur (सिरपुर) in Chhatisgarh is, however, comparatively modest in size. Like the Daśāvatāra (दशावतार) temple at Deogaṛh (देवगढ़), this brick temple rests on a high massive platform. The temple is approached by flights of steps provided at the north and the south of the platform. The temple consists of the *garbha-gṛha*, the *antarāla* (अन्तराल) and the *maṇḍapa* (मण्डप) built in a single axis. The intricately carved doorframe depicts figures of Śeṣaśāyī Viṣṇu (शेषशायी विष्णु) along with his different incarnations.

The basic temple architecture of the Gupta period underwent much modification from the eighth century onwards and many regional variations emerged in Madhya Pradesh, Orissa, Andhra Pradesh, Karnataka, Maharashtra, Gujarat and Rajasthan. Peripheral regions like Kashmir, Himachal Pradesh, Assam, Bengal and Kerala also witnessed many regional variations. The emphasis was laid more on elaboration of each component part of the temple architecture than on the serenity in the ambience. Elaboration also called for excellence in carving of images and a large variety of decorative motifs. It also called for perfection in architectural engineering — a science that kept on developing through the ages. Measurements of each and every part in relation to one above and one below, is prescribed. The post-Gupta or Early Medieval period witnessed the birth of several *śilpa* (शिल्प) texts on temple architecture. For example, the *Śilpaprakāśa* (शिल्पप्रकाश), an early text on Orissan temple architecture describes the various temple types of Orissa.

3

Central Indian Temples

THE decline of the Gupta (गुप्त) Age by the end of the sixth century witnessed the birth of a paramount power in north India under the Vardhanas (वर्धन) of Thāneśvar (थानेश्वर). Harṣavardhana (हर्षवर्धन), the prominent ruler of this dynasty, however, for most part of his life ruled from Kannauj (कन्नौज). Soon after them, i.e. by the second half of the seventh century, smaller kingdoms emerged in north, central and north-western India. These royal houses played a very important role in the further development of Nāgara (नागर) style of temple architecture which was introduced by the Guptas in the fifth–sixth centuries. The major dynasties that flourished at different periods of time between seventh and eleventh centuries, and which gave immense patronage to temple building activities, were the Gurjara–Pratihāras (गुर्जर–प्रतिहार, eight–eleventh century), the Kaḷacuris (कळचुरि),

Pl. 31 : Telī-kā-Mandir, Gwalior

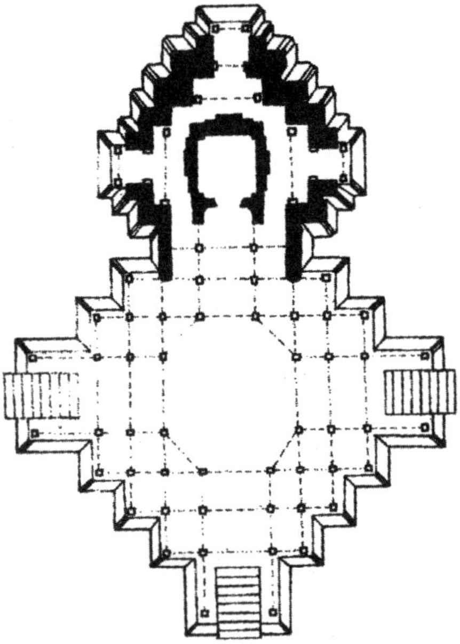

Fig. 33 : General plan of the north Indian temple

eighth–thirteenth century), the Paramāras (परमार, ninth–fourteenth century), the Solaṅkīs (सोलंकी, tenth–thirteenth century) and the Candelas (चन्देल, tenth–thirteenth century). They, individually and collectively, contributed greatly to the growth of the Nāgara architectural tradition but with regional variations.

The early Pratihāra temples at Gwalior, Gyāraspur (ग्यारसपुर) and Barolī (बरोली) in Madhya Pradesh show various stages of the development of central Indian temple architecture. For example, the Telī-kā-Mandir (तेली का मन्दिर, *c.* ninth century) dedicated to Śakti (शक्ति) cult at Gwalior, is the oldest Pratihāra temple in this region (*Pl.* 31). It has a rectangular *mūla-prāsāda* (मूल-प्रासाद) (*mūla* means "root," "original," etc. the main shrine where deity is consecrated) with the oblong *śikhara* (शिखर) or spire. It is also significant to note that here the Drāviḍa (द्राविड) style of *śikhara* penetrated somewhat strangely in this heartland of India at this early stage. The topmost part of the *śikhara* (शिखर) has the barrel-vaulted or wagon-top roof called *śālā śikhara* (शाला-शिखर) — the reminiscent of the Draviḍian order. The stepped-pyramidal roof, also called as *phaṁsana* (फंसन) roof," built above the porch, is also peculiar to this early temple in this region. The sides of the temple wall have three projections with intermediate recessions. Rudimentary form of "Latina" *śikhara*s (*śikhara*s resembling "sugar loaf" mass), *kuḍu* (कुडु) window arches and lotus medallions decorate the exterior. From this simple style of architecture developed Latina *mūla-prāsāda*s (मूल-प्रासाद) with *pradakṣiṇāpatha*s (प्रदक्षिणापथ), balconies with *chajjā*s (छज्जा) or overhanging eaves, *maṇḍapa*s (मण्डप) or halls with open *vedikā* (वेदिका, railing) for free transmission of air and light. The *phaṁsana,* or gable roofs, were adorned with *pūrṇa-kalaśa* (पूर्ण-कलश) or *padma-kumbha* (पद्म-कुम्भ) capitals or finials fixed along the long axis of the gable roof.

The later Pratihāras (प्रतिहार) further developed the *mūla-prāsāda* and its superstructure (*figs.* 33, 34, 35a, 35b & 36). This development can be seen in the temples of Barolī and Gyāraspur in Madhya Pradesh. The early tenth-century Ghaṭesvara (घटेश्वर) temple at Barolī has a stepped-pyramidal roof over its square portico (*ardha-maṇḍapa* अर्ध-मण्डप). Its parapets are beautifully decorated in the Drāviḍa (द्राविड) manner (but not with Drāviḍa elements of *kūṭa* (कूट), *pañjara* (पञ्जर) and *śālā vimāna,* शाला विमान), with smaller shrines (aedicules) and miniature Latina *śikhara*s (शिखर) at the corners. The Barolī temples, it may be noted, have taller *śikhara*s with elegantly curved profile than those of the usual Pratihāra temples.

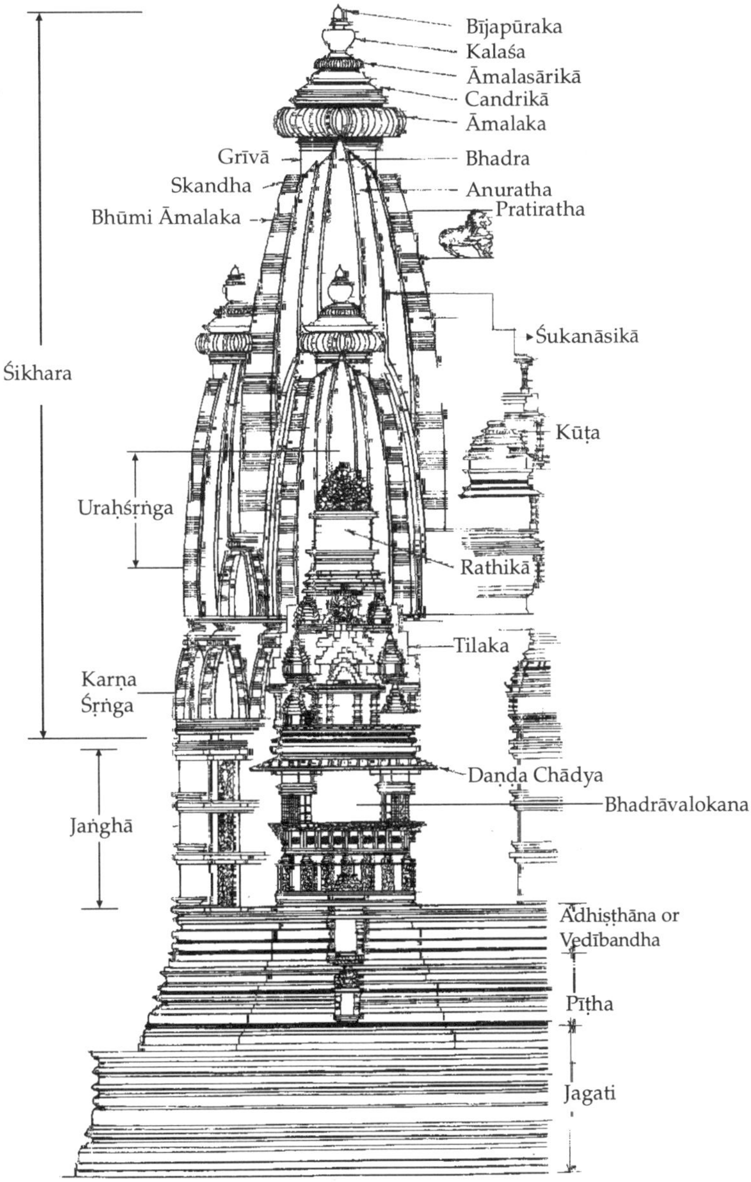

Fig. 34 : Elevation of the north Indian temple

The *rāha-paga*s (राह-पग) or central bands, called *jālī*s (जाली) or screens because of intricate geometric designs carved in stencil techniques in which while the central part of the figure is scooped out the outlines, in the linear form, are left out on a single smooth plain. These *jālī*s or *jāla*s (जाल), forming the *rāha-paga*s, project in the form of human tongue, somewhat triangular and pointed, a little beyond the *gaṇḍī* (गण्डी) or neck and reach the base of the larger *āmalaka* (आमलक) which is the characteristic feature of the central Indian *śikhara*.

The *āmalaka,* and, over it, the *pūrṇa-kalaśa* crown the *śikhara*. Now in front of the *garbha-gṛha* (गर्भ-गृह) was added an *antarāla* (अन्तराल) (a small vestibule) whose superstructure carried a variety of miniature shrines. The *śikhara* (शिखर) of the temple is crowned by not one but two *āmalaka*s (आमलक) where a smaller one is placed over a larger *āmalaka*. The small *āmalaka* supports the *kalaśa* (कलश).

The temples of Gyāraspur (*c*. eighth–ninth centuries) take us a step further in the development process (*Pl.* 32). They are more advanced than those of Barolī. The Gyāraspur temple has *pradakṣiṇāpatha* (प्रदक्षिणापथ), *antarāla* (अन्तराल), *maṇḍapa* (मण्डप) with balconies or *chajjā*s (छज्जा) (*chādya*, छाद्य) and *mukha-maṇḍapa* (मुख-मण्डप, porch) (*fig*. 37). This temple provides the earliest known example of Śekharī (शेखरी) style, a typical central Indian temple architectural tradition. Here miniature "latina" *śikhara*s are clustered about the base of the main *śikhara* of the *mūla-prāsāda* (मूल-प्रासाद). The roofs of both, the halls (*maṇḍapa*) and the porch (*mukha-maṇḍapa*), are stepped pyramidal or *phaṁsana* (फंसन) type. From these early temples of the eighth and ninth centuries evolved the later ones at Khajurāho (खजुराहो).

The Kaḷacuris (कळचुरि) were also a great power in central India. During their reign, around tenth century, the central Indian temple architecture witnessed the Transitional Phase whose developments can be seen in the temples at Amarkaṅṭaka (अमरकंटक) and the Virāṭeśvara (विराटेश्वर) Temple at Sohāgpur (सोहागपुर). For example, the plan of the Keśavanārāyaṇa (केशवनारायण) temple at Amarkaṅṭaka consists of the *garbha-gṛha* (गर्भ-गृह), *antarāla* and the *maṇḍapa*, all aligned in one axis, i.e. the *maṇḍapa* leads to *antarāla* which in turn opens to the *garbha-gṛha*, all are aligned along a single line. The *śikhara*, along with its *garbha-gṛha*, is *pañca-ratha* (पञ्च-रथ) in its plan and has the same fivefold projections in its vertical axis or elevation (*Pl.* 33). The *rāha-pagas* (राह-पग) project beyond the *gaṇḍī* (गण्डी) and the double *āmalakas* (आमलक) crown the superstructure. The *antarāla* is covered by a gabled *śikhara*. The *maṇḍapa*, square in plan, has *kakṣāsanas* (कक्षासन) (*kakṣa*, कक्ष = room; *āsana*, आसन = seat; stone seats with decorated back-rests) and *chajjās/chādyas* (छज्जा/छाद्य, overhanging eaves or sun-shades).

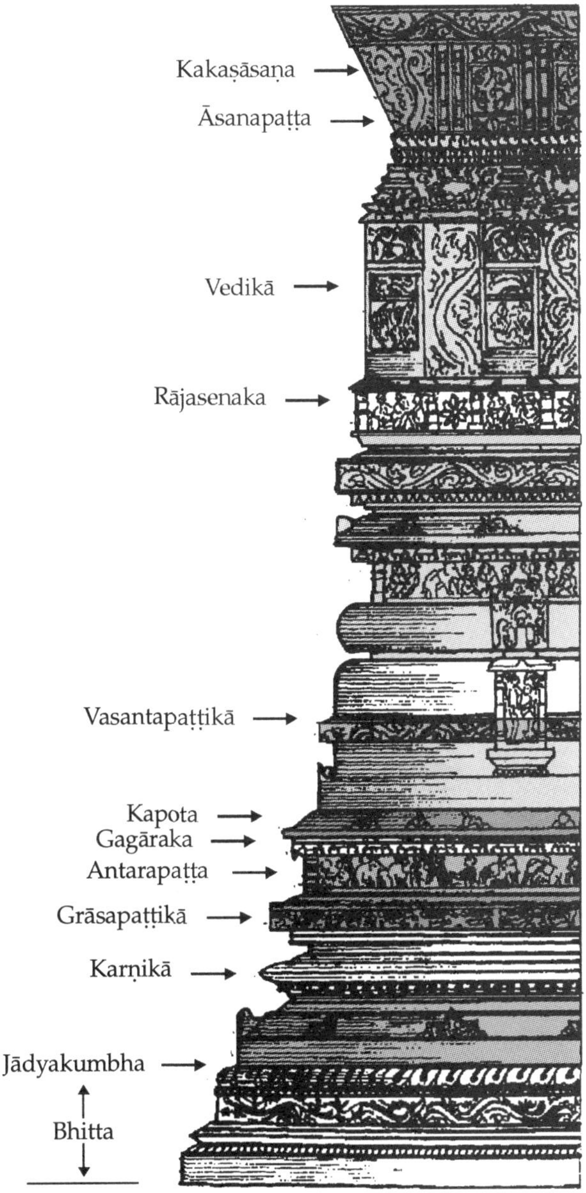

Fig. 35a : Base mouldings of the north Indian temples

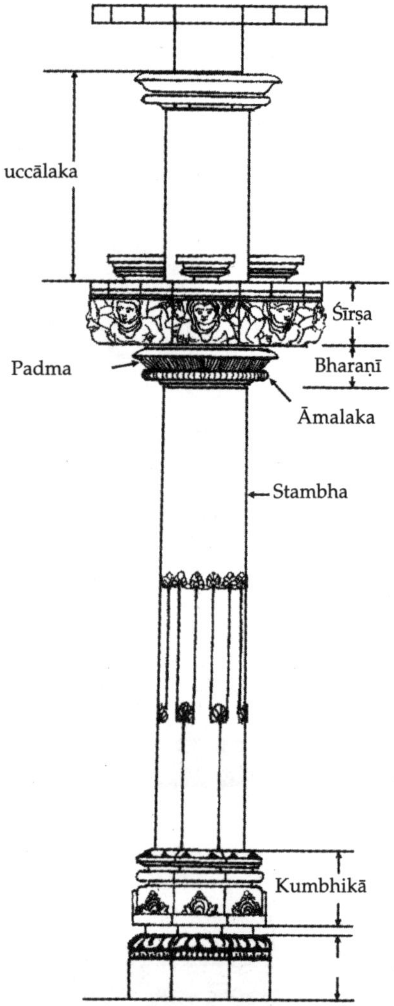

Fig. 35b : Different components of the north Indian temple pillar

The Virāṭeśvara (विराटेश्वर) temple at Sohāgpur (सोहागपुर) represents the still further developmental stage in the central Indian temple types with the addition of an *ardha-maṇḍapa* (अर्ध-मण्डप) in front of the *mūla-maṇḍapa* (मूल-मण्डप), or main *maṇḍapa* (also called *gūḍha-maṇḍapa,* गूढ-मण्डप). Thus, now the temple plan consists of the *garbha-gṛha, antarāla, mahāmaṇḍapa* and *ardha-maṇḍapa,* all aligned in one axis. It may be noted that the whole temple, consisting of these four structures, stands on a common platform or *adhiṣṭhāna* (अधिष्ठान). The *śikhara* (शिखर) over the *mūla-prāsāda* (मूल-प्रासाद) is *saptaratha* (सप्त-रथ) type, in its elevation and plan, i.e. having seven projections on each of the four faces (*Pl.* 34). Two *bandhana*s (बन्धन) or horizontally running mouldings divide the *jaṅghā* (जंघा) into three sections. The *rāha-paga*s (राह-पग) with triangular ends project beyond the *gaṇḍī* (गण्डी) or neck, as usual.

This is to be noted that here the *śikhara* is crowned by three *āmalaka*s (आमलक) instead of two. This tradition of multiple *āmala*s (आमल) or *āmalaka*s, also called *āmalakasāra*s (आमलकसार), inspired the architects of the Orissan temples also which we will be discussed later.

The Candelas (चन्देल) are known in Indian history not so much for any great empire but for art, architecture and literature. In fact, at one time they were feudatories of the Gurjara–Pratihāras (गुर्जर–प्रतिहार), but became independent by the tenth century. Their capital city of Khajurāho (खजुराहो) witnessed the zenith of central Indian temple architecture with magnificent temples of artistic and architectural excellence. Most of the Khajurāho temples were built of high quality sandstone in different hues ranging from buff to pink or pale yellow. It was quarried at Pannā (पन्ना) on the east coast of the River Ken nearby. However, some early temples like the Causaṭha-Yoginī (चौसठ-योगिनी, sixty-four *yoginīs*), Lālaguān-Mahādeva (लालगुआँ-महादेव) (*fig.* 38) and Brahmā (ब्रह्मा) (*fig.* 39) temples were built either wholly or partially of granite also. Their architecture also has some elements of the Pratihāra temples of the earlier period. For instance, the Lālaguān and Brahmā temples, like so many earlier Pratihāra temples, consist of a stepped pyramidal superstructure and shallow portico in the form of an *ardha-maṇḍapa* (अर्ध-मण्डप) or else *mukha-maṇḍapa* (मुख-मण्डप) raised over a plain platform. The wall is divided into two registers below the entablature or parapet, i.e. cornice (*chādya*).

The Causaṭha-Yoginī (*Pl.* 35, *fig.* 40) temple, dedicated to

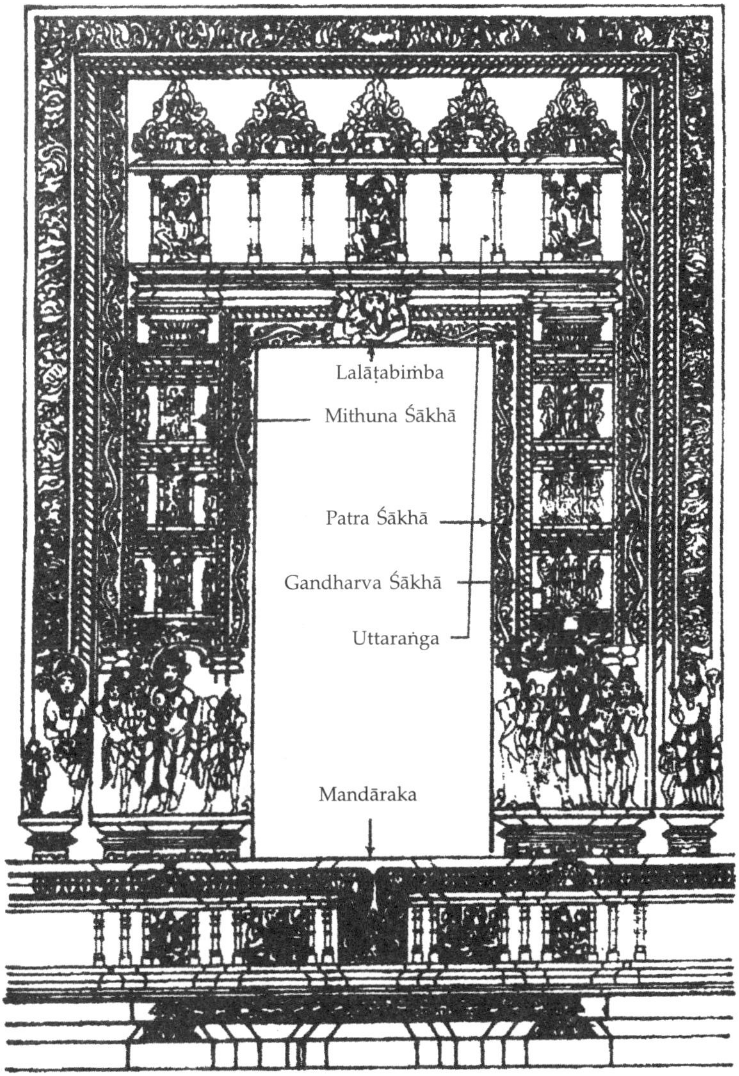

Fig. 36 : Gateway of the north Indian temple

sixty-four goddesses, oriented on a north-east–south-west direction, is among the oldest temples of Khajurāho, probably belonging to the late ninth century CE. It is the only temple complex of Khajurāho built entirely of granite. The temple complex is raised on a high *jagati* (जगति) built of huge blocks of granite. Originally, sixty-five shrines of this rectangular temple complex opened to the central courtyard. At present, there are only thirty-four smaller shrines in this complex. The square shrines, built of dressed stones, have monolithic doorjambs and lintels. They are surmounted by the embryonic forms of Nāgara *śikhara* (नागर शिखर).

Another temple depicting the early stage of the central Indian Nāgara style is the Brahmā (ब्रह्मा) temple. It is originally dedicated to Viṣṇu (विष्णु) as is indicated by the *lalāṭa-bimba* (ललाट-बिम्ब) on the lintel of the sanctum doorway. The temple stands on a high *jagati* (platform). The *jagati* is plain with twelve prominent mouldings. The temple consists of a small *garbha-gṛha* (गर्भ-गृह) fronted by the *mukha-maṇḍapa* (मुख-मण्डप, entrance porch), the latter is now completely lost. The *bāḍa* (बाड) of the temple is built of granite but the *śikhara* is of sandstone. The temple wall is devoid of any decoration. Externally, the shrine is cruciform with *ratha* (रथ) projections on each side. The central *ratha* projections on the north and south contain latticed

Pl. 32 : Mālā-Devī temple, Gyāraspur

windows. The *garbha-gṛha* is surmounted by the stepped pyramidal (*phaṁsana*, फंसन) *śikhara*.

In course of time temples with more architectural members and artistic elements appeared at Khajurāho. There are temples with *uraḥśṛṅga* (उर:श्रृङ्ग), equivalent to the Orissan *aṅga* (अङ्ग) or subsidiary *śikhara*s, built around the main *śikhara*. Such *śikhara*s were classified as of Śekharī (शेखरी) style. Similarly, there are temples of *nirandhāra* and *sandhāra* types. The *nirandhāra* (निरन्धार) type temples will not have a *pradakṣiṇāpatha* (प्रदक्षिणापथ) or circumambulatory passage around the *garbha-gṛha* whereas in the *sandhāra* (सन्धार) type there is a circumambulatory passage around the sanctum. The *sandhāra* temples have the famous balconied windows with *chajjā*s/*chādya*s (छज्जा / छाद्य, sloping sun-shades), projecting from the main body of the temple which are the most important characteristic feature of the Khajurāho temples. These balconies, like the antechambers, or sideways, extending *maṇḍapa*s (मण्डप), have the decorated short pillars and projecting *chajjā*s. On plan it becomes a cross. It may keep on repeating as one moves from the *ardha-maṇḍapa* (अर्ध-मण्डप) to *maṇḍapa* (मण्डप), *mahāmaṇḍapa* (महामण्डप), etc.

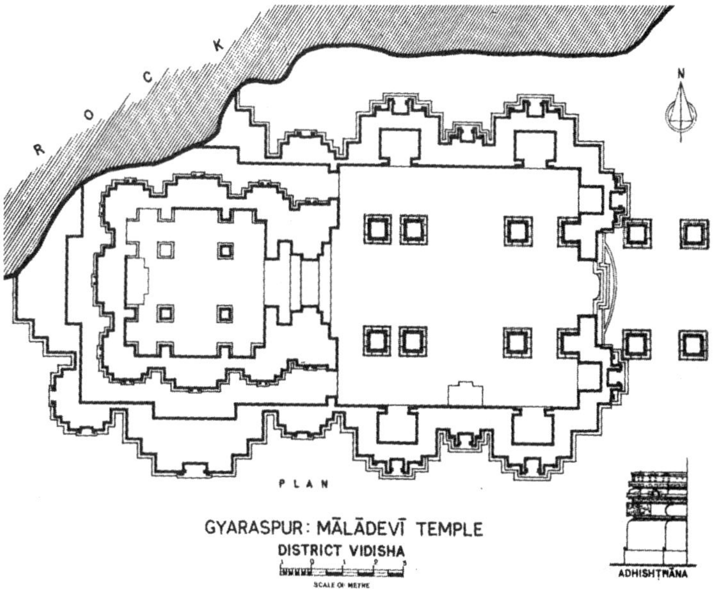

Fig. 37 : Plan of the Mālā-Devī temple, Gyāraspur

The largest and the typical Nāgara (नागर) style temples at Khajurāho (खजुराहो)

Pl. 33 : Keśavanārāyaṇa temple, Amarkaṅṭaka

Pl. 34 : Virāṭeśvara temple, Sohagpur

are the Lakṣmaṇa (लक्ष्मण) (*Pl.* 36, *fig.* 41), Viśvanātha (विश्वनाथ) (*Pl.* 37, *fig.* 42) and Kandarīya-Mahādeva (कन्दरीय-महादेव) (*Pl.* 38, *fig.* 43) temples. These are *pañcāyatana* (पञ्चायतन) temples (i.e. a main shrine with four subsidiary smaller shrines at its four corners standing on one and the same platform). They all, however, share some common features in their plan and elevation. The horizontal axis lies to the east-west direction with many halls or *maṇḍapa*s standing on a common *adhiṣṭhāna* (अधिष्ठान) aligned in a single axis. However, each compartment or *maṇḍapa* has its own superstructure or *śikhara* (शिखर). As one enters into the temple through an elaborately carved *makara-toraṇa* (मकर-तोरण), the first hall, known as the *ardha-maṇḍapa* (अर्ध-मण्डप), provides *kakṣāsana*s (कक्षासन, seats with back-rests) on its sides meant for the devotees to take rest on them. The *ardha-maṇḍapa* is open on three sides and its pillars support the roof and the overhanging *chajjā* (छज्जा, eaves or sun-shade). The *ardha-maṇḍapa* opens into a larger *maṇḍapa.* This *maṇḍapa* also has openings and *kakṣāsana*s on both sides and pillars supporting the roof. These openings provided ample light and air to the interior. The *maṇḍapa* opens into the *mahāmaṇḍapa* (महामण्डप) which is an enclosed hall with projecting balconies attached on both lateral sides. These balconies are accessible from the *mahāmaṇḍapa*. These added balconies provide the cross shape ground plan to the *mahāmaṇḍapa.*

At the centre of the *mahāmaṇḍapa* there are four columns that support the architraves and the ceiling. The *garbha-gṛha* (गर्भ-गृह) of these larger temples, of what is called *sandhāra* (सन्धार) type, i.e. one with circumambulatory passage or *pradakṣiṇāpatha* (प्रदक्षिणापथ) round the sanctum or *garbha-gṛha*, is, therefore, not the closed end of the temple. These *sandhāra* sanctums were also provided with outward projecting balconies on their three sides. This gives the plan the shape of a double-arm, what is generally called "Latin Cross," a form of cross in which three upper arms — the top and the side ones are of equal length, only the lower arm is longer than the rest. The balconied windows and the *kakṣāsanas* provide sufficient air and light to the *ardha-maṇḍapa, maṇḍapa, mahā-maṇḍapa* and the *pradakṣiṇāpatha* so that the devotees will not get suffocated inside the temple. Aesthetically and functionally, these elements made the temples get rid of not only the monotonous heavy and closed look but also the mysterious darkness surrounding of the end-part of the temple, i.e. the *garbha-gṛha* (गर्भ-गृह). In between the *mahāmaṇḍapa* (महामण्डप) and *garbha-gṛha* there is the *antarāla* (अन्तराल), i.e. a small and narrow vestibule or *maṇḍapa* (मण्डप), the place up to which the devotees could go and have a *darśana* (दर्शन) of the deity from close quarters.

Contrary to the Orissan temples which are as a

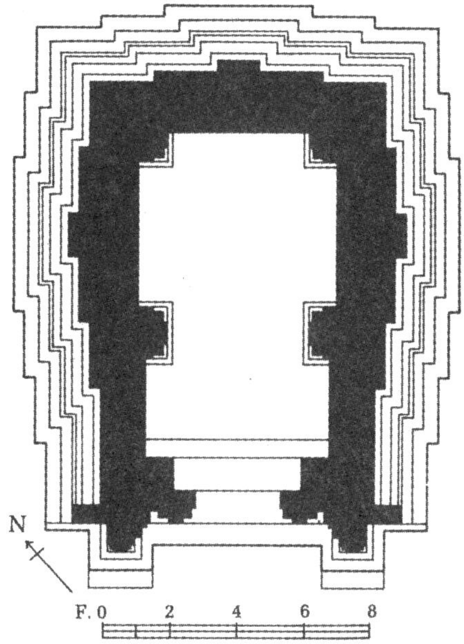

Fig. 38 : Plan of the Lalguan Mahādeva temple, Khajurāho

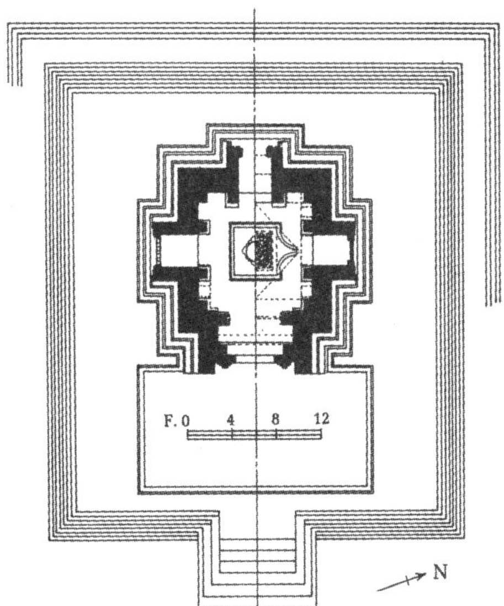

Fig. 39 : Plan of the Brahmā temple, Khajurāho

Pl. 35 : Causaṭha-Yoginī temple, Khajurāho

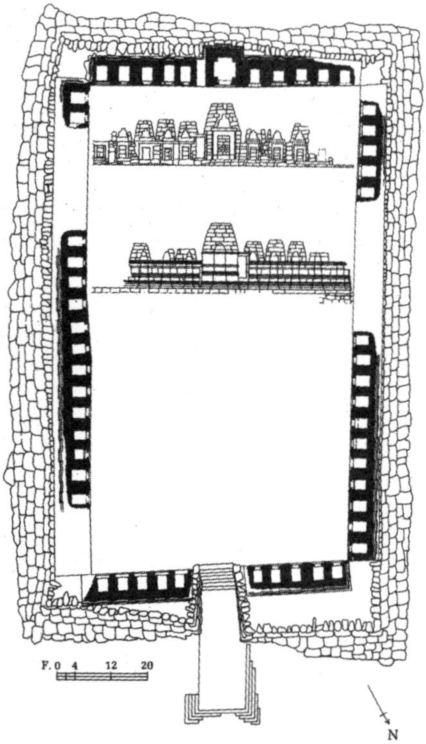

Fig. 40 : Plan and elevation of the Causaṭha-Yoginī temple, Khajurāho

rule plain, the interior of the Khajurāho (खजुराहो) temples are richly carved with beautiful sculptures. The walls, the pillars, the pilasters, the main entrance, the doorway of the sanctum as well as the splayed-out half-height walls of the balconies, which carried the seats for the relaxation of the visitors, are the virtual art-galleries of our museums, a lot to see and enjoy and also learn in terms of iconography of gods and goddesses besides geometric and floral motifs.

The vertical axis or elevation of the *śikhara*s (शिखर) of the central Indian temples, like that of the Orissan temples, has many divisions. The *saptaratha* (सप्तरथ) temples, especially, have magnificent sculptures on each *ratha* (रथ) or storey. The *mūla-prāsāda* (मूल-प्रासाद) and its *maṇḍapa*s stand on a common platform, called *jagati* or the lowest platform of the temple. Over the *jagati* (जगति), a series of highly ornamental mouldings form a high *adhiṣṭhāna* (अधिष्ठान) whose outward slope gives the impression that the temple comfortably sits on a compressed cushion seat. Over the *adhiṣṭhāna* rises the *bāḍa* (बाड, or cube or main temple walls). The *jaṅghā* (जंघा) part of the *bāḍa* is

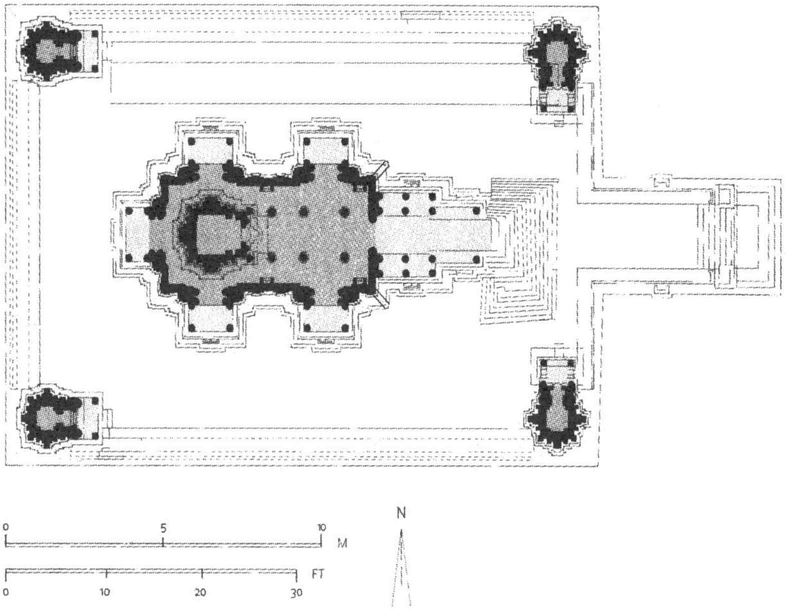

Fig. 41 : Plan of the Lakṣmaṇa temple, Khajurāho

divided by two *bandhana*s (बन्धन) (horizontally running mouldings) making it into seven vertical sections, called *saptāṅga-bāḍa* (सप्ताङ्ग-बाड). On the contrary, in the Orissan temple the *jaṅghā* is divided into two sections by only one *bandhana*. Thus, the central Indian *bāḍa* consists of seven parts or *saptāṅga*, namely, *pābhāga* (पाभाग), *jaṅghā*, *bandhana*, *jaṅghā*, *bandhana*, *jaṅghā* and *baraṇḍa* (बरण्ड), from bottom upwards. The division of *bāḍa* into seven sections

Pl. 36 : Lakṣmaṇa temple, Khajurāho

provided ample space to adorn the temple wall with marvellous sculptural representations. The provision of richly carved balconied windows and *kakṣāsanas* (कक्षासन) further enhances the beauty and dignity of the Khajurāho temples.

The *saptāṅga-bāḍa* (सप्ताङ्ग·-बाड़ा) supports the lofty superstructure or *śikharas* (शिखर), i.e. spire of the temple. The *garbha-gṛha* (गर्भ-गृह) and its *maṇḍapas* (मण्डप), it may be noted, have separate *śikharas* marking the importance of the halls. As per the status, the lowest *śikhara* appears over the *ardha-maṇḍapa* (अर्ध-

Pl. 37 : Viśvanātha temple, Khajurāho

मण्डप), the higher one over the *maṇḍapa*, one still higher over the *mahāmaṇḍapa* (महामण्डप), while the lofty crowning *śikhara* covers the *garbha-gṛha*. This ascending order of the *śikharas* provides a marvellous view to the temple which is composed with the rising peaks of the mountains. It also emphasizes the fact that a Hindu temple is supposed to represent the highest mountain, the Meru Parvata (मेरु पर्वत) or Meru Mountain with peak-over-peak and peak-behind-peak look. Each peak represents one stage in the long upward journey of the soul. It also represents "pilgrim's progress" crossing hurdle after hurdle. The *dharma-yātrās* (धर्म-यात्रा) to the temples, located in the most difficult locations of the mountains of the Himalayas and beyond Kedārnātha (केदारनाथ), in fact represent the basic concept of the rising *śikharas*.

In Orissan temple of the *rekhā* (रेखा) style *śikhara* takes its curvilinear profile towards the topmost part only whereas in the central Indian style the tall *śikhara* takes its graceful curvilinear form from its base or cornice or *chajjā* (छज्जा) itself. It is because of this that the *śikhara* gives not the sleek look but somewhat huge

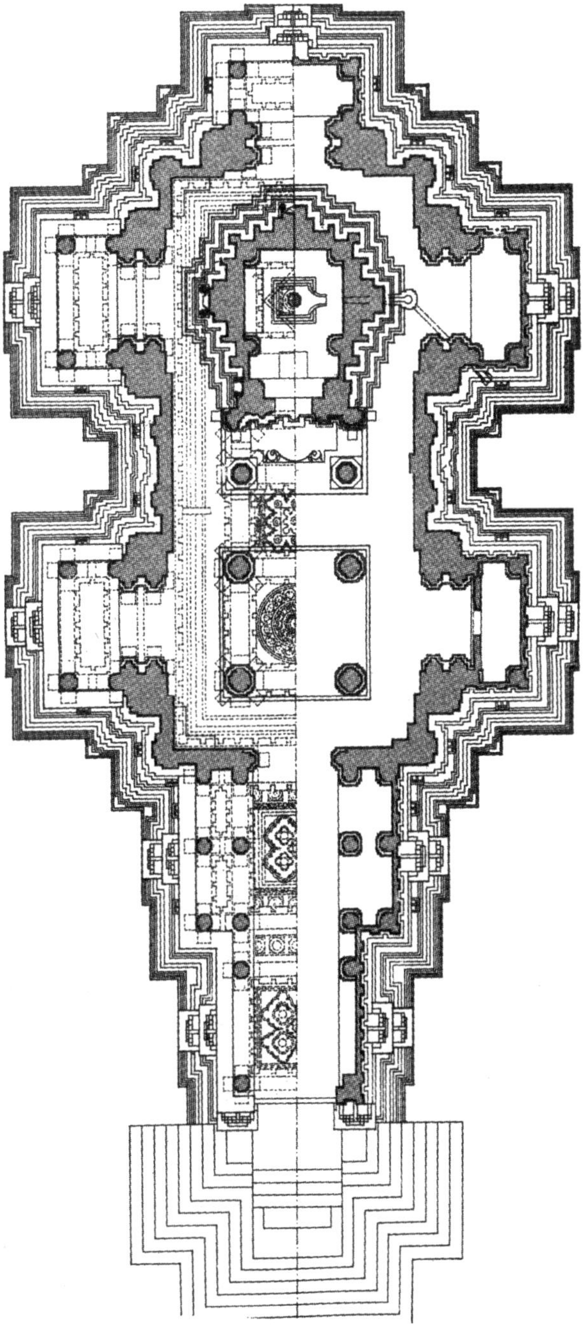

Fig. 42 : Plan of the Viśvanātha temple, Khajurāho

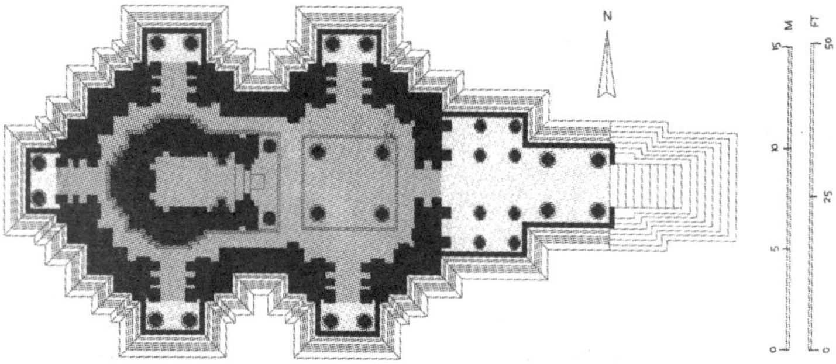

Fig. 43 : Plan of the Kandarīya-Mahādeva temple,

Pl. 38 : Kandarīya-Mahādeva temple, Khajurāho

and bulbous look. The central bands, known as the *rāha-pagas* (राह-पग), project beyond the *śikhara* and end in a tongue like triangular form, reaching almost to the base of the lower *āmalaka* (आमलक). The tall *śikhara* is surrounded by a cluster of miniature *śikharas*, known as *uraḥśṛṅga* (उर:शृङ्ग·), that are equivalent to the Orissan *aṅga-śikharas* (अङ्ग·-शिखर). Instead of one, in central India, usually two *āmalakas* appear above the *bekī* (बेकी or *grīvā* ग्रीवा, neck). The upper and smaller *āmalaka* supports the *pūrṇa-kalaśa* (पूर्ण-कलश), over which appears the *āyudha* (आयुध) (or main weapon or mark of cognizance of the enshrined deity). These features distinctively characterize the central Indian Nāgara (नागर) temples and make them belong to a somewhat separate category from the Orissan counterparts. In short, while the Orissan *śikhara* is of "Latina" type, i.e. *śikhara* with curvilinear profile (Liṅgarāja लिङ्गराज temple and Mukteśvara मुक्तेश्वर temple, Bhubaneswar भुवनेश्वर), the central Indian

Pl. 39 : Sekharī Śikhara of the Kandarīya-Mahādeva temple

śikhara (शिखर) is of Śekharī (शेखरी) type, in which a number of smaller *śikhara*s arranged one above the other form the clustered look about the dominant central *śikhara,* for example, Khandarīya-Mahādeva (कन्दरीय-महादेव) and Viśvanātha (विश्वनाथ) temples of Khajurāho (खजुराहो) (*Pl.* 39).

4

Temples of Orissa

ORISSAN temples stand among the finest examples of Nāgara (नागर) style architecture. It flourished between the seventh and the thirteenth centuries CE. The earliest among the typical Orissan temples are, however, dated in the middle of the eighth century CE. These are concentrated in Bhubaneswar and Purī (पुरी). The Orissan temple architecture reached its zenith during the most elaborate construction of the Sun Temple at Koṇārk (कोणार्क) in the middle of the thirteenth century.

There are several variations in the plan as well as the elevation adopted by the Orissan master-architects, the *sthapatis* (स्थपति), engaged in constructing temples called in local language *deul*; the term emerged from Sanskrit term *devālaya* (देवालय) (house of *deva* देव). There are three types of these temples: (1) *rekhā-deul* (रेखा-देउल), (2) *pīḍhā-deul* (पीढा-देउल) and (3) *khakhāra-deul* (खखार-देउल). One of these is called *rekhā-deul*, since its *śikhara* (शिखर) or spire is linear, *rekhā* (रेखा) meaning linear or straight and *deul* (देउल) meaning temple. The two together means "the temple with spire or *śikhara* designed in straight linear form" as opposed to the central Indian types where the *śikhara* was curvilinear. In the *rekhā-deul* the *śikhara* was straight, like a vertical line, almost up to the top, only at the top-end it took an inward

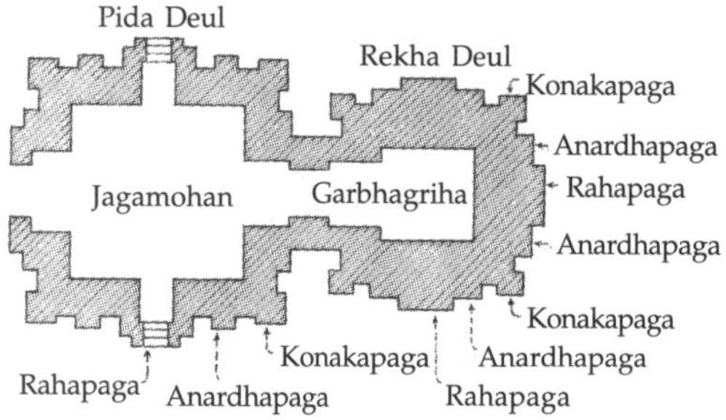

Fig. 44a : Plan of the Orissan temple

curvature to touch the *grīvā* (ग्रीवा) or neck. In the *pīḍhā-deul* (*pīḍhā* means *caukī* चौकी, a low flat wooden tablet to sit on) the *śikhara* has tiers of diminishing *pīḍhā*s or platforms. It is also called *jagamohana* (जगमोहन). It is in fact the *maṇḍapa* (मण्डप) raised in front of the sanctum as a separate but connected structure. In the *khakhāra-deul* [the word *khakhāra* (खखार) has been derived from *kakharū* (कखरू) (pumpkin, gourd)], the top looks like a gourd or barrel-shaped roof. It may, therefore, be seen that the classification is based only upon the plan and shape of the *śikhara* (शिखर) of the temples and not so much on the basal platform, the *pīḍhā* (पीढा), etc.

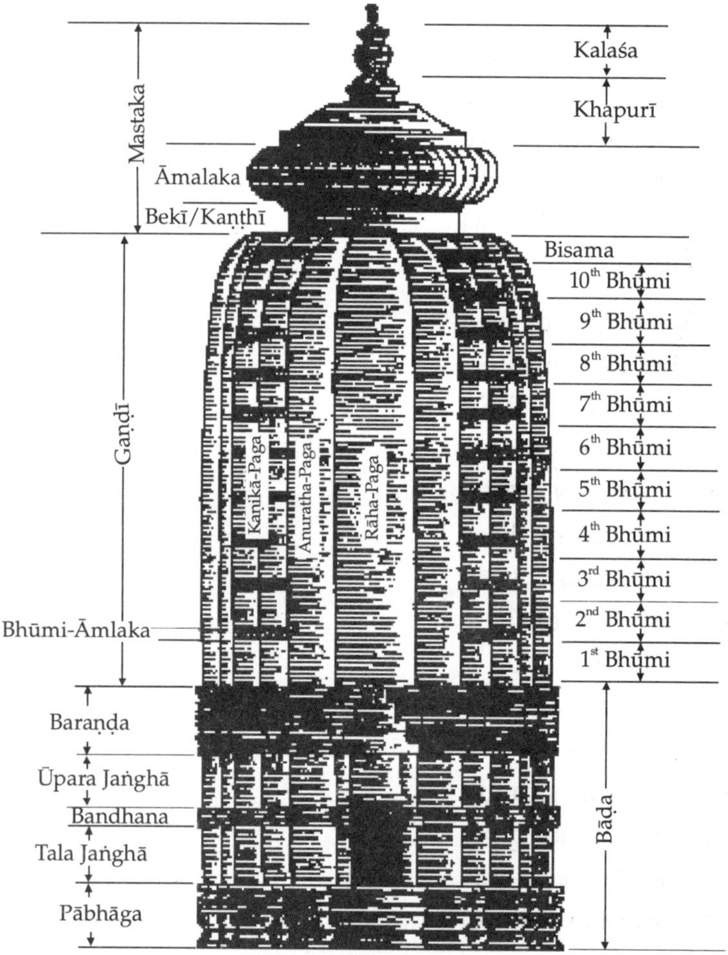

fig. 44b: Elements of Rekhā Deul

The *rekhā* and *pīḍhā-deul* stand on a common platform known as *piṣṭa* (पिष्ट), same as *pīṭha* (पीठ). It is, when large and high, called *adhiṣṭhāna* (अधिष्ठान), which is decorated with some mouldings. The Orissan temple architects used terms for different parts of a temple which are derived from the human body. Thus, the Orissan temple has the following major parts from base to top (*figs.* 44a, 44b & 44c).

(i) *pābhāga* (पाभाग) or foot-part, *pā* (पा) or *pāga* (पाग) (in

Hindi *paira* पैर), means foot, and *bhāga* (भाग) means part. The term is applied to the basal platform or low *adhiṣṭhāna* (अधिष्ठान) on which the temple stands.

(ii) *jaṅghā* (जंघा) or thigh. This term is applied to the vertical part of the temple which houses the *garbha-gṛha* (गर्भ-गृह), *antarāla* (अन्तराल) and the *mahāmaṇḍapa* (महामण्डप).

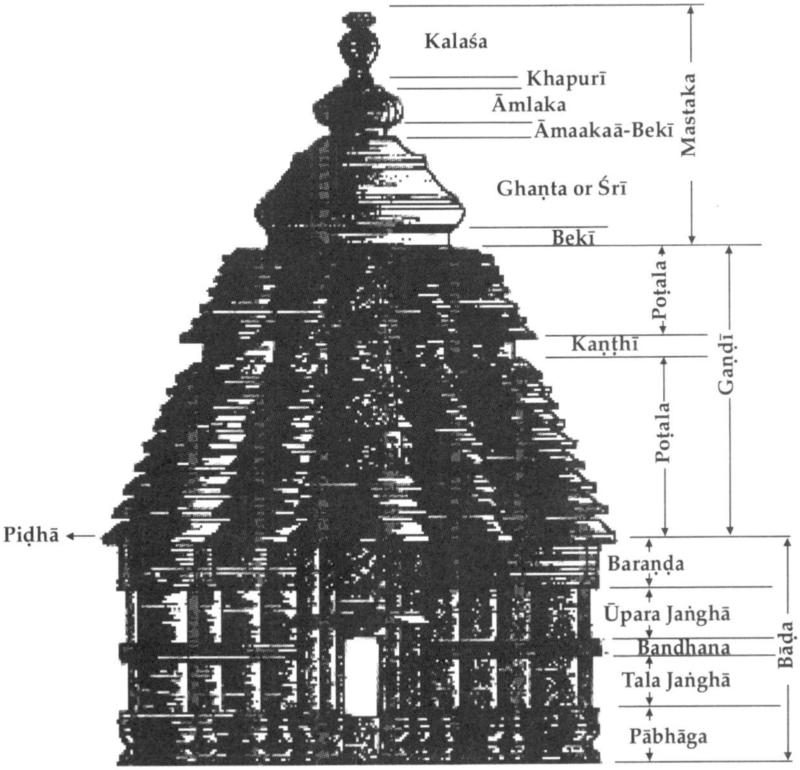

Fig. 44c : Elements of Pīḍhā-Deul

(iii) *gaṇḍī* (गण्डी) or trunk. The term stands for *śikhara*.

(iv) *mastaka* (मस्तक) or forehead. It stands for the top front part of the temple on the *śikhara*.

(v) *khapurī* (खपुरी) means skull-top or head. The term stands for the rounded stone placed above the *śikhara* which looks like the top of the skull.

(vi) *śīrṣa* (शीर्ष) or top-most part of the head represented by the finial.

Elevation of the Temple

The body or shell of the temple, from *adhiṣṭhāna* or

basal platform to the *śīrṣa* or finial, has the following elements:

1. *Piṣṭa* — This is the local Oṛiyā (ओड़िया) term for the *adhiṣṭhāna* or the basal platform or podium of the temple. It is generally much lower in height than those in central India. However, this is also profusely decorated with mouldings and sculptural panels.
2. *Bāḍa* (बाडा) — This is the local term for the main or vertical part of the temple. The term represented the portion below the *śikhara*, from cornice lower down up to the *piṣṭa*. *Bāḍa* meaning big and large. It has many elements arranged from bottom upwards. They are:
   - (i) *pābhāga* (पाभाग) or *pīḍhā* (पीढा) or *adhiṣṭhāna* (अधिष्ठान), the bottom platform of the *bāḍa* (बाडा).
   - (ii) *tāla jaṅghā* (ताल जंघा) or lower part of the *bāḍa*.
   - (iii) *bandhana* (बन्धन) or horizontally laid mouldings which run between *tāla jaṅghā* and *ūpara jaṅghā* (ऊपर जंघा). They hold the *jaṅghā* parts together architecturally and also visually.
   - (iv) *ūpara jaṅghā*, i.e. upper part of the *bāḍa*.
   - (v) *baraṇḍa* (बरण्ड), i.e. the topmost mouldings of the *bāḍa*, separating the *bāḍa* from the *gaṇḍī* (गण्डी). The word meaning is "an overhanging or projecting wall," also "moulding of a pillar," etc.
3. *Gaṇḍī* — The *gaṇḍī* or *śikhara* (शिखर). It has the following components:

(i) *bhūmi* (भूमि) (same as *tala* तल/storey/section into which the *gaṇḍī* of the *rekhā-deul* (रेखा-देउल) is divided); thus, *dvi-bhūmi gaṇḍī* (द्वि-भूमि गण्डी) will mean two-storeyed temple, and so on.

(ii) *bhūmi-āmalā* (भूमि-आमला) (same as *āmalaka* आमलक) is a small section of a ribbed disc-shaped stone which crowns the *bhūmi śikharas*, i.e. the *śikhara*s marking different storeys; *bhūmi* is storey.

(iii) *bisama* (बिसम), a local term for the flat stone slab, which caps the *gaṇḍī* or *śikhara* over which some further elements of architecture are placed.

4. *Mastaka* (मस्तक) — literally, the term *mastaka* means forehead. It starts from *bisama* upwards. This part of the temple-top incorporates the following elements:

(i) *bekī* (बेकी), the local term for neck, same as *grīvā*, (ग्रीवा), which rests on the *bisama*. It is cylindrical in shape which supports the topmost *āmalā-śīla*, (आमला-शील).

(ii) *āmalā* (आमला) (it is a ribbed-disc shaped stone which might have more than one section joined together to form a single *āmalā*). Same as *āmalaka* (आमलक).

(iii) *khapurī* (खपुरी, skull-cap shaped stone which rests over the *āmalā*).

(iv) *kalaśa* (कलश, a vase-shaped stone placed on top of the *khapurī*).

(v) *āyudha* (आयुध, i.e. weapon, or mark of cognizance of a god, placed over the *kalaśa* which denotes the presiding deity

Pl. 40 : Paraśurāmeśvara temple, Bhubaneswar

of the shrine, for example, if it is a Śiva (शिव) temple it will be *triśūla* (त्रिशूल) or trident but if it is a Viṣṇu (विष्णु) temple it will be *cakrā* चर्क or wheel).

Plan of the Rekhā-deul

The ground plan of the *rekhā-deul* (रेखा-देउल) is square whereas the exterior face of the shrine raised over it has many projections and offsets. The projections are known as *paga*s (पग). These are made in the middle of each of the four outer faces of the *bāḍa* (बाडा), i.e the main shrine below the *śikhara* (शिखर).

On the *gaṇḍī* (गण्डी) or *śikhara* these projections of the *bāḍa* are seen extending up to the top. These are called *rāha* (राह) in short and *rāha-paga*s (राह-पग) in full. The projection in the centre is large and prominent and complete in all respects. It is generally called *rāha-paga*. On either side of this *rāha* are two *anu-rāha-paga*s (अनु-राह-पग), *anu* means secondary, small, and narrow, almost pilaster-type, etc. At two corners are two *koṇaka-paga*s (कोणक-पग), *koṇaka* means *koṇa* (कोण), angle, i.e. corner of the *śikhara*. The central projection or *rāha* on each of the four sides is punctured with big rectangular recesses created one above the other, from one to three to five to seven or more. These niches are indicative of the storeys which constituted the *gaṇḍī* or *śikhara* hence temple as a whole. Thus, a temple could be *triratha* (त्रिरथ) (three storeyed) type, or still taller, *pañcaratha* (पञ्चरथ) (five storeyed) type or still more elevated, *saptaratha* (सप्तरथ) (seven storeyed) type. Each one of these niches represents one storey, called *ratha* (रथ) or *bhūmi* (भूमि). These *ratha*s are indicated on the *anu-rāha*s (अनु-राह) by *bhūmi* or *ratha-āmalā*s (रथ-आमला).

HOW TO COUNT RATHAS?

If there are two side projections, i.e. *anu-rāha*s (अनु-राह) on the left as well as right of the central *rāha*, it will be *pañcaratha* (पञ्चरथ) (2+2+1), but if 3 projections on either side of the main *rāha* it will be *saptaratha* (सप्तरथ), and so on.

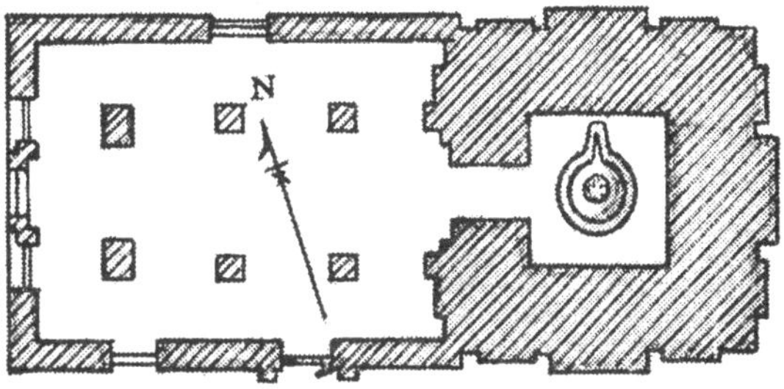

Fig. 45 : Plan of the Paraśurāmeśvara temple, Bhubaneswar

Elevation of the Pīḍhā-deul

Pīḍhā-deul (पीढा-देउल) possesses elements similar to those of the *rekhā-deul* (रेखा-देउल) but only up to the *baraṇḍa* (बरण्ड), i.e. a series of moulded strings. Beyond the *baraṇḍa* the form and shape of the *gaṇḍī* (गण्डी) or *śikhara* (शिखर) is totally different from that of the *rekhā-deul*. The *gaṇḍī* of the *pīḍhā-deul* is stepped pyramidal or layered as if one platform is sitting over the other in necessarily smaller size. In order to break their monotony, a certain number of *pīḍhā*s or platforms were grouped and separated from each other by a recess or gap called *kaṇṭhī* (कण्ठी), i.e. neck. These two or more sections or groups are called *poṭala*s (पोटल). Each *poṭala* is thus

Pl. 41 : Mukteśvara temple, Bhubaneswar

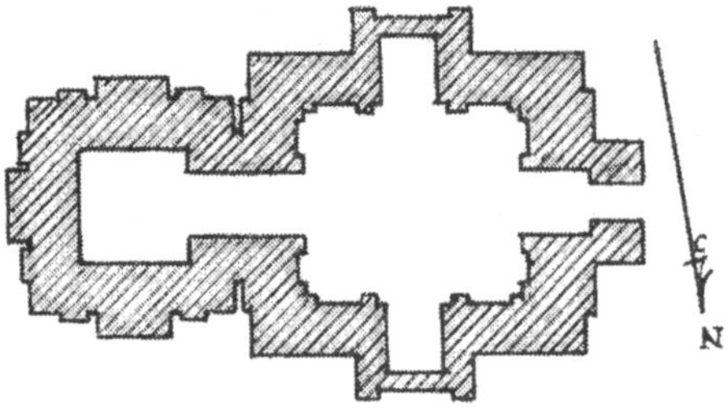

Fig. 46 : Plan of the Mukteśvara temple, Bhubaneswar

composed of a number of horizontal platforms or *pīḍhās*. In between the *poṭalas* there is a *kaṇṭī* or *kaṇṭhī, kaṇṭha* (कण्टी, कण्ठी या कण्ठ), i.e. neck separating each *poṭala* from the one above it. The crowning elements like *āmalā, khapurī* (खपुरी), *kalaśa* (कलश) and *āyudha* (आयुध), however, resemble those of the *rekhā-deul*, except that the *ghaṇṭā* (घण्टा), a bell-shaped member, intervenes between the *bekī* (बेकी) or neck and the *āmalā* (आमला).

Additional Maṇḍapas

The plan of the later or developed types of the Orissan temples has two more additional halls, but each one separately constructed, namely *nāṭya-maṇḍapa* (नाट्य-मण्डप, hall of dance) and *bhoga-maṇḍapa* (भोग-मण्डप, hall of offerings). The *rekhā-deul, pīḍhā-deul, nāṭya-maṇḍapa* and *bhoga-maṇḍapa*, it may be noted, are placed in one axial alignment and placed facing the *garbha-gṛha* (गर्भ-गृह).

Pl. 42 : Rājarānī temple, Bhubaneswar

Decoration

In Orissan temples the ornamental decorations and sculptural elements are concentrated more on the exterior wall than the interior; the latter is generally plain and featureless — which was also a tradition in central Indian temple architecture.

Similarly, the addition of a *toraṇa-dvāra* (तोरण-द्वार) (in central Indian temples it is *makara-toraṇa* मकर-तोरण), as an independently standing arched gateway in front of the temple is considered unique in Nāgara (नागर) style temples.

Pl. 43 : Megheśvara temple, Bhubaneswar

Evolution of the Orissan Temple Architecture

Among the earliest extant temples of the Orissan style are at Bhubaneswar (*c.* eighth century CE). The Paraśurāmeśvara (परशुरामेश्वर) temple is one of them (*Pl.* 40, *fig.* 45). The temple has the *triratha* (त्रिरथ) type *rekhā-deul* (रेखा-देउल), i.e. with one projection on each of the four sides. The *gaṇḍī* (गण्डी) or body of the *śikhara* (शिखर) of the *rekhā-deul* is short in height. Unlike the later period temples, in which the curve of the *śikhara* or *gaṇḍī* takes place only at the top-end, the *gaṇḍī* in this temple takes its curvilinear shape right from the base of the *gaṇḍī*. It is of course, an exception. However, it includes the *rāha* (राह), *anurāha* (अनुराह) and *koṇaka pagas* (कोणक पग). Over the *bisama* (बिसम), the stone over the *śikhara*, rest *dopīcha-siṁhas* (दोपीछ-सिंह, one-headed and two bodied lions) which supported the large *āmalaka* (आमलक). These types of typical figures above the *bisama* are generally known as *deul-cāriṇīs* (देउल चारिणी), *cāriṇī* (चारिणी) means

Pl. 44 : Brahmeśvara temple, Bhubaneswar

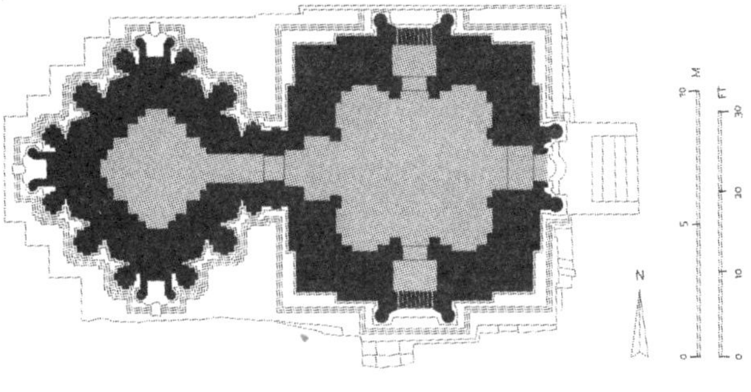

Fig. 47 : Plan of the Rājarānī temple, Bhubaneswar

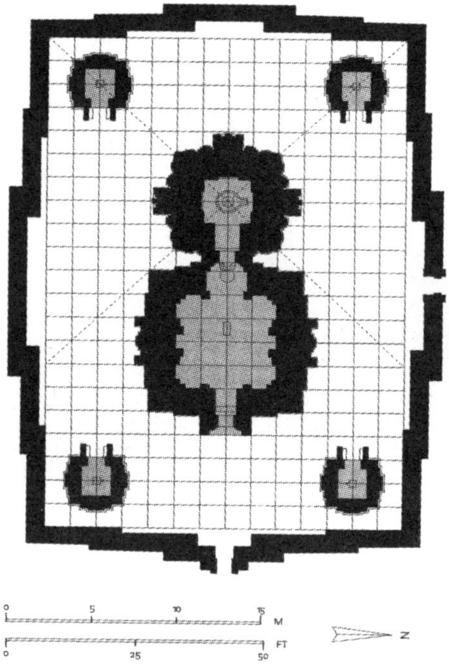

Fig. 48 : Plan of the Brahmeśvara temple, Bhubaneswar

serving or supporting something, in this case the *siṁhas* (सिंह). The *jagamohana* or the frontal porch, i.e. *mukha-maṇḍapa* (मुख-मण्डप), is not fully developed with typical tiered-roofs of the *pīḍhā-deul* (पीढा-देउल) variety. However, it has two-tiered sloping roofs that seem to have led to the later period *pīḍhā*s (पीढा).

The second stage of development in the Orissan temples can be seen in the early tenth century Mukteśvara (मुक्तेश्वर) temple in Bhubaneswar (*Pl.* 41, *fig.* 46). The temple has fully developed *gaṇḍī* or *śikhara* of the *rekhā-deul* and *jagamohana* of the *pīḍhā-deul*. The architectural members of this temple are well proportioned and harmoniously blended. Because of its architectural perfection, the Mukteśvara is considered "a gem of Orissan architecture." The *rekhā-deul*, here is *pañcaratha* (पञ्चरथ) type, with two extensions on each of the four sides. Both the *rekhā* and *pīḍhā-deul*s stand on a single low platform. The *pīḍhā-deul* has a stepped pyramidal roof typical of the Orissan style. However, the richly carved interior in this example is not characteristic of the Orissan temples since it is usually plain. Figures of the Saptamātṛkās (सप्तमातृका) and Vīrabhadra (वीरभद्र) adorn the ceiling. Similar architectural features have found in Rājarānī (राजरानी), Megheśvara (मेघेश्वर), and Brahmeśvara (ब्रह्मेश्वर) temples of Bhubneswar (*Pls.* 42, 43 & 44, *figs.* 47 & 48).

In course of time, the temple plan and elevation became more complex and a number of elements were added to the basic plan. The *triratha* (त्रिरथ) type *rekhā-deul* (रेखा-देउल) got enlarged to the *pañcaratha* (पञ्चरथ), *saptaratha*, and finally to the *navaratha* (नवरथ) type. In earlier temples, the *bāḍa* (बाडा) or the main body of the temple had only three sections, namely *pābhāga* (पाभाग or *pīḍhā* पीढा, platform), *jaṅghā* (जंघा or *bāḍa* बाडा, i.e. main body with *garbha-gṛha*) and *baraṇḍa* (cornice) but now the *bāḍa* has five sections or parts. This was done by placing a *bandhana* (बन्धन, moulding) around the middle portion of the *jaṅghā* which divides the latter into *tala* (lower) *jaṅghā* and the *ūpara* (ऊपर) (upper) *jaṅghā*. The mouldings on the *pābhāga* and *baraṇḍa* (बरण्ड) also increased.

As time passed, more and more *bhūmi*s (भूमि) or *tala*s, i.e. storeys, were added to the superstructure as a result of which the *śikhara* (शिखर) became taller, hence more slender. While the ratio between the height of the *śikhara* and the length of the sanctum is three to one in the early temples, like the Paraśurāmeśvara (परशुरामेश्वर), those of the second or middle period (tenth century CE) have a ratio of five to one, and still later (thirteenth century CE) examples like the Sun Temple at Koṇārk (कोणार्क), seven to one, meaning thereby that the height became seven times higher than the length of the sanctum, hence very tall. It provided a very imposing look to the temple. Being on the shore of the

Pl. 45 : Ananta-Vāsudeva temple, Bhubaneswar

Pl. 46 : Liṅgarāja temple, Bhubaneswar

Bay of Bengal, the ships coming from Indonesia, etc. could see them from a long distance.

By the tenth century, miniature replicas of the *śikhara*, known as *aṅga-śikhara*s, *aṅga* (अङ्ग) means supplementary or auxiliary, i.e. secondary, make their appearance on the *anurāha-paga*s (अनुराह-पग) or secondary *rāha*s (राह). The *gaja-siṁha* (गज-सिंह) (the rampant figure of a lion sitting on a crouching elephant) often projected from the *rāhapaga* of the *gaṇḍī* (गण्डी) or *śikhara.* All the four structures of the great Orissan temples, the *rekhā* and *pīḍhā-deul*, the *nāṭya* (नाट्य) and *bhoga-maṇḍapa* (भोग-मण्डप), lie along the same axis as noted earlier. These features, characteristic of the later Orissan types, mark the final development of temple architecture in this region.

Further development in the Orissan temple architecture can be seen in the Ananta-Vāsudeva (अनन्त-वासुदेव) and Liṅgarāja (लिङ्गराज) temples in Bhubaneswar (*Pls.* 45 & 46) and the Jagannātha (जगन्नाथ) temple at Purī (पुरी), contemporary of the Liṅgarāja temple (*fig.* 49) of the eleventh century, is of *pañcaratha* (पञ्चरथ) type with a *rekhā-deul* (रेखा-देउल) rising to a height of 214 ft from the ground level. A 20 ft high wall encloses the shrine. The entire temple-complex has four gateways at the eastern, southern, western and northern sides, called Lion Gate, Horse Gate, Tiger Gate and the Elephant Gate, respectively. Like the Liṅgarāja, the Jagannātha temple has two *deul*s and two *maṇḍapa*s (मण्डप), four in total, namely, *rekhā-deul, pīḍhā-deul, nāṭya-maṇḍapa* (नाट्य-मण्डप) and *bhoga-maṇḍapa* (भोग-मण्डप). The temple-complex covers an area of 4,00,000 sq ft. However, the Jagannātha temple does not incorporate any new element in the development of the temple architecture of Orissa.

The grandest achievement of the Orissan style is, however, the Sun Temple at Koṇārk in Purī District (*Pl.* 47, *figs.* 50a & 50b). This temple, built from CE 1238 to 1264 by the Gaṅga (गंग) king

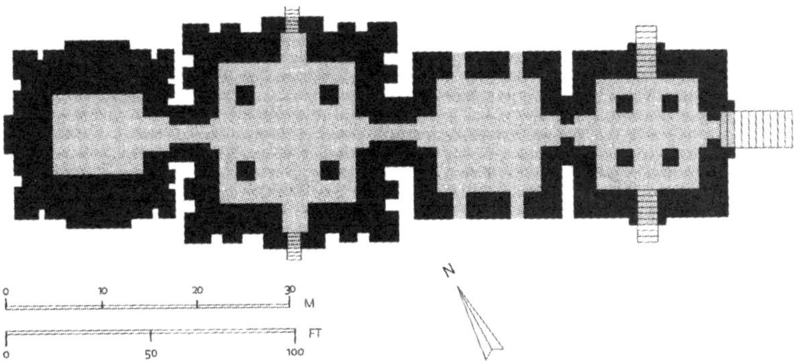

Fig. 49 : Plan of the Liṅgarāja temple, Bhubaneswar

Pl. 47 : Jagamohana of the Sūrya temple, Koṇārk

Narasiṁhadeva (नरसिंहदेव) I on the sea-shore of the Bay of Bengal was referred to as the "Black Pagoḍā" (पगोडा) by the early European writers because of its dark colour which it assumed due to the continuous plastering and subsequent blackening of the surface over many centuries. The temple was originally built of khondalite stone, like all other temples of Orissa, since this was the locally available pink coloured stone with yellow streaks.

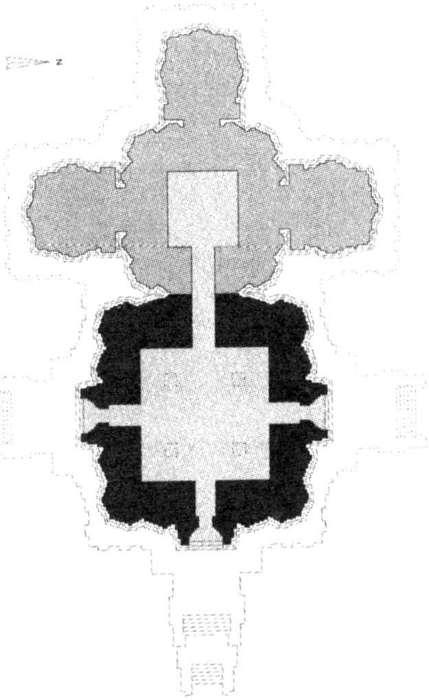

Fig. 50a : Plan of the Sūrya temple, Koṇārk

The alignment of the temple is east-west, with the *rekhā-deul* rising to a height of 229 ft and the *pīḍhā-deul* to a height of 128 ft. The plan of both the *rekhā* and *pīḍhā-deul* is *pañcaratha*, which means the temple consists of two *anurāha pagas* (अनुराह-पग), two *koṇaka pagas* (कोणक पग) and one *rāha paga* (राह-पग).

The *rekhā-deul* is presently dilapidated since it was struck by lightning, while the *jagamohana* (जगमोहन) is intact. A huge *āmalaka* (आमलक) crowns the pyramidal roof of the *pīḍhā-deul* (पीढा-देउल). The latter is composed of three *poṭalas* (पोटल). Only a small portion of the *nāṭya-maṇḍapa* (नाट्य-मण्डप) and *bhoga-maṇḍapa* (भोग-मण्डप) are extant, the rest have collapsed long time back. Conservation was done and still being done but the new stones are jarring to look at. There were, it may be mentioned, four Sūrya (सूर्य) images inside the temple, one of these is now in the National Museum, New Delhi.

The entire temple has been conceived as a chariot of the sun god Sūrya. It has 12 pairs of wheels, each about 10 ft in diameter, with a set of spokes and elaborate carvings. Seven horses are shown in the posture of moving, seven is the number prescribed for the chariot of the sun in the medieval texts, although in sculptural representations of the early historical period in north India only four horses were depicted. Still earlier there were only two, in the Śuṅga (शुंग) period, for example. It is said that the temple of Koṇārk (कोणार्क) represented seven rays

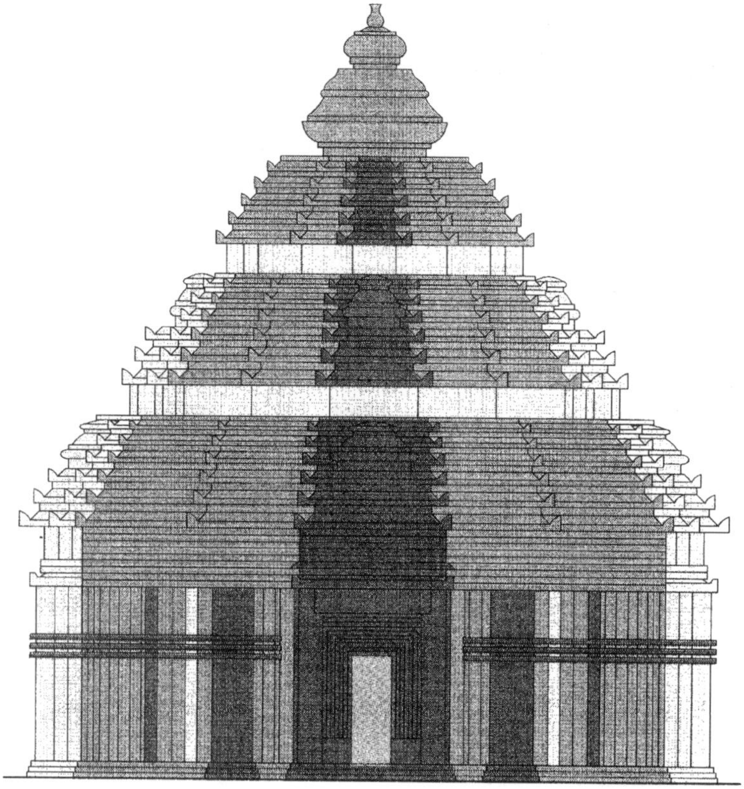

Fig. 50b : Elevation of the Jagamohana of the Sūrya temple, Koṇārk

of the sun. The entrance of the temple is guarded by two lions crushing elephants. Each elephant in turn lies on top of a human body. A flight of steps leads to the main entrance.

The *nāṭya-maṇḍapa*, built independently but located in front of the *jagamohana* (जगमोहन), is also intricately carved. Thousands of images which adorn the temple surface include deities, celestial and human musicians, dancers, lovers, and scenes of courtly life, ranging from hunts and battles to the pleasures of the worldly life. The base of the temple, the walls and the roof depict human, divine and semi-divine figures, often in sensuous poses and postures. There are also images of animals, birds, foliage, warriors on horses as well as geometrical patterns depicted in relief and also image-in-the-round. Thus, every inch of the exterior face of the temple is intricately carved with large and miniature figures with great sense of beauty and joy. It is indeed a jewel in the crown of Indian temple architecture.

5

Temples of Gujarat

ALTHOUGH Gujarat, like Orissa, also falls in the category of Nāgara (नागर) or north Indian style of temple architecture, yet, like Orissa, Gujarat also developed some features which are not found in the typical Nāgara temples of central India, such as those located at Khajurāho. The structural temple activities with newer elements start in the post-Gupta period in Gujarat. It started with the emergence of a new and powerful royal house, known as Maitrakas (मैत्रक) (CE 470–784) of Valabhī (वलभी). The Maitraka temple architecture, however, started flourishing greatly towards the end of the sixth century CE. Also known as the "Saurāṣṭra (सौराष्ट्र) style" it had four types of superstructures, namely, (i) the *kuṭina* (कुटिन) resembling the Drāviḍa *śikhara* (द्राविड शिखर), (ii) the *valabhī* (wagon-vault/*śālā-śikhara*, शाला-शिखर), (iii) the *phaṁsana* (फंसन)

Pl. 48 : Old temple, Gop, Gujarat

(literally, wedge-shaped; stepped pyramidal), and (iv) the latina (single *śikhara* variety with curvilinear profile). By the end of the seventh century the first two forms, i.e. the *kuṭina* and *valabhī*, became less popular whereas the latina *śikhara*s gained popularity.

The plan and elevation of the early Maitraka temples were simple. The temples consisted of the square *garbha-gṛha* (गर्भ-गृह) with or without the *mukha-maṇḍapa* (मुख-मण्डप). However, the *mukha-maṇḍapa*s are not found in the majority of the Maitraka temples. There were both *sandhāra* (सन्धार)and *nirandhāra* (निरन्धार) temples. Some of the important Maitraka temples of sixth-seventh century are the old temple at Gop (गोप) (*Pl.* 48, *fig.* 51); the Viṣṇu (विष्णु) temple at Kadvar (कदवर); the Bilvanātha (बिल्वनाथ) temple at Bileśvara (बिलेश्वर) (*Pl.* 49, *fig.* 52); the Temple nos. 1, 2, 5 & 6 at Bhanasara (भनसर) (*fig.* 53); Temple nos. 1 & 2 at Khīmeśvara (खीमेश्वर) (*fig.* 54); Temple no. 1 at Ghumlī (घुम्ली) and the Sūrya (सूर्य) temples at Pasnavaḍa (पस्नवड), Srinagar and Jhamra (झमर).

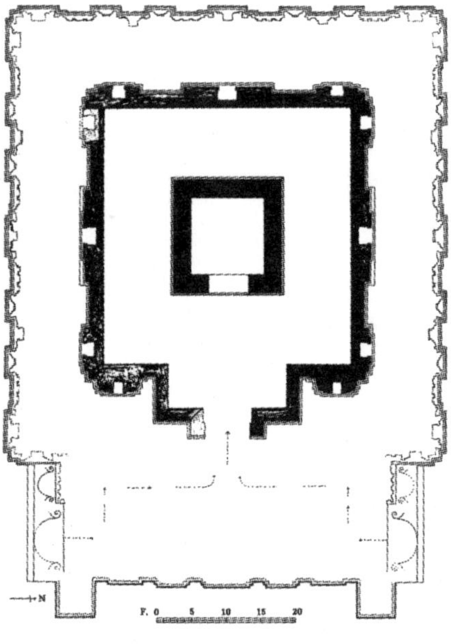

Fig. 51 : Plan of the Old temple, Gop, Gujarat

Among the Maitraka temples of Gujarat, the sixth–seventh century temple of Gop, known as Zinavari Gop, in Jāmnagar (जामनगर) district of Kāṭhiāwāṛ (काठियावाड़), shows a square *sandhāra vimāna* (सन्धार विमान) with stepped pyramidal (*phaṁsana* (फंसन) *śikhara* (शिखर) built on a moulded *adhiṣṭhāna* (अधिष्ठान). However, the temple is devoid of a frontal *maṇḍapa* (मण्डप). The lower course of the *śikhara* of this temple is decorated with two projected *caitya* (चैत्य)-windows as *nāsikā*s (नासिका) and the upper course with one. The *phaṁsana śikhara,* it may be noted, is crowned by a Drāviḍa type domical finial and not the *āmalaka*s (आमलक), etc. of the Nāgara type.

The temple wall shows *ratha* (रथ) projections with *deva-koṣṭhas* (देव-कोष्ठ) in between. Following the Gupta (गुप्त) tradition, the whole temple stands on a *jagati* (जगति, platform).

Pl. 49 : Bilvanātha temple, Bilesvar

Further development in the Maitraka architecture can be seen in the Viṣṇu temple at Kadvar. This *sandhāra* temple consists of a rectangular *mūla-prāsāda* (मूल-प्रासाद), a square *gūḍha-maṇḍapa* (गूढ-मण्डप) and a *mukha-maṇḍapa* (मुख-मण्डप). Here also the temple stands on a *jagati* which supports the *adhiṣṭhāna* or the *pīṭha* (पीठ) of the structures. However, these basal mouldings are not elaborate and show the continuation of the Gop style. This temple is characterized by the covered *pradakṣiṇāpatha* (प्रदक्षिणापथ) with two-tiered *phaṁsana*-roof, decorative *gavākṣas* (गवाक्ष), the images of the Varāha (वराह) and the Kumāra (कुमार), *jāla* (जाल) patterns, and a partially decorated doorframe depicting figures of Gaṅgā (गंगा) and Yamunā (यमुना) at the bottom. Unlike the Gop (गोप) temple, the doorframe of this temple shows different receding jambs, known as the *dvāra-śākhās* (द्वार-शाखा), such as *ratna-śākhā* (रत्न-शाखा), *stambha-śākhā* (स्तम्भ-शाखा), *padma-śākhā* (पद्म-शाखा), and the *bāhya-śākhā* (बाह्य-शाखा). Interestingly, all these Maitraka (मैत्रक) temples of Saurāṣṭra show one or more Draviḍian elements such as the stepped pyramidal roof, cornice depicting the *kutu* (कुतु) motifs, covered *pradakṣiṇāpatha* with multi-tiered roofs, *caitya* (चैत्य) dormers and *kūṭas* (कूट) of the *hāra* (हार) elements. It

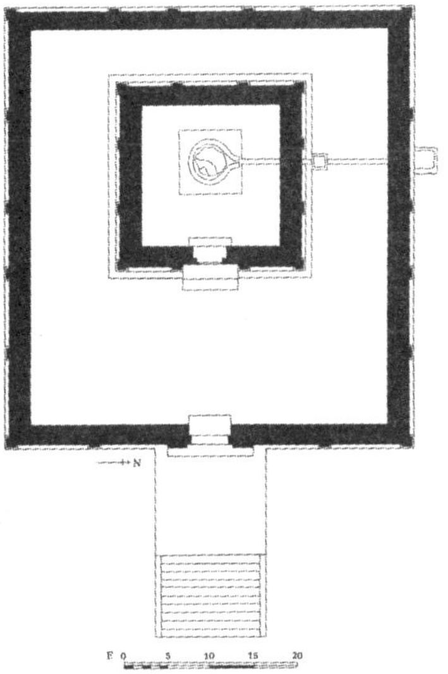

Fig. 52 : Plan of the Bilvanātha temple, Bileśvara

indicates that the Maitraka architecture was greatly influenced by the architecture of the Deccan.

By the early eighth century, a transition from the Saurāṣṭra style to the real Nāgara style takes place in the temple architecture of Gujarat. For example, the temples of Varāha (वराह) at Kadvar (कदवर) and Sūrya (सूर्य) at Sūtrapada (सूत्रपद) (*fig.* 55), near Somnātha (सोमनाथ), in the Jūnāgaṛh (जूनागढ़) district, exhibit a rudimentary *śikhara* (शिखर) in the *triratha* (त्रिरथ) form, a *garbha-gṛha* (गर्भ-गृह) with a *pradakṣiṇā-patha* (प्रदक्षिणापथ), and a closed *maṇḍapa* (मण्डप) with a porch and a sloping roof.

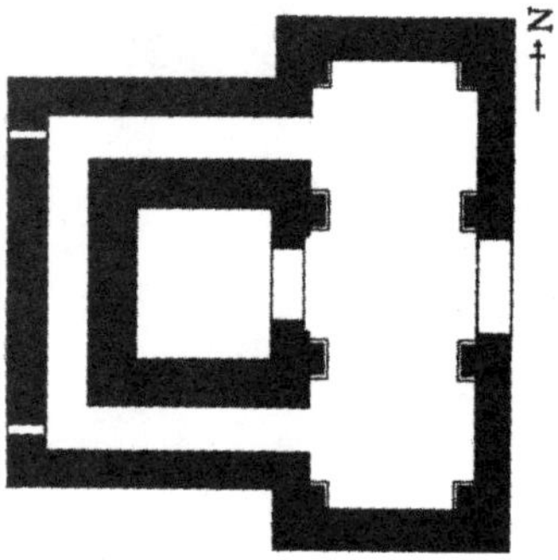

Fig. 53 : Plan of the temple no. 5, Bhanasara

The next development in the temple architecture can be seen at Roḍā (रोडा). Here the developed latina *śikhara*s with *triratha* (त्रिरथ) or *pañcaratha* (पञ्चरथ) projections rest over the *garbha-gṛha*. Though the *śikhara* over the sanctum was of the latina type, yet the superstructure over the *maṇḍapa*s were of pyramidal variety. We can, therefore, a kind of hybridization of styles as in Karnataka.

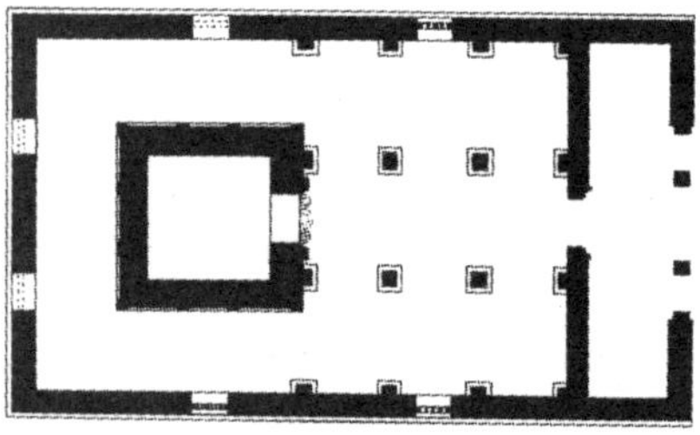

Fig. 54 : Plan of the temple no. 1, Khīmeśvara

The establishment of the Solaṅkī (सोलंकी) dynasty by the tenth-century Gujarat witnessed several new features introduced by the temple architects. A new impetus in temple architecture was given by its rulers. The architecture that flourished during this period in Āṇartta (आणर्त्त), Saurāṣṭra (सौराष्ट्र), Kaccha (कच्छ) and Lāṭa (लाट), is termed as "Maru–Gurjara" (मरु–गुर्जर) style. It was, however, not a new creation of the Solaṅkīs. This style had already been there since the eighth century which was the mixture of two regional traditions, known as "Mahā–Maru" (महा–मेरु) and "Mahā-Gurjara" (महा–गुर्जर) styles. But it was not perfected then. However, under Solaṅkīs

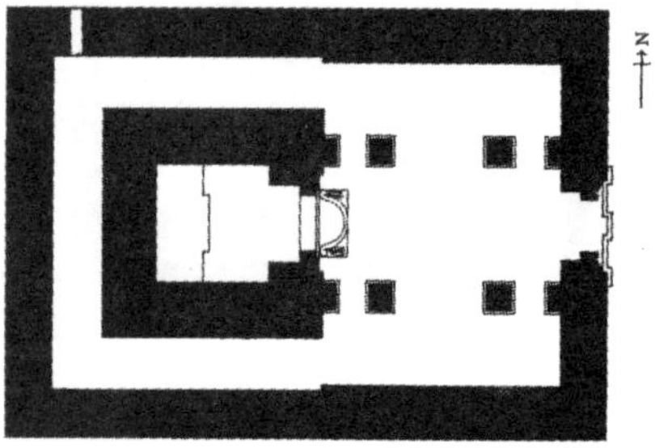

Fig. 55 : Plan of the Sūrya temple, Sutrapada

the Maru–Gurjara style attained its architectural perfection.

The developed Maru–Gurjara style temples comprise of the *garbha-gṛha/mūla-prāsāda* (गर्भ-गृह/मूल-प्रासाद), the *gūḍha-maṇḍapa* (गूढ-मण्डप) (closed hall or *mahāmaṇḍapa* महामण्डप), and a porch in front of the *gūḍha-maṇḍapa*, like *antarāla* (अन्तराल) of the Nāgara (नागर) temple. In several examples a semi-open *raṅga-maṇḍapa* (रंग-मण्डप) or *nṛtya-maṇḍapa* (नृत्य-मण्डप) (dance hall) or a *sabhā-maṇḍapa* (सभा-मण्डप) (assembly hall) was also added. This feature really distinguished it. These *garbha-gṛha* and *maṇḍapa*s were, as usual, aligned in a single axis.

In later temples the *maṇḍapa*s were fronted by a free-standing *kīrti-toraṇa* (कीर्ति-तोरण, decorated entrance with its own pair of pillars) and a temple tank (*kuṇḍa* कुण्ड). This made Gujarat style a unique one.

There were, however, some *pañcāyatana* (पञ्चायतन) temples where the main temple was surrounded by four subsidiary shrines (*karma-prāsāda*s कर्म-प्रासाद) at its four corners as in central India. The larger temples had *pradakṣiṇāpatha* (circumambulatory passage) around the *garbha-gṛha* (गर्भ-गृह).

The *mūla-prāsāda* (मूल-प्रासाद), same as *vimāna* (विमान) or *śikhara* (शिखर), of the Maru–Gurjara/Solaṅkī (मरु-गुर्जर/सोलंकी) type temples have three divisions in their elevation, namely, (i) the *pīṭha* (base) (*fig.* 56), (ii) the main hall called *maṇḍovara*

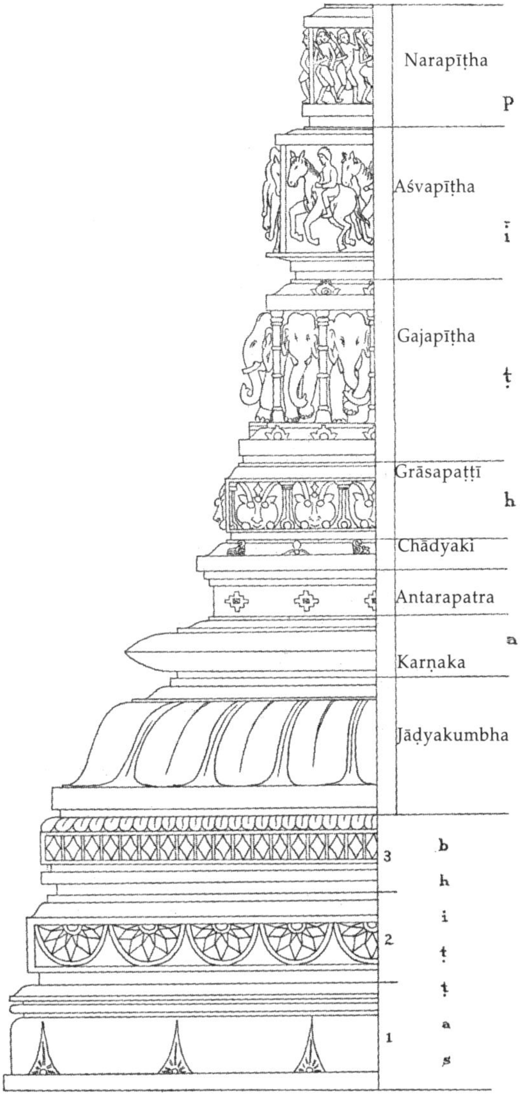

Fig. 56 : Pīṭha or base of the Solaṅkī temple (after Pramod Chandra)

(मण्डोवर) (i.e. the wall surface up to the *prastara* (प्रस्तर)/ entablature/cornice) (*fig.* 57), and (iii) the *śikhara* (spire). The whole temple stands on a *khara-śilā* (खर-शिला, paved terrace) which is almost similar to the *jagati* (जगति) of the central Indian temples, though not prominent like that of the latter.

Over the *khara-śilā* rises the *bhitta* (भित्त) which becomes the plinth of the entire structure. Over the *bhitta* rests the *pīṭha* (base) which in developed temples comprises a series of seven or eight mouldings with repeating motifs shown in relief. The lowermost moulding of the *pīṭha* is *jaḍyakumbha* (जड्यकुम्भ) whose design looks like inverted lotus petal.

The next course of moulding is called *karṇaka* (कर्णक), which is a knife-edged moulding. The third one, known as *antarapatra* (अन्तरपत्र) or *antarapaṭṭa* (अन्तरपट्ट), is a recessed flat band. *Kapotāli* or *kapotakī,* (कपोतालि या कपोतकी) or *chādyaki* (छाद्यकि), resembling a sloppy eave or sun-shade (*chādya,* छाद्य) appears over the recessed band. Above the *chādyaki* is the *paṭṭika* (पट्टिक) or *grasapaṭṭī* (ग्रसपट्टी) which displays a series of horned-heads like *kīrtimukha*s (कीर्तिमुख).

Over the *grasapaṭṭī* appears *gajapīṭha/gajaṭhāra* (गजपीठ/गजठार) with elephant-band reliefs, *aśvapīṭha/ aśvaṭhāra* (अश्वपीठ/अश्वठार) with horse-band reliefs and *narapīṭha/naraṭhāra* (नरपीठ/नरठार) with human-band reliefs, respectively, from bottom upwards. The *pīṭha*, as a whole, supports the *maṇḍovara* (the temple wall).

Maṇḍovara

The *maṇḍovara* (मण्डोर) is a term which is hardly 300 years old in the literature dealing with Gujarat temples. It is the temple wall of the Maru–Gurjara temple which is the most important element of Gujarat temples. Much attention was paid to it. It corresponds to the Orissan *bāḍa* (बाड). It is the main part or hall of the temple. Special attention was given to decorate it with beautiful relief sculptures.

The *maṇḍovara* has three major sections, namely, (i) the *vedi-bandha* (वेदि-बन्ध), which is a series of binding mouldings around the lower portion of the wall, (ii) the *jaṅghā* (जंघा) (the main part of the wall) and (iii) the *varāṇḍikā* (वराण्डिका) (a series of mouldings in the form of cornices) respectively, from bottom upwards.

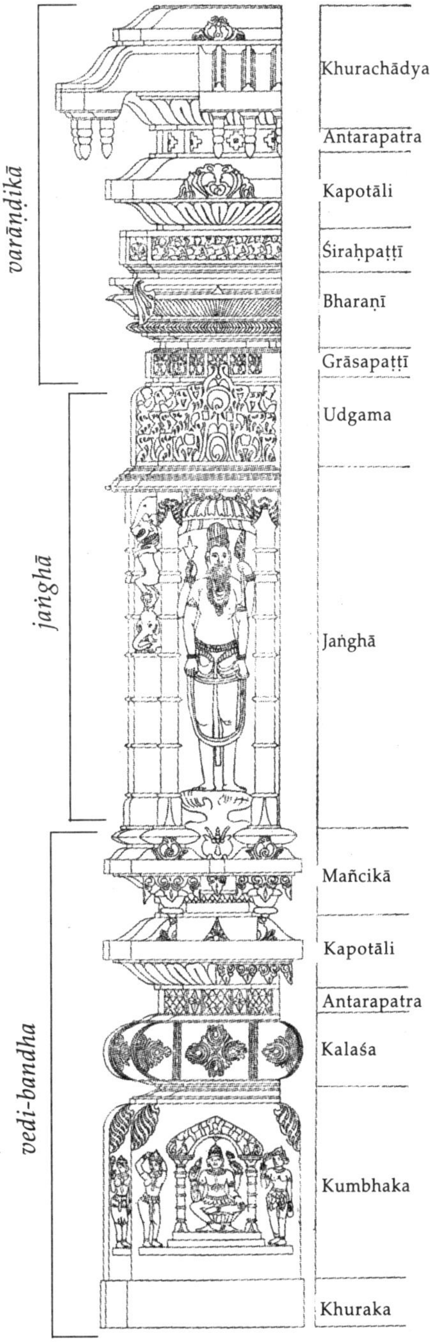

Fig. 57 : Diffenrent elements of the Maṇḍovara (after Pramod Chandra)

The *vedi-bandha* (वेदि-बन्ध) of the *maṇḍovara* (मण्डोवर) consists of four or five mouldings: (a) the *khuraka* (खुरक, hoof-shaped lowest moulding where the wall proper rests), (b) *kumbhaka* (कुम्भक, pot representing the water-element) surmounted by small *kalaśa* (कलश, pitcher), (c) *antarapatra* (अन्तरपत्र, a recessed flat band with motifs), and (d) *kapotāli* (कपोतालि, cornice-like moulding). *Kumbha* (कुम्भ) is generally decorated with half-diamond, half lotus, *candraśālā* (चन्द्रशाला) (*gavākṣa/caitya* (गवाक्ष/चैत्य) window; *kuḍu* (कुडु) arches in Tamil for Drāviḍa style), and other relief motifs. The *kalaśa* (कलश) may be decorated with intricate designs and carved bands.

The *vedi-bandha* is topped by an ornate moulding, resembling the *kapotāli*. It is called as *mañcikā* (मञ्चिका). It serves as the function of the pedestal for the *jaṅghā*. The *jaṅghā* has a series of framed niches, called *rathikā*s (रथिका). The *rathikā*s bear the images of deities. A crowning element on top of each niche is called as *udgama* (उद्गम). It adds elegance to the *jaṅghā*.

The *udgama* is followed by a fluted element in the form of a pot, known as *bharaṇī* (भरणी). The *bharaṇī*, in turn, is topped by a projecting band, known as *śīrṣapaṭṭika/śiraḥpaṭṭī* (शीर्षपट्टिका/शिर:पट्टी). The *śīrṣapaṭṭika*, in turn, is followed by a series of cornice-mouldings, known as *varāṇḍikā*. The *varāṇḍikā* is finally topped by a projecting sun-shade, known as *khurachādya* (खुरछाद्य). Its roof has the shape of ribbed tiles. The *varāṇḍikā*, i.e. the series of cornices, tie the temple walls with the roof.

Śikhara

The *śikhara* (शिखर), as usual in all Nāgara (नागर) temples, starts on top of the *varāṇḍikā* or cornice. Like those of the central Indian temples, *uraḥśṛṅga* (उर:शृङ्ग), in most cases, cluster about the main *śikhara* of the Maru–Gurjara temples. At the base of the middle *uraḥśṛṅga* in the front row is a *rathikā* (niche) bearing an image of a deity. The curvilinear *śikhara*

Pl. 50a : Sun temple, Moḍherā

is topped by a massive *āmalaka/āmalasaraka* (आमलक/आमलसरक) over which rests the *candrikā* (चन्द्रिका) (capstone) and *kalaśa* (pot finial).

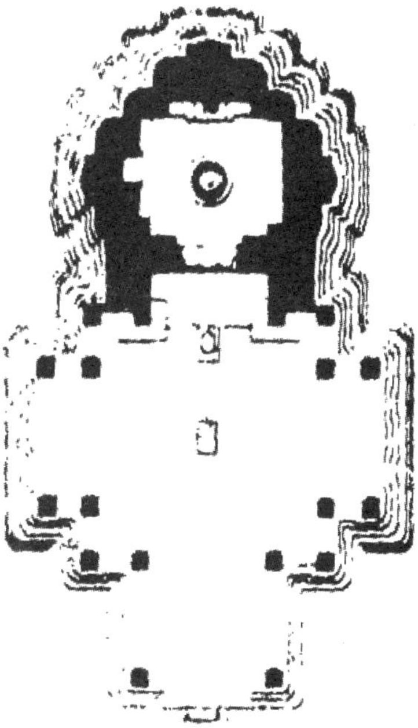

Fig. 58 : Plan of the Sūrya temple, Moḍherā

Gūḍha-maṇḍapa (गूढ-मण्डप)

The term *gūḍha-maṇḍapa* is given in Gujarat to the *mahāmaṇḍapa* (महामण्डप) of the Nāgara style. Significantly, in some temples the *gūḍha-maṇḍapa* is attached to the *mūla-prāsāda* (मूल-प्रासाद) or *garbha-gṛha* (गर्भ-गृह). If the *gūḍha-maṇḍapa* is attached to the *mūla-prāsāda,* the elevational elements of both the structures are similar up to the level of the *khurachādya* (खुरछाद्य), i.e. the cornice. If the *raṅga-maṇḍapa* (रंग-मण्डप) is attached with the *mūla-prāsāda,* the features above the *pīṭha* (पीठ) levels of both the structures will be different. This is very significant since it helps distinguish the *raṅga-maṇḍapa* (रंग-मण्डप) from the *gūḍha-maṇḍapa* (गूढ-मण्डप).

Unlike the *gūḍha-maṇḍapa*, the *raṅga-maṇḍapa* is open and half-walled which allows free passage of air and light. The *raṅga-maṇḍapa* has decorated *kakṣāsanas* (कक्षासन, stone-seats with decorated back rests) for the audience and devotees as in central Indian temples of Khajurāho (खजुराहो). The columns of these *maṇḍapas*, in many cases, are square or octagonal at the base, turning sixteen-sided in the middle section and *vṛtta* (वृत्त) (circular) at the top.

These pillars have many divisions starting from bottom upwards, *kumbha* (कुम्भ), *kevala* (केवल), *stambha* (स्तम्भ), *bharaṇī* (भरणी), *śira* (शिर), and *ṭekī* (टेकी).

The roof of the *maṇḍapa* is either of the *phaṁsana* (फंसन, stepped-pyramidal) or, more frequently, the *saṁvaraṇa* (संवरण, bell-roof) class.

Among the Solaṅkī (सोलंकी) type Maru–Gurjara temples the Sun temple at Moḍherā (मोढेरा) (1026-27) is most famous (*Pl.* 50a, *fig.* 58). Though it is partially ruined, the temple gives a clear picture of the typical Solaṅkī type temple with all its characteristic features. Moreover, its artistic elaboration is harmoniously blended with its architectural magnificence which is rare in Gujarat. This east-facing temple, built of golden-brown sandstone, stands on a broad terrace, known as the *khara-śilā* (खर-शिला), which is made of solid brick faced with stone.

The whole temple complex is fronted by a temple tank, known as *kuṇḍa* (कुण्ड), or stepped well. It encompasses a number of miniature shrines on its smaller steps. A broad flight of steps in the middle of the western side of the tank lead to the decorated archway, known as *kīrti-toraṇa*, standing in front of the *nṛtya-maṇḍapa/sabhā-maṇḍapa*.

Immediately behind the *kīrti-toraṇa* (कीर्ति-तोरण), begins the temple complex. It consists of the *sabhā-maṇḍapa* (सभा-मण्डप), *gūḍha-maṇḍapa* (गूढ-मण्डप) and *garbha-gṛha* (गर्भ-गृह), all aligned in a single axis, though these are separately built ones. These structures have all the three basic parts, namely, the *pīṭha* (पीठ), *maṇḍovara* (मण्डोवर) and the *śikhara* (शिखर).

The *sabhā-maṇḍapa,* rising immediately behind the *kīrti-toraṇa,* is a pillared hall with *kakṣāsana*s (कक्षासन) around (*Pl.* 50b). It is a very important element of a Gujarat temple. It has four entrances at its four sides with a flight of steps. Eight central pillars support the roof. Short pillars over the half-wall support the

Pl. 50b : Richly carved Raṅgamaṇḍapa of the Sun temple, Moḍherā

chajjā (छज्जा). Above the *chajjā* has a triple cornice from which the stepped pyramidal roof begins.

The *sabhā-maṇḍapa* leads to the *gūḍha-maṇḍapa*, leaving an empty space in between. The latter is a closed hall which forms one unit with the *garbha-gṛha*. Compared to the *sabhā-maṇḍapa*, the *gūḍha-maṇḍapa* is simpler and less decorated. The wall of the *maṇḍapa* contains many niches incorporating the images of the Sun-god. The *gūḍha-maṇḍapa* has only one entrance at its eastern side which is fronted by a portico. *Gavākṣākāra*s (गवाक्षाकार) (balconied windows) project from the northern and southern sides of the *gūḍha-maṇḍapa*. A set of eight pillars support the roof of the *maṇḍapa*.

The *mūla-prāsāda* is of *sandhāra* (सन्धार) type, i.e. with a *pradakṣiṇāpatha* (प्रदक्षिणापथ). The *gavākṣākāra*s (balconied windows), projecting from the northern and southern sides of the *mūla-prāsāda*, provide light and air to the *pradakṣiṇāpatha*. The *śikhara* of the *mūla-prāsāda* is highly damaged, though it may be assumed from the contemporary temples that the temple once had the Śekharī (शेखरी) type of the superstructure with *uraḥśṛṅga*s (उरःशृङ्ग) clustered about the base of the main *śikhara*.

The construction of the Rudra Mala temple at Siddhapur (सिद्धपुर), during the time of Jayasiṁha Siddharāja (1094–1142), indicates that the Solaṅkī style architecture continued in the twelfth century. Towards the end of the thirteenth century the Muslim rulers of Delhi invaded Gujarat and put an end to the Solaṅkī dynasty as well as their magnificent architectural activities.

6

Temples of Rajasthan

THE temple architecture of Rajasthan came into prominence during the time of the Gurjara–Pratihāras (गुर्जर–प्रतिहार) of Mandore (मण्डोर) (eighth–tenth century). They built numerous temples at Osian (ओसियन), Jagat (जगत्) and Kirāḍu (किराड़ु). These *pañcāyatana* (पञ्चायतन) temples, built in Nāgara (नागर) style, consist of the *mūla-prāsāda* (मूल-प्रासाद) or main temple in the centre which is surrounded by four smaller shrines at four corners. A richly carved open *maṇḍapa* (मण्डप) usually stands in front of the *garbha-gṛha* (गर्भ-गृह), which in turn, is fronted by the *mukha-maṇḍapa* (मुख-मण्डप). However, many of these early temples do not have *antarāla* (अन्तराल, vestibule) and *pradakṣiṇāpatha* (प्रदक्षिणापथ, circumambulatory path). Some of the best examples of the eighth-ninth-century temples are the Hari-Hara (हरि-हर) group of temples located at two different places, Sūrya I and Pīplā Mātā (पीपला-माता) temple at Osian in Dist. Jodhpur, and the Ambikā Mātā (अम्बिकामाता) temple at Jagat in Dist. Udaipur. However, the ninth-century Ambikā Mātā temple shows the *pañcaratha mūla-prāsāda* with the *pradakṣiṇāpatha*. The *gūdha-maṇḍapa* (गूढ-मण्डप, main enclosed hall) in front of the *garbha-gṛha* is fronted by the smaller *mukha-maṇḍapa* with projecting *chajjā*s (छज्जा) or eaves. This temple is more elaborately built than those of the eighth-century temples of Osian, although comparatively smaller in size.

Pl. 51 : Jaina temple, Nāgdā, Rajasthan

During the late tenth century, a group of Jaina temples emerged at Nāgdā (नागदा), near Udaipur (*Pl.* 51). The main temple at Nāgdā shows a curvilinear *śikhara* (शिखर) with *aṅga-śikhara*s (अङ्ग-शिखर), an *antarāla* (अन्तराल) and a hypostyle *maṇḍapa* (मण्डप) provided with lateral porticos at its three sides. The *maṇḍapa* is surmounted by a *phaṁsana* (फंसन, pyramidal) *śikhara*. These early temples show definite influence of the central Indian temple architecture. However, unlike the central Indian temples, the early temples of Rajasthan have only three horizontal divisions in their *bāḍa/bāṛā* (बाड), such as *pābhāga* (पाभाग), *jaṅghā* (जंघा) and *baraṇḍa* (बरण्ड).

Pl. 52 : Hari-Hara 1, Osian, Rajasthan

From tenth century onwards, the temples of Rajasthan show the influence of the Solaṅkī (सोलंकी) architectural style of

Gujarat which is otherwise known as the Maru–Gurjara (मरु–गुर्जर) style. Such temples, belonging to tenth–twelfth century are found at Kirāḍu (किराडु) in Bāṛmer (बाड़मेर) and Dilwāṛā (दिलवाड़ा) in Mount Abu (माउट आबु). It may be noted that these later period temples have largely influenced the architecture of the fifteenth-century Jaina temples of Ranakpur (रनकपुर) near Udaipur (उदयपुर).

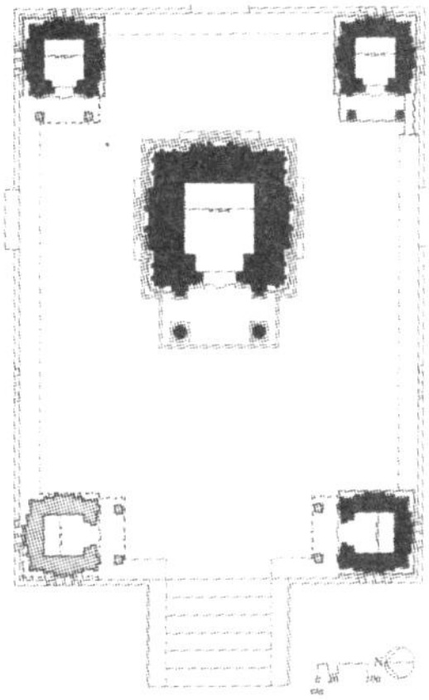

Fig. 59 : Plan of the Hari-Hara No. 1, Osian (after Michael W. Meister)

Osian, anciently known as Ukeśapura (उकेशपुर), was the religious city of the Gurjara–Pratihāras (गुर्जर–प्रतिहार) between eighth and eleventh centuries. It is situated in the Mārwāṛ (मारवाड़) region about 65 km north-west of Jodhpur (जोधपुर). More than fifteen imposing temples of both Brāhmanical and Jaina faiths adorn the landscape of Osian. Temples dedicated to Viṣṇu (विष्णु), Sūrya (सूर्य) and Śakti (शक्ति) and Jaina *tīrthaṁkara*s (तीर्थंकर) flourished here. They have been divided into two groups: those belonging to the Early Phase (eighth–ninth century) and Later Phase (tenth–twelfth century).

Pl. 53 : Hari-Hara 2, Osian, Rajasthan

A group of 11 temples, belonging to the Early Phase lie in and around the Osian village. The temples of the Later Phase are located on the nearby hill. These temples are located

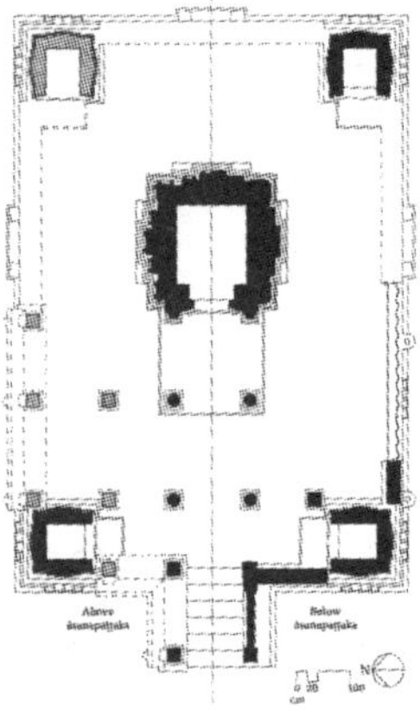

Fig. 60 : Plan of the Hari-Hara No. 2, Osian (after Michael W. Meister)

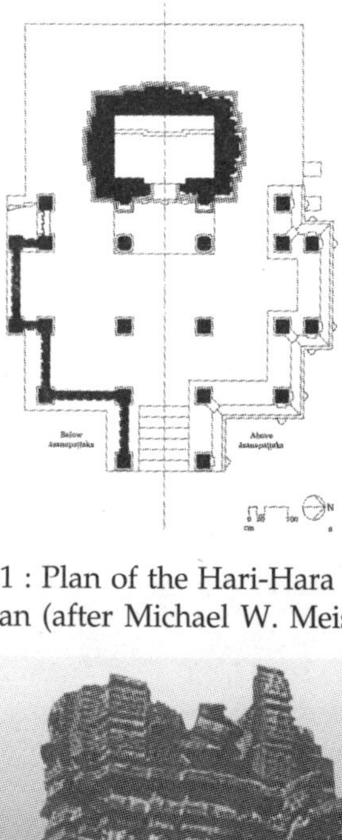

Fig. 61 : Plan of the Hari-Hara No. 3, Osian (after Michael W. Meister)

in the north, west and south of the Osian village. The south group of temple includes the eighth–ninth century Hari-Hara (हरि-हर) I, II & III (*Pls.* 52, 53, & 54, *figs.* 59, 60 & 61). The west group contains the eighth–ninth-century temples dedicated to Sūrya, Viṣṇu, Mahiṣāsuramardinī (महिषासुरमर्दिनी) (locally known as Pīplā Mātā, पीपला माता), (*Pl.* 55) and Mahāvīra (महावीर). The Mahāvīra temple is unique among the various Osian temples, with the vaulted design of its *maṇḍapa* (मण्डप) ceiling, hence very significant.

The south group includes the Sūrya temple (early eighth century) and the Sacīya Mātā (सचीय माता) temple of twelfth century. The latter has a *śikhara* (शिखर) clustered by two rows of *uraḥśṛṅgas* (उरःशृङ्ग), a *pradakṣiṇāpatha* (प्रदक्षिणापथ) and a large *sabhā-maṇḍapa* (सभा-मण्डप) with an elaborate ceiling. The Sūrya temple in the Sacīya Mātā temple complex is the oldest temple of the group. Its doorway is regarded as one of the finest temple doorways in India. It is indeed extremely beautiful with jewel-like fine carvings.

Like the Orissan temples, the temples of Osian were also built on a broad *piṣṭa* (पिष्ट, platform). Over this *piṣṭa* was built the *pīṭha* (पीठ, *adhiṣṭhāna* अधिष्ठान/socle) consisting of many mouldings, such as *khura* (खुर, hoof-shaped), *kumbha* (कुम्भ, pot-shaped), *kalaśa* (कलश, pitcher-shaped) and *kapota/kapotāli* (कपोत/कपोतालि,

Pl. 54 : Hari-Hara 3, Osian, Rajasthan

inverted lotus-petal shaped). These mouldings were arranged in accordance with the *ratha* (रथ) projections of the *vimāna* (विमान). The mouldings of the early temples like Hari-Hara (हरि-हर) group of temples and Sūrya (सूर्य) are plain without any decoration. However, the *kapota* is generally carved with *kuḍu* (कुडु) arches.

Above the *pīṭha* rests *maṇḍovara* (मण्डोवर, the wall) which is moderately decorated in early temples. All the *pagas* (पग) of the *maṇḍovara* of these *pañcaratha* (पञ्चरथ) temples contain *devakoṣṭhas* (देवकोष्ठ), or niches for images, surmounted by miniature *śikharas* (शिखर). These temples do not have *chajjā/ chādya* (छज्जा/छाद्य, eaves) to protect them

Pl. 55 : Piplā Mātā temple, Osian

Pl. 56 : Śikhara of the Ambikā Mātā temple, Jagat

Pl. 57 : Mūlaprāsāda of Someśvara temple, Kirāḍu, Rajasthan

from the scorching sun. Over the *maṇḍovara* starts the curvilinear *śikhara* which is crowned by an *āmalaka* (आमलक).

The *garbha-gṛha* (गर्भ-गृह) of the eighth-century temples is fronted by a small open *maṇḍapa* (मण्डप) which has flat roof. The *maṇḍapa*s of the temples like Hari-Hara II and III and the Pīplā Mātā (पीपला माता) are provided with *kakṣāsana*s (कक्षासन) or seat with back-rests. Moderately carved pillars with *pūrṇa-kalaśa*s (पूर्ण-कलश) support the ceilings. Since the main *maṇḍapa*s themselves are simple, the features of the narrow *mukha-maṇḍapa* (मुख-मण्डप) (portico) are not prominent in early temples. During the later period the Pratihāras (प्रतिहार) built many imposing temples with *antarāla* (अन्तराल), *pradakṣiṇāpatha* (प्रदक्षिणापथ) and projecting *gavākṣa*s (गवाक्ष) (balconies). Such features can be seen in the Sacīya Mātā (सचीय माता) temple of Osian (ओसियान).

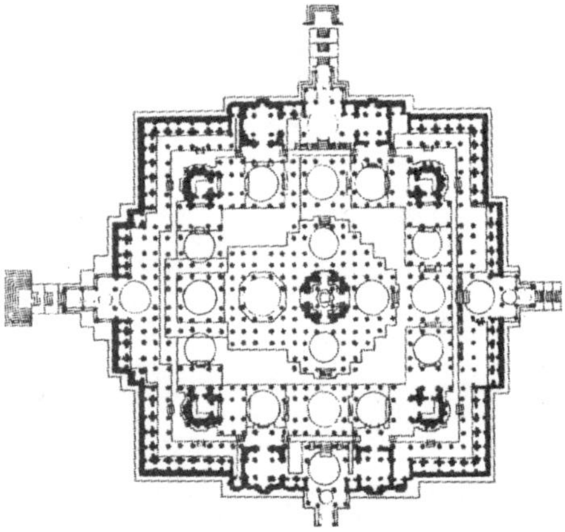

Fig. 62 : Plan of Vimala Vasāhī, Dilwāṛā, Rajasthan

Further developments in the temple architecture can be seen in the Ambikā Mātā (अम्बिका माता) temple of Jagat (जगत्) (*Pl.* 56). This temple, assignable to tenth century, consists of a *garbha-gṛha,* a *gūḍha-maṇḍapa* (गूढ-मण्डप, main enclosed hall) and a *mukha-maṇḍapa* with projecting *chajjā*s or eaves. The walls of the *garbha-gṛha* and the *maṇḍapas*, doorways and ceilings are adorned with fine carvings. The *garbha-gṛha* is

Pl. 58 : Maṇḍapa of Vimala Vasahi, Mount Abu, Rajasthan

Pl. 59 : Ādinātha temple, Ranakpur, Rajasthan

surmounted by the *śekharī śikhara* (शेखरी-शिखर) while *maṇḍapa*s are supporting the *phaṁsana* (फंसन, pyramidal) *śikhara*.

The zenith of the Gurjara-Pratihāra architecture can be seen in the Kirāḍu (किराडु) group of temples situated near the village Hathma (हथ्म), about 43 km away from Bāṛmer (बाड़मेर) in Rajasthan. These temples were built after tenth century, incorporating both the late Gupta (गुप्त) and the Solaṅkī (सोलंकी) architectural elements. All, except five temples in ruined condition, are completely dilapidated leaving the *adhiṣṭhāna* (अधिष्ठान) alone for our close study. Mutilated sculptures of gods and goddesses, animals, celestial nymphs and broken pieces of carvings are spread around them.

Among the earliest of the temples of Kirāḍu is the ruined Pañcaratha Viṣṇu (पञ्चरथ विष्णु) temple resting on the moulded *adhiṣṭhāna*. The plan consists of the *garbha-gṛha* (गर्भ-गृह), *nṛtya-maṇḍapa* (नृत्य-मण्डप) and the *mukha-maṇḍapa* (मुख-मण्डप). However, only the *maṇḍovara* of the *garbha-gṛha* and the *stambhas* (स्तम्भ) of the central octagonal nave of the *nāṭya-maṇḍapa* exist to date. The pillars are richly carved with *pūrṇa-kalaśa* (पूर्ण-कलश) motifs and celestial nymphs (*apasaras*es, अपसरस्) in dancing postures. The multi-loop arches joining the pillars added to the beauty of the interior. Unlike those of the early Osian temples, this temple shows the *śekharī* (शेखरी) variety of *śikhara* (शिखर) with

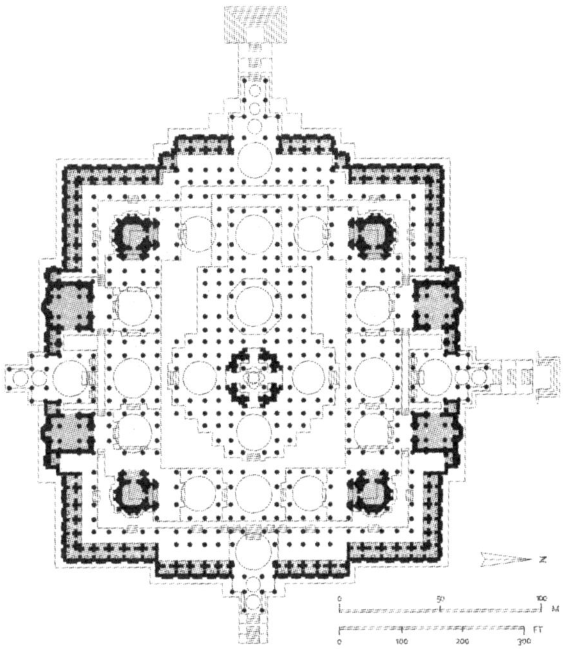

Fig. 63 : Plan of Ādinātha temple, Ranakpur, Rajasthan

miniature spires placed at different levels.

At Kirāḍu the best example is the Someśvara (सोमेश्वर) temple, dedicated to Śiva (*Pl.* 57). It is finely sculpted and has a *bahu-tala* (बहु-तल, multi-storeyed) *śikhara*. This temple shows the increasing trend of architectural elaboration and ornamentation. The *pañcaratha mūla-prāsāda* (मूल-प्रासाद) stands on a moulded *adhiṣṭhāna* (*pīṭha* पीठ) showing many *thāra*s (थार, panels). Each *thāra* depicts horned heads, elephants (*gaja-thāra*, गज-थार), horses (*aśva-thāra*, अश्व-थार) and humans (*nara-thāra*, नर-थार) respectively from bottom upwards. The *jaṅghā* (जंघा) (middle portion of the temple wall) is lavishly decorated, which also supports the *devakoṣṭha*s (देवकोष्ठ). The *śekharī śikhara* is adorned with *uraḥśṛṅga* (उर:श्रृङ्ग).

The octagonal *nāṭya-maṇḍapa* in front of the *garbha-gṛha* is exceptionally well decorated. However, the huge pillars of this pavilion are mostly plain at the base but carved with the most elegant *pūrṇa-kalaśa* (पूर्ण-कलश) motifs topped by the cross-shaped bracket capital. The *toraṇa*s (तोरण) or decorated arches spanning over the spaces between the pillars are not seen here. The pillars support the shallow domed ceiling of the *nāṭya-maṇḍapa* (नाट्य-मण्डप). The decoration on the exterior of the *maṇḍapa* (मण्डप) includes the scenes of battle, everyday life, palace life, rituals and also scenes from the *Rāmāyaṇa* (रामायण). The *maṇḍapa* walls have perforations to serve as windows thereby allowing free passage of light and air.

The other three remaining temples are smaller in size but consisting of the same architectural features such as *pīṭha* (पीठ), *maṇḍovara* (मण्डोवर) and *śikhara* (शिखार) — all lavishly ornamented with sculptures and other kinds of carvings such as the *jālī*s and floral designs. *Śikhara*s are also decorated with *aṅga-śikhara*s (अङ्ग-शिखर) which cluster about the central main *śikhara*. The temples of Kirāḍu (किराडु), thus, share many architectural features with the temples of Gujarat as well as central India.

The temples of eighth–ninth century were in the style of central Indian temples, while the later temples demonstrate the fusion of indigenous and Solaṅkī (सोलंकी) architectural styles. This is because many of the Jaina temples of Rajasthan, built during this period, were under the Solaṅkī architectural

Pl. 60 : Sūrya temple, Ranakpur, Rajasthan

influence. For example, the Jaina temple complex of Dilwāṛā (दिलवाड़ा) at Mount Abu (माउंट-आबु), particularly the Vimala Vasāhī (विमल वसाही) and the Lūṇa Vasāhī (लूण वसाही), show the happy blending of many regional variations with stupendous sculptural ornamentation suggesting a strong Maru–Gurjara (मरु–गुर्जर) and central Indian influence mingled in a most harmonious fashion. These Jaina temples, mostly made of white marble with beautiful *toraṇa*s (तोरण), carved ceilings with lotus motifs, female bracket-figures, and also open backyards with *deva-kulika*s (देव-कुलिक), i.e. niches with images of gods and goddesses, are superb in their artistic rendition.

However, in plan there is no difference between a Brāhmanical and a Jaina temple, even at Khajurāho (खजुराहो). The east facing Vimala Vasāhī, built between *c.* CE 1031 and 1045 by Vimala Shāh (विमल शाह), dedicated to Ādinātha (आदिनाथ), consists of the *mūla-prāsāda* (मूल-प्रासाद) built of black stone, *gūḍha-maṇḍapa* (गूढ-मण्डप, closed hall), *sabhā-maṇḍapa* (सभा-मण्डप, assembly hall), and *deva-kulika* (देव कुलिक, subsidiary shrines) (*fig.* 62).

The entrance porch of the Vimala Vasāhī (विमल वसाही) has a false dome. It leads into an octagonal *maṇḍapa* (मण्डप), whose pillars support an imposing corbelled dome decorated with sixteen celestial nymphs (*apsaras*es अप्सरस्). The lintels supporting the dome were reinforced by the system of triangulated supports with their intricately carved brackets which also enhanced the beauty of the interior (*Pl.* 58). This type of ceiling arrangements and depictions were adopted in many later period temples both at Mount Abu (माउंट आबु) and at Ranakpur (रनकपुर). To the north–east of the Vimala Vasāhī is another temple, dedicated to Neminātha (नेमिनाथ), known as the Lūṇa Vasāhī (लूना वसाही). It was built around CE 1230 by two brothers Tejapāla (तेजपाल) and Vasupāla (वसुपाल). It also shares the similar architectural and artistic elements with the Vimala Vasāhī. Both the temples are intricately carved on their doorways, pillars, walls and ceilings. The most fascinating decorations are found in the inner surface of the shallow domes surmounting octagonal nave and supported by highly sculpted pillars. The eight pillars of the assembly hall are loftier and of different types. The ceiling of this hall is magnificently carved with figures of dancers, animals, mythological figures and processions of horsemen. From the centre of the ceiling hangs a clustered and finely carved marble pendant in the shape of a lotus bud.

These later period temples are among the finest examples of Indian temple architecture where architectural members metamorphosed into a single sculptural unit. Each nook and corner of these marble edifices, including their pillars, ceilings, walls and floors excel in sculptural details. Jaina mythology, saints, gods and goddesses, monks, devotees, flora, fauna or just good old religious motifs, such as the diamond and bell, all find their way in these sculptural edifices. The poetic sense of the sculptors is evidenced from the depiction of a marble maiden as having just emerged from her bath, and, the droplets falling from her long hair are shown being drunk by a swan sitting by her feet, a motif the history of which goes back to the Kuṣāṇa (कुषाण) period *stūpa* (स्तूप)-railings.

The magnificent Jaina temple at Ranakpur (रनकपुर), dedicated to Ādinātha (आदिनाथ) in 1439, is another stupendous creation of art in marble (*Pl.* 59, *fig.* 63). The temple built on *caumukha* (चौमुख) or four-faced plan has cruciform structural arrangement in the interior. The *mūla-prāsāda* (मूल-प्रासाद) has four subsidiary shrines at its four corners, making it a *pañcāyatana* (पञ्चायतन) temple. Balconies buttress the main *śikhara* (शिखर) of *mūla-prāsāda.* The temple is surrounded by porticoed courtyards. The richly carved hypostyle *sabhā-maṇḍapa*s (सभा-मण्डप) and the interior of the corbelled domes receive enough light to project their sculptural marvel from the openings of the superlative internal spaces. Here also specially arranged columns supported the domes but the lintels are no more supported by the triangulated brackets. The Sūrya (सूर्य) temple at Ranakpur is another architectural marvelous of the period (*Pl.* 60). It also shows the characteristic features of the fifteenth-century temples of Rajasthan. Thus, the architectural grandiose shown by the temples of Mount Abu (माउंट आबु) and Ranakpur are unique which distinguish them from the central Indian and western Indian Nāgara temples. Still, the fact remains that the temples of Rajasthan belong to the north Indian or Nāgara (नागर) style of temple architecture.

7

Early Western Cāḷukyan Temples

THE Early Western Cāḷukyas (चाळुक्य) (CE 535–757), who ruled over the entire Karnataka and parts of Maharashtra and Andhra Pradesh not only initiated rock-cut architecture in the Deccan but also built structural temples at their capitals at Aihoḷe (ऐहोळ), Bādāmī (बादामी) and Paṭṭaḍakal (पट्टडकल) and also at Mahākūṭ (महाकूट), Nagaraḷ (नगरळ) and Siddhanakoḷḷa (सिद्धनकोळ्ळ) — all in the Bagalkoṭ (बगलकोट) district of modern Karnataka. In Andhra Pradesh, they erected many structural temples at Ālampur (आलमपुर), Kuḍaveli (कुडवेलि), Paṇyam (पण्यम्) Mahānandī (महानन्दी),

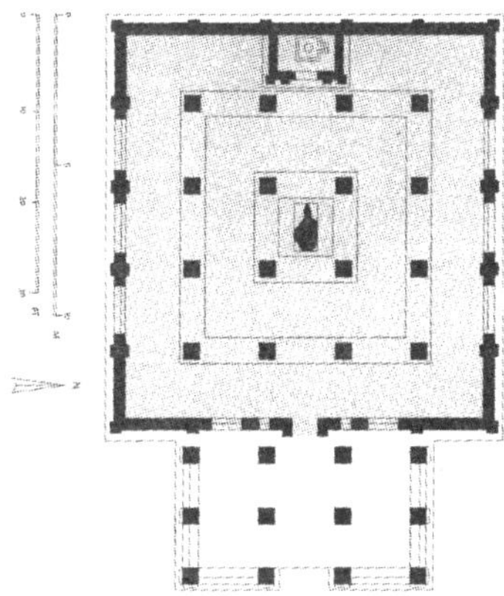

Fig. 64 : Plan of the Lāḍh Khañ temple, Aihoḷe, Karnataka

Pl. 61 : Lāḍh Khañ temple, Aihoḷe

Pl. 62 : Durgā temple, Aihoḷe

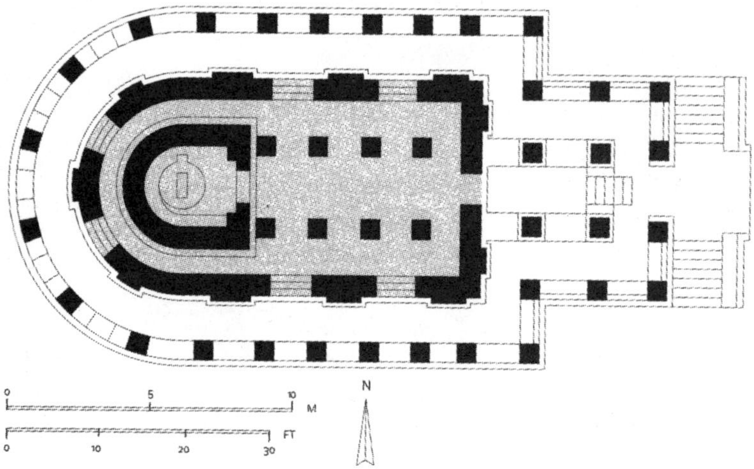

Fig. 65 : Plan of the Durgā temple, Aihoḷe

Satyavoḷu (सत्यवोळु) and Kadamarakalava (कदमरकलव) with Latina (लटिन) form of temple superstructures.

In addition to Drāviḍa (द्राविड), and Nāgara (नागर) styles, a third one which is the hybrid form of the above two styles, known as Vesara (वेसर), originated in the Deccan during this early period.

However, neither true Nāgara, nor true Drāviḍa, nor true Vesara form is found in the Early Western Cāḷukyan architecture. What we see are merely the edifices of combinations and contradictions since they do not follow any particular style of Indian temple architecture. However, this free spirit of experimentations had great potential to evolve into a full-fledged Vesara style, only at a later period during the time of the Hoyasaḷa (होयसळ) administration.

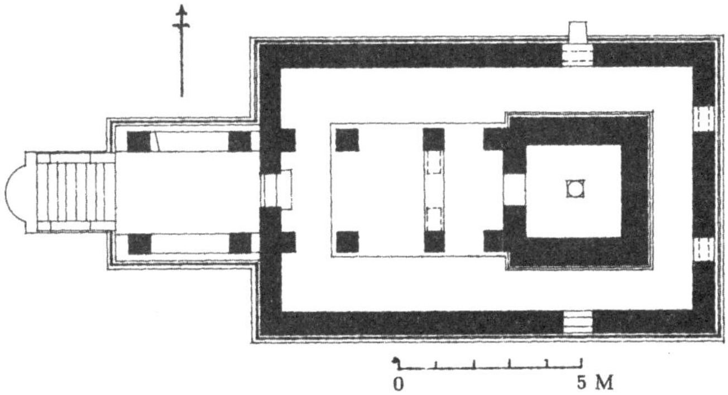

Fig. 66 : Plan of Hucchimalliguḍi temple, Aihoḷe

Pl. 63 : Hucchimalliguḍi temple, Aihoḷe

Aihoḷe, the first capital of the Early Western Cāḷukyas, has several examples of initial attempts made towards the making of structural temples. These early abodes of gods, modest in their appearance, were generally *maṇḍapa* (मण्डप) type structures with pillared halls and flat roofs. They also followed the basic concept of the Hindu temple architecture, i.e. the *garbha-gṛha* (गर्भ-गृह) fronted by the pillared *maṇḍapa*, though, in different style. In course of time, this simple plan was elaborated and the *garbha-gṛha* was developed into a full-fledged *mūla-prāsāda* (मूल-प्रासाद) with its distinct *śikhara* (शिखर). However, the *śikhara*, in many examples, lacks originality and also elegance. More structural elements were added to the *mūla-prāsāda* in the form of an *antarāla* (अन्तराल), closed *sabhā-maṇḍapa* (सभा-मण्डप) and *mukha-maṇḍapa* (मुख-मण्डप). The sanctum was provided with a *pradakṣiṇāpatha* (प्रदक्षिणापथ) making it the *sandhāra* (सन्धार) type.

Among the earliest temples at Aihoḷe, the temples of the Koṇṭi-guḍi (कोण्टिगुडि) group and the Lāḍh Khaṅ (लाढ खाँ) Temple exhibit simplest plan and

Pl. 64 : Meguti temple, Aihoḷe

elevation (*Pl.* 61, *fig.* 64). The Koṇṭi-guḍi group, consisting of three individual shrines, has the *garbha-gṛha*s (गर्भ-गृह) attached to the rear wall and the pillared open verandahs in front. It is, therefore, much different from the central Indian Nāgara (नागर) temples. Massive pillars support the roofs of the shrines. Since the sanctum was attached to the rear wall these shrines do not have *pradakṣiṇāpatha*s (प्रदक्षिणापथ, circumambulatory passages). Therefore, they are known as the *nirandhāra* (निरन्धार) shrines.

Pl. 65 : Upper Śivālaya, Bādāmī

The Lāḍh Khañ Temple, which stands on a moulded *adhiṣṭhāna* (अधिष्ठान), comprises the *garbha-gṛha* abutting the rear wall, the *maṇḍapa* (मण्डप) enshrining the Nandī (नन्दी) (the bull vehicle of Śiva), and the pillared portico in front. The *maṇḍapa* walls in front of the sanctum have latticed windows which allow free passage of light and air. Over the Nandī *maṇḍapa* is a small shrine with high reliefs of the deities on the outer walls.

A stone ladder from the pillared *maṇḍapa* leads to the roof-top shrine, which is not seen in the central Indian temples of Nāgara style. The temple has a two-tiered sloping roof with long flat slabs whose joints were covered by long narrow stone strips.

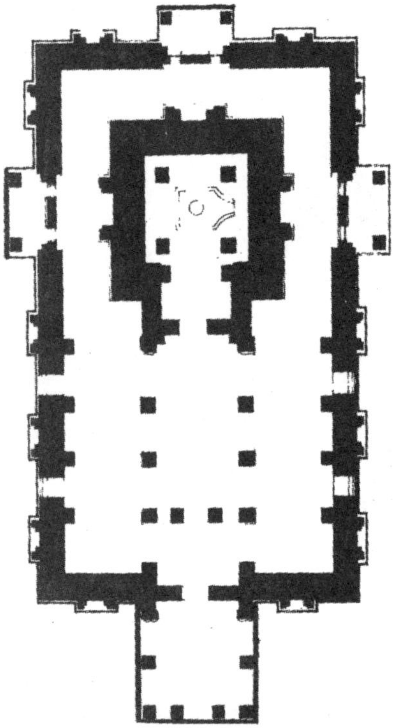

Fig. 67 : Plan of Malegiṭṭi Śivālaya, Bādāmī

It may be noted that the monolithic square pillars of the *maṇḍapa* stand directly on the floor without any pillar bases. Over the pillars have capitals with wavy brackets. For the first time in the Deccan the cushion capital (i.e. capitals with flattish round with or without ribbed forms) appears on the pillars of the Lāḍh Khañ temple. It was later adopted by the Pallavas and the cushion capitals became the integral part of the Draviḍian temple architecture. The pillars of the portico depict the images of the river goddesses, Gaṅgā (गङ्ग) and Yamunā (यमुना). The portico is also provided with the *kakṣāsana* (कक्षासन, stone-seat with back-rest) which is the first of its kind in the Cāḷukyan (चाळुक्य) territory although it was common in the temples of Khajurāho (खजुराहो).

The next development in the Early Cāḷukyan temple architecture can be seen in the famous "Durga (दुर्ग) Temple" at Aihoḷe (ऐहोळ) which derives its name from Durgaguḍi, (दुर्गगुडि) meaning "temple near the fort" (*Pl.* 62, *fig.* 65). The temple, dedicated to Viṣṇu (विष्णु), stands on a high, well-moulded *adhiṣṭhāna* (अधिष्ठान). It is apsidal in plan which consists of the *mukha-maṇḍapa* (मुख-मण्डप), *sabhā-maṇḍapa* (सभा-मण्डप) and the *garbha-gṛha* (गर्भ-गृह) with a *pradakṣiṇāpatha* (प्रदक्षिणापथ). The Buddhist *caitya* (चैत्य) architecture

Pl. 66 : Malegiṭṭi Śivālaya, Bādāmī

might have influenced the plan of this temple although Early Historic Hindu temples were also built on this type of apsidal platforms. This apsidal plan and barrel vaulted structure, is classified in the Vāstu-śāstras (वास्तुशास्त्र), as the *hasti-pṛṣṭha* (हस्ति-पृष्ठ) or "elephant-back" type. The temple appears to be of a late seventh- or early eighth-century construction.

Pl. 67 : Lower Śivālaya, Bādāmī

The pillars are square, massive and with cushion capitals. They are decorated with relief panels and medallions. The roof of the portico is supported by four square pillars. From the porch, a highly decorated doorway leads to the *sabhā-maṇḍapa*. The temple exhibits an unsuccessful copy of the north Indian Maru–Gurjara (मरु-गुर्जर) latina *śikhara* (शिखर) over the *garbha-gṛha*. But it lacks the elegance of a typical Nāgara (नागर) style *rekhā śikhara* (रेखा शिखर) in its plan, elevation and proportion with the rest of the structure.

Further development in the temple architecture is witnessed at Huccīmallī-guḍi (हुच्चीमल्ली-गुडि) temple at Aihoḷe (*Pl.* 63, *fig.* 66). It has a rectangular plan consisting of a square sanctum with a curvilinear *śikhara*. The temple also encloses a covered *pradakṣiṇāpatha*, an *antarāla* (अन्तराल, vestibule), a pillared hall (*maṇḍapa*) and a porch (*mukha-maṇḍapa*). The *mukha-maṇḍapa* has *kakṣāsanas* (कक्षासन) on both sides which are decorated with vase and foliage designs.

The Meguti (मेगुति) temple of the Jainas, built in CE 634 during the reign of Pulakeśin II (पुलकेशिन् II), is the most developed of the *maṇḍapa* style temples at Aihoḷe (*Pl.* 64). The temple stands on a high platform on a hillock. The *mūla-prāsāda* (मूल-प्रासाद),

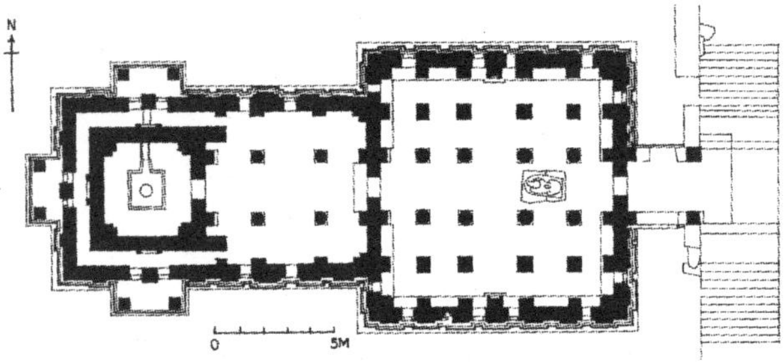

Fig. 68 : Plan of the Pāpanātha temple, Paṭṭaḍakal

square in plan, resembles a closed *maṇḍapa*. The temple includes the *garbha-gṛha*, an *antarāla*, and a large *mukha-maṇḍapa*. Though the *pradakṣiṇāpatha* (प्रदक्षिणापथ) was provided, it was intercepted by cross-walls which prevent circumambulation. A flight of steps leads to the *mukha-maṇḍapa*. Over the *garbha-gṛha* is a smaller shrine which is accessible by a flight of stairs.

At Bādāmī (बादामी), the second capital of the Early Cāḷukyas, mainly south Indian style temple architecture is found with Drāviḍa *vimāna* (द्राविड विमान). For example, early *vimāna* temples like the upper Śivālaya (शिवालय), the lower Śivālaya, and the Malegiṭṭi Śivālaya exhibit the Drāviḍa characteristics in their architecture.

The upper Śivālaya consists of a *sandhāra garbha-gṛha* (सन्धार गर्भ-गृह) with a closed *pradakṣiṇāpatha*

Pl. 68 : Pāpanātha temple, Paṭṭaḍakal

(प्रदक्षिणापथ) (*Pl.* 65). In front of it is a pillared *maṇḍapa* (मण्डप). The *kuḍu* (कुडु) arches decorate the *chajjās* (छज्जा, eaves). The multi-storeyed square *vimāna* rises in diminishing order. The *sukanāsikās* (सुकनासिका), the characteristic feature of the Early Cāḷukyan architecture, decorate each side of the square *grīvā* (ग्रीवा) and the *śikhara* (शिखर).

The Malegiṭṭi Śivālaya is a *nirandhāra* (निरन्धार) shrine fronted by a closed *maṇḍapa* (*Pl.* 66, *fig.* 67). The first *tala* (तल, storey) of the *vimāna* is decorated with *karṇakūṭas* (कर्णकूट) and *śālās* (शाला). The *nāsikās* (नासिका) adorn the four cardinal faces of the *grīvā*. The octagonal *śikhara* is crowned by a heavy dome.

The Lower Śivālaya, unlike the Malegitti Śivālaya, has a *pradakṣiṇāpatha* (*Pl.* 67). It is smaller than the former. All the *talas* (तल) of the *vimāna* have the *hāra* (हार) elements while the octagonal *grīvā* and *śikhara* have *kūṭas* (कूट). The octagonal *grīvā* and *śikhara* with *hāra* elements are the typical Draviḍian style.

At Paṭṭaḍakal (पट्टडकल), the third Cāḷukyan (चाळुक्य) capital, one can see the most developed form of the Early Cāḷukyan temple architecture. Both Nāgara (नागर) and Drāviḍa traditions of temple architecture flourished here. The four main temples at Paṭṭaḍakal are the Pāpanātha (पापनाथ), Saṅgameśvara (संगमेश्वर), Virūpākṣa (विरूपाक्ष), and Mallikārjuna (मल्लिकार्जुन). Of these, the first one exhibit Nāgara features while the rest are in Drāviḍa style.

It may be noted that even in north India, the Nāgara architecture had not developed before the seventh century in its full-fledged form. It might be a reason that while dealing with the Nāgara *rekhā prāsāda* (रेखा प्रासाद) or *śikhara* the Early Cāḷukyan

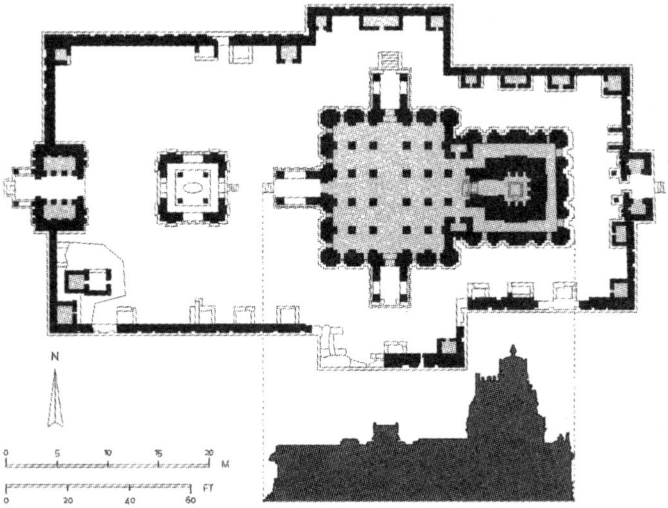

Fig. 69 : Plan of Virūpākṣa temple, Paṭṭaḍakal

architects reveal their inexperience in basic details. For example, the plan of the Pāpanātha temple lacks harmony in its structural arrangements (*Pl.* 68, *fig.* 68). Further, the height of the *śikhara* (शिखर) is out of proportion with the length of the temple. The *antarāla* (अन्तराल) is also out of proportion with the *garbha-gṛha* (गर्भ-गृह). In front of the *antarāla* is a large pillared *maṇḍapa* (मण्डप) enshrining the Nandī (नन्दी).

The Saṅgameśvara (संगमेश्वर) temple, built by Cāḷukya Vijayāditya (चाळुक्य विजयादित्य) in Drāviḍa (द्राविड) style, does not show the characteristic *sukanāsikā* (सुकनासिका) of the Cāḷukyan tradition. The *tritala vimāna* (त्रितल विमान, three-storeyed) is square in plan from the base to top. The temple is *sandhāra* type with a closed *pradakṣiṇāpatha* (प्रदक्षिणापथ) around the *garbha-gṛha*. The sanctum is fronted by a *mahāmaṇḍapa* (महामण्डप) and in turn by an *ardha-maṇḍapa* (अर्द्ध-मण्डप). The whole temple complex stands on a common *adhiṣṭhāna* (अधिष्ठान). The first and second *talas* (तल) of the *vimāna* have *śālās* (शाला) and *kūṭas* (कूट) while the topmost *tala* has only *śālās*. The *prastara* (प्रस्तर, entablature, i.e. parapet) over the *prākāra* (प्राकार, outer wall) carries *kūṭas* and *śālās*. The *śikhara* is crowned by a *kalaśa* (कलश). Latticed windows on the exterior walls allow passage of air and light to the *mahāmaṇḍapa* and the *pradakṣiṇāpatha*.

The final developments in the Early Cāḷukyan

temples can be witnessed in the Virūpākṣa (विरूपाक्ष) and Mallikārjuna (मल्लिकार्जुन) temples. These temples were influenced by the architecture of the Kailāsanātha (कैलासनाथ) temple at Kāñcīpuram (कांचीपुरम्). It may be noted that since the Cāḷukyans and the Pallavas (पल्लव) were the contemporaries, their respective architectural traditions were also influenced by each other's peculiar structural elements.

The Virūpākṣa temple (known as Śrī Lokeśvara-Mahā-Śilā-prāsāda श्री लोकेश्वर-महा-शिला-प्रासाद), built by Lokamahādevī (लोकमहादेवी), one of the queens of Vikramāditya II (विक्रमादित्य II, CE 733-45), in commemoration of her husband's victory over the Pallavas of Kāñcīpuram, closely resembles the Kailāsanātha temple at Kāñcīpuram on plan and elevation and represents a well-developed stage of

Pl. 69 : Virūpākṣa temple, Paṭṭaḍakal

Pl. 70 : Mallikārjuna temple, Paṭṭaḍakal

the Karnataka Draviḍian architecture (*Pl.* 69, *fig.* 69). The temple consists of the *garbha-gṛha* with a *pradakṣiṇāpatha*, an *antarāla* (अन्तराल), a *sabhā-maṇḍapa* (सभा-मण्डप) with entrances on the east, north and south and a separate Nandī-*maṇḍapa* (नन्दी-मण्डप) in front. The whole temple complex is enclosed by a high *prākāra* or boundary wall.

The temple stands on a high moulded *adhiṣṭhāna* (अधिष्ठान). The *garbha-gṛha* (गर्भ-गृह), square in plan, from base to *śikhara* (शिखर), has three storeys. It is a *sandhāra* (सन्धार) temple with a *pradakṣiṇāpatha* (प्रदक्षिणापथ) around the sanctum. From the third storey of the *vimāna* (विमान) projects the *sukanāsikā* (सुकनासिका) over the *antarāla* (अन्तराल), a characteristic feature of the Early Cāḷukyan (चाळुक्य) architecture. The *hāra* (हार) elements such as *śālā*s, *kūṭa*s and *pañjara*s of the Drāviḍa style adorn the *tala*s (तल) of the *vimāna*. The *vimāna* is crowned by a round finial over which rests the *kalaśa* (कलश). The outer faces of the *prākāra* wall have so many projections interspersed with recesses. These projections have niches incorporating the images of various deities like Bhairava (भैरव), Narasiṁha (नरसिंह), Hari-Hara (हरि-हर) and Lakulīśa (लकुलीश). The recesses are filled with latticed windows.

The pillars of the *sabhā-maṇḍapa* (सभा-मण्डप) are highly decorated with relief panels depicting stories from *Rāmāyaṇa* (रामायण) and *Mahābhārata* (महाभारत). Aesthetically carved amorous couples, flowers, leafy scrolls, birds, animals, geometrical designs, etc. also adorn the interior of the temple.

The Mallikārjuna (मल्लिकार्जुन) temple (known as Śrī Trailokeśvara Mahā Śaila Prāsāda, श्री त्रैलोकेश्वर महा शैल प्रासाद), built by queen Trailokyamahādevī (त्रैलोक्यमहादेवी) of Vikramāditya II (CE 733-45) in commemoration of her husband's victory over the Pallavas of Kāñcīpuram (कांचीपुरम्), resembles the Virūpākṣa (विरूपाक्ष) temple in plan, elevation, decoration and sculptural art (*Pl.* 70, *fig.* 70). The temple consists of a sanctum (*garbha-gṛha*) with circumambulatory passage (*pradakṣiṇāpatha*) an antechamber (*antarāla*), a *sabhā-maṇḍapa* with entrance porches on the east, north and south and a separate Nandī-*maṇḍapa* (नन्दी-मण्डप) in front.

The temple stands on a high moulded *adhiṣṭhāna*. Like the Virūpākṣa temple, the outer projections on the *prākāra* wall accommodate the images of divinities. The recesses in between these projections are filled with latticed windows.

The topmost *tala* of the three-storeyed *vimāna* is devoid of any *hāra* element. The first and second *tala*s are adorned with *śālā*s and *kūṭa*s. A *sukanāsikā*, incorporating the image of the Naṭarāja (नटराज), projects from the *vimāna* over the *antarāla*.

Like the Virūpākṣa (विरूपाक्ष) temple, the Mallikārjuna (मल्लिकार्जुन) also depicts the stories from the ancient Indian scriptures like the *Rāmāyaṇa* (रामायण) and the *Mahābhārata* (महाभारत). The *adhiṣṭhāna* (अधिष्ठान) of the Nandī-*maṇḍapa* (नन्दी-मण्डप) has beautifully carved figures of elephants and other animals. Human figures, flora and fauna also adorn various parts of the temple. The interior decoration

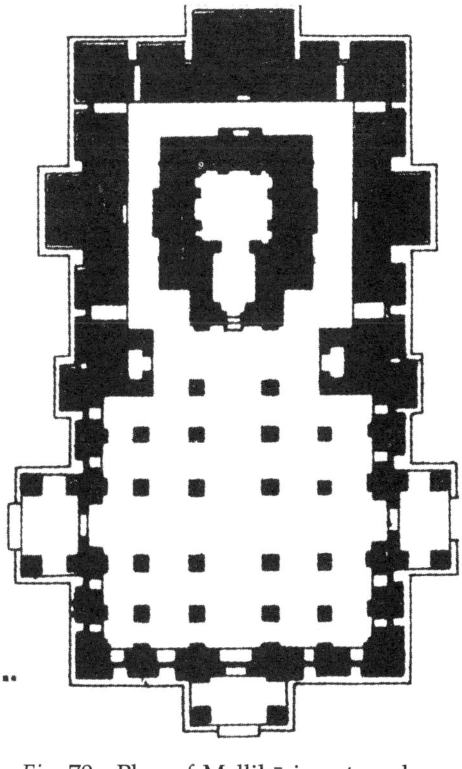

Fig. 70 : Plan of Mallikārjuna temple, Paṭṭaḍakal

of the Virūpākṣa and Mallikārjuna temples attests that the Early Cāḷukyans (चाळुक्य) were not only interested in the splendid look of the divine edifices but also took special care in the embellishment of the structural work with sculptural art.

At Ālampur, District Mahaboobnagar, Andhra Pradesh, the Bādāmī Cāḷukyans constructed a group of nine temples (known as Nava Brahmā (नव ब्रह्मा) temples, dedicated to Lord Śiva) on the bank of the River Tuṅgabhadrā (तुंगभद्रा). They are the Svarga Brahmā (स्वर्ग ब्रह्मा), Padma Brahmā (पद्म ब्रह्मा), Arka Brahmā (अर्क ब्रह्मा), Viśva Brahmā (विश्व ब्रह्मा), Garuḍa Brahmā (गरुड ब्रह्मा), Bāla Brahmā (बाल ब्रह्मा), Tāraka Brahmā (तारक ब्रह्मा), Kumāra Brahmā (कुमार ब्रह्मा), and Vīra Brahmā (वीर ब्रह्मा). According to the temple inscriptions the Nava Brahmā group of temples has been dated between the last quarter of the sixth century and the first half of the eighth century CE.

Except Tāraka Brahmā all other temples have similar plan and elevation. In plan they are provided with a rectangular pillared *maṇḍapa* (मण्डप) with a *sanctum sanctorum* at one end. In some shrines such as the Svarga Brahmā and the Kumāra Brahmā the rectangular *maṇḍapa* is fronted by a small pillared porch or *mukha-maṇḍapa* (मुख-मण्डप). The pillar arrangement of the *mukha-maṇḍapas* follows the typical Gupta inter-columnation. In elevation, the temples consist of a moulded *adhiṣṭhāna* (अधिष्ठान), *bhitti* (भित्ति), *prastara* (प्रस्तर, entablature), and a curvilinear *śikhara* (शिखर). The *bhitti* is interspersed with latticed windows and *devakoṣṭhas* (देवकोष्ठ). The *prastara* is not developed with projecting *chajjās* (छज्जा). However, it is provided with water spouts. The interior of these temples resembles the rock-cut temples of the Deccan. However, the *śikhara* of the Nava Brahmā temples (except Tāraka Brahmā) resembles those of the eighth-century temples of Osian (Rajasthan) and Bhubaneswar (Orissa). In all the examples the *śikhara* takes its curvilinear form right from the bottom. There are no aedicules or miniature shrines to adorn the *śikhara*s. The *paga*s (पग) are interspersed with *bhūmi-āmalaka*s (भूमि-आमलक). A huge *āmalaka* (आमलक) crowns the superstructure. The *sukanāsikā* (सुकनासिका) appears at the base of the *raha-paga* (रह-पग) above the *maṇḍapa.* In the Svarga Brahmā temple the *sukanāsikā* depicts dancing Śiva. Like the Hari-Hara (हरि-हर) 1 temple at Osian, the Nava Brahmā temples also bear *devakoṣṭha*s on the outer walls.

The Tāraka Brahmā, a ruined temple, consists of *garbha-gṛha* (गर्भ-गृह), *antarāla* (अन्तराल) and *mukha-maṇḍapa.* It lacks any significant decorations except the presence of *devakoṣṭha*s (देवकोष्ठ) on the walls of the *sanctum sanctorum* and a standing Lakṣmī (लक्ष्मी) on the *antarāla* (अन्तराल) doorway. The presence of *hārāntara* (हरन्तर) elements such as *śālā* (शाला), *kūṭa* (कूट) and *pañjara* (पञ्जर) easily differs it from the best of the group.

The Early Western Cāḷukyas not only built their finest monuments of worship at Ālampur but also meaningfully embellished them with relief panels depicting the temporal and spiritual life. While the Cāḷukyan architects adopted Nāgara style for their temples at Ālampur, the sculptors tried to retain the grace of Gupta art in their own creations. The figures on the exterior walls, pillars, doorframes and ceilings of the temples attest to a high level of artistic endeavour. The figures in round and in relief display delicacy, softness, vitality and motion.

The temples depict various forms of Śiva, gods, goddesses, flying *vidyādhara*s (विद्याधर), *bhūta*s (भूत), *garuḍa* (गरुड) faces, *dvārapālikā*s (द्वारपालिका), *cauri-* (चौरि) bearers, *ṛṣi*s (ऋषि), Purāṇic (पुराणिक) themes, floral motifs, birds, animals and amorous couples. The graceful faces of *mithuna*s (मिथुन) draw a narrow line between lust and love. The dynamic representations of Liṅgodbhavamūrti (लिङ्गोद्भवमूर्ति), Tripurasaṁhāra-mūrti (त्रिपुरसंहारमूर्ति), Gaṅgāvataraṇamūrti (गङ्गावतरणमूर्ति) and Tāṇḍavamūrti (ताण्डवमूर्ति) display the vigorous cosmic energy and motion. Thus, Cāḷukyan sculptors succeeded in infusing a high level of philosophical thoughts into tangible creations of beauty.

8

Later Western Cāḷukyan Temples

THE Later Western Cāḷukyas (चाळुक्य) (the descendants of the Bādāmī Cāḷukyas बादामी चाळुक्य), established themselves in the tenth century and ruled until thirteenth century, first from Mānyakheta (मान्यखेत) (modern Malkheḍ मलखेड) and later from Kalyāṇī (कल्याणी). Their temples were also influenced by the architectural traditions of the north and south. Unlike the early Cāḷukyas, the Later Cāḷukyas relied more on fine-grained dark marble like smooth and soapy chloritic schist than sandstone for their temples.

Pl. 71. Kalleśvara temple, Kukkanur

They retained the multi-storeyed *vimāna* (विमान) with embellishments around the cella and

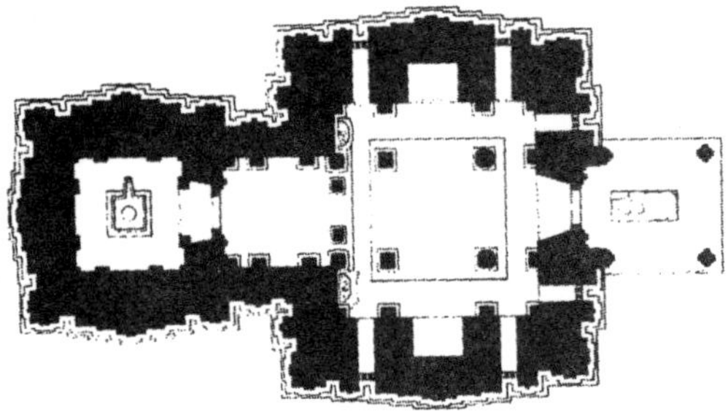

fig. 71. Plan of Kalleśvara temple, Kukkanur

śikhara (शिखर). The *hāra* elements like *śālā* (शाला), *kūṭa* (कूट) and *pañjara* (पञ्जर) began to disappear gradually from the *prastara* (प्रस्तर) and *śikhara* with the modification of the plan and elevation of the *mūla-prāsāda* (मूल-प्रासाद). The temples are usually oblong without a *pradakṣiṇāpatha* (प्रदक्षिणापथ) around the sanctum. The broad *adhiṣṭhāna* (अधिष्ठान) extended beyond the temple walls provide a path for circumambulation around the whole temple complex. Often the main entrance was attached to the sides of the *mahāmaṇḍapa* (महामण्डप) rather than in the front of the *mukha-maṇḍapa* (मुख-मण्डप). Similarly, subsidiary porches were attached to the *maṇḍapas* which were projected from the sides of the latter.

Pl. 72: Kāśīviśveśvara temple, Lakkuṇḍī

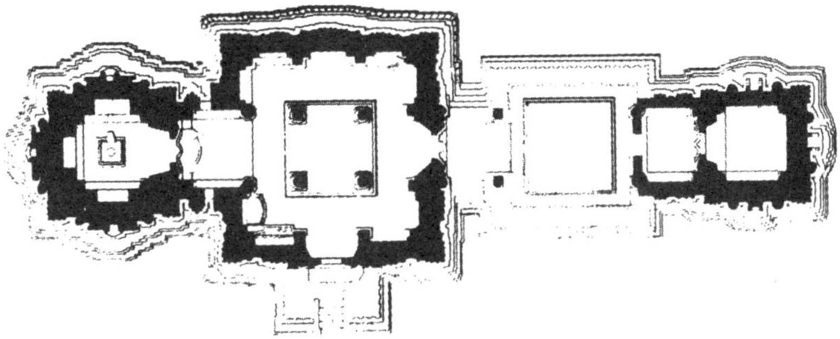

fig. 72: Plan of Kāśīviśveśara temple, Lakkuṇḍī

The Jaina temple at Lakkuṇḍī (लक्कुण्डी) near Gaḍag (गडग) is among the earliest temple styles of the Later Cāḷukyans which has been tentatively dated in the latter half of the eleventh century. Built on fine-grained chloritic schist, the temple rises to five storeys. It is square in plan from the base to the *śikhara*. The *garbha-gṛha* (गर्भ-गृह) is fronted by a close square *maṇḍapa*, known as *navaraṅga* (नवरंग). A *sukanāsikā* (सुकनासिका) projects from the *śikhara*. The *nāsikā* motifs in between the pairs of slender pilasters adorn the temple walls.

Pl. 73: Mukteśvara temple, Chauḍadampur

The Kalleśvara (कल्लेश्वर) temple at Kukkanur (कुक्कनुर) is a three-storeyed *vimāna* (विमान)

which is fronted by a *navaraṅga* (नवरंग) (a square closed *maṇḍapa* which has nine *aṅkanas* (अंकन) or divisions, i.e. a central *aṅkana* surrounded by eight smaller *aṅkanas*) (*Pl.* 71 & *fig.* 71). The temple wall has projections and recesses that are almost empty without any decoration. The *talas* (तल) of the *vimāna* lack the typical forms. The *śikhara* (शिखर) of the temple is crowned by a square cupola over which rests the *kalaśa* (कलश).

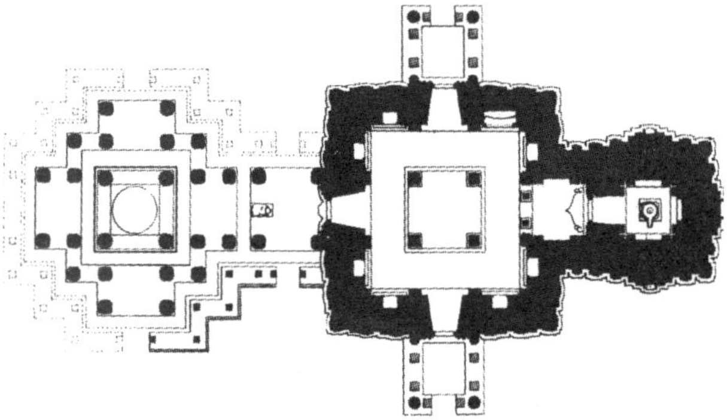

fig. 73: Plan of Mahādeva temple, Iṭṭagi

The maturity of the Later Cāḷukyan (चाळुक्य) style was achieved by the end of the eleventh century at several sites including Haṅgal (हंगल), Kuruvatti (कुरुवत्ति), Iṭṭagi (इट्टगि) and Lakkuṇḍī (लक्कुण्डी). Now the temples have well-defined, highly ornate moulded *adhiṣṭhāna* (अधिष्ठान), *jaṅghā*

Pl. 74: Mahādeva temple, Iṭṭagi

(जंघा) (main part of the wall), highly developed *prastara* (प्रस्तर) with projecting *chajjās* (छज्जा) and multi-storeyed diminishing *śikhara* towards the top. The middle of each *tala* of the *śikhara* exhibits a *kīrtimukha* (कीर्तिमुख) arch enshrining the relief image of the deity. The projected sloping *chajjā* appearing from below the *prastara* protected temple walls and relief panels from heavy rains and scorching sun. Such projecting eaves are one of the characteristic features of the Later Cāḷukyan style. Temples like the Kāśīviśveśvara (कशीविश्वेश्वर) at Lakkuṇḍī (*Pl.* 72, *fig.* 72), the Mukteśvara (मुक्तेश्वर) at Chauḍadampur (छौडदमपुर) (*Pl.* 73), the Mahādeva (महादेव) at Iṭṭagi (*Pl.* 74, *fig.* 73), and the Mallikārjuna (मल्लिकार्जुन) at Kuruvatti (*Pl.* 75a & 75b, *fig.* 74) provide examples for the projecting *chajjās*. The pillar shafts and capitals are intricately carved with delicate jewel motifs, scalloped designs, arches, leafy scrolls, floral designs and divinities.

Pl. 75a: Mallikārjuna temple, Kuruvatti

The outer face of the *vimāna* wall has many projections and niches. The central and two corner projections of each side of the temple wall exhibit a miniature relief shrine crowned by a *śikhara* imitating the *śikhara* of the *mūla-prāsāda* (मूल-प्रासाद). Interestingly, even these miniature relief shrines projecting from the temple walls are provided with a projecting *chajjā* immediately below the duplicate *śikhara* which imitates the main *śikhara* of the temple proper.

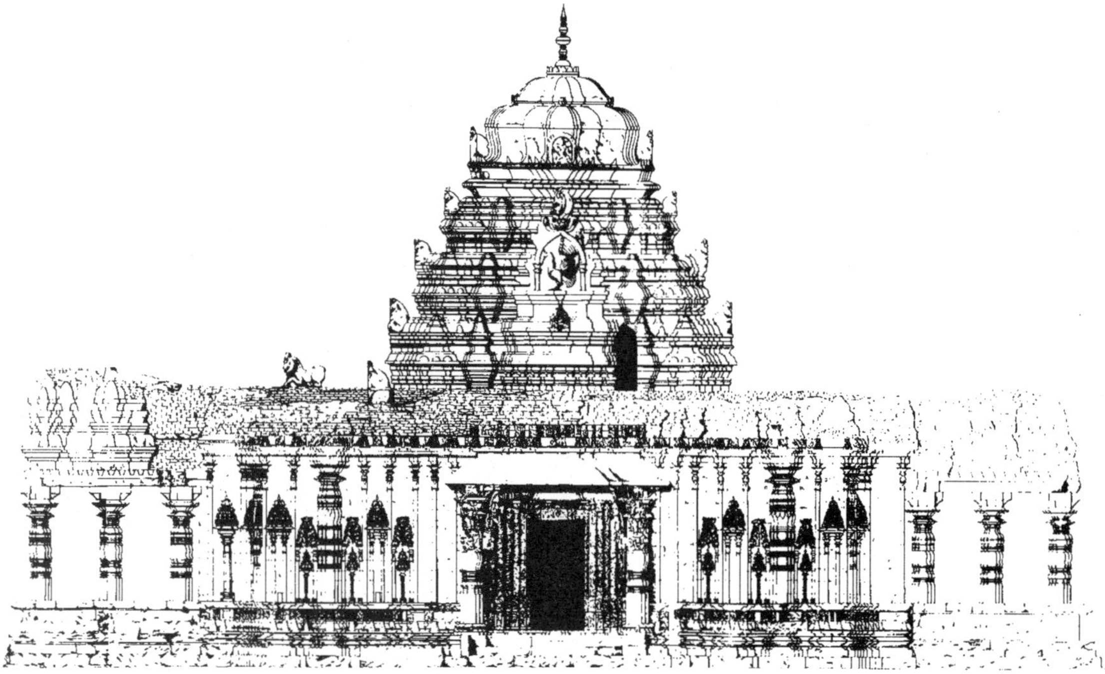

Pl. 75b: Frontal elevation of Mallikārjuna temple, Kuruvatti

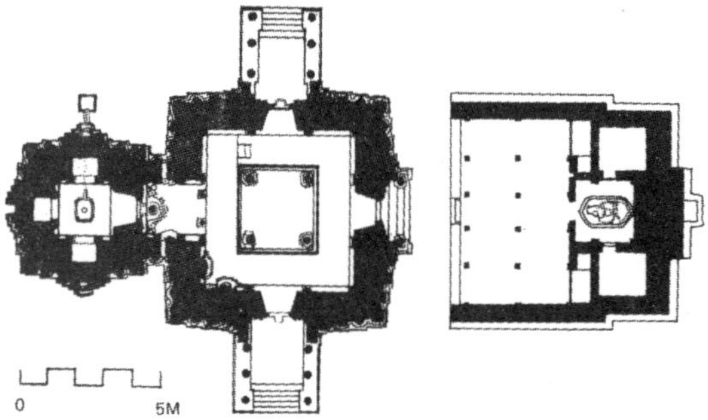

fig. 74: Plan of Mallikārjuna temple, Kuruvatti

In short, unlike the Early Western Cāḷukyas, the Later Cāḷukyas gave more attention to the development of the hybrid form of the Deccan temple architecture by adopting and modifying new elements from the north and south as well as incorporating indigenous styles and artistic elements into the existing hybrid architectural tradition. To achieve this perfection, the Later Cāḷukyans first provided a symmetrical appearance to the whole body of the temple complex, and different structural units in proper proportions were erected in their suitable places. Imposing *vimāna*s (विमान) decorated with typical *kīrtimukha* (कीर्तिमुख) arches and beautifully carved *adhiṣṭhāna* (अधिष्ठान) mouldings, pillars and pilasters are noteworthy.

9

Pallava Temples

Pl. 76 : Shore Temple, Mamallapuram

THE south Indian temple architecture is represented by the Draviḍian order, or else, the mixture of Drāviḍa (द्राविड) and Nāgara (नागर), called Vesara (वेसर) style. This classification is based on the shape of the *vimāna* (विमान) including its *śikhara* (शिखर) and *grīvā* (ग्रीवा). A temple is considered of Nāgara type if its *vimāna* or spire, i.e. *śikhara,* is four-sided, square or oblong; Drāviḍa if six- or eight-sided; Vesara if bell-shaped. However, in a mixed variety, if the lower part of the *vimāna* differs from the *śikhara* and *grīvā* in plan, normally the shape of the latter is taken into consideration for classification.

Pallava Structural Temples

Pallava (पल्लव) rule (seventh–ninth century CE) is

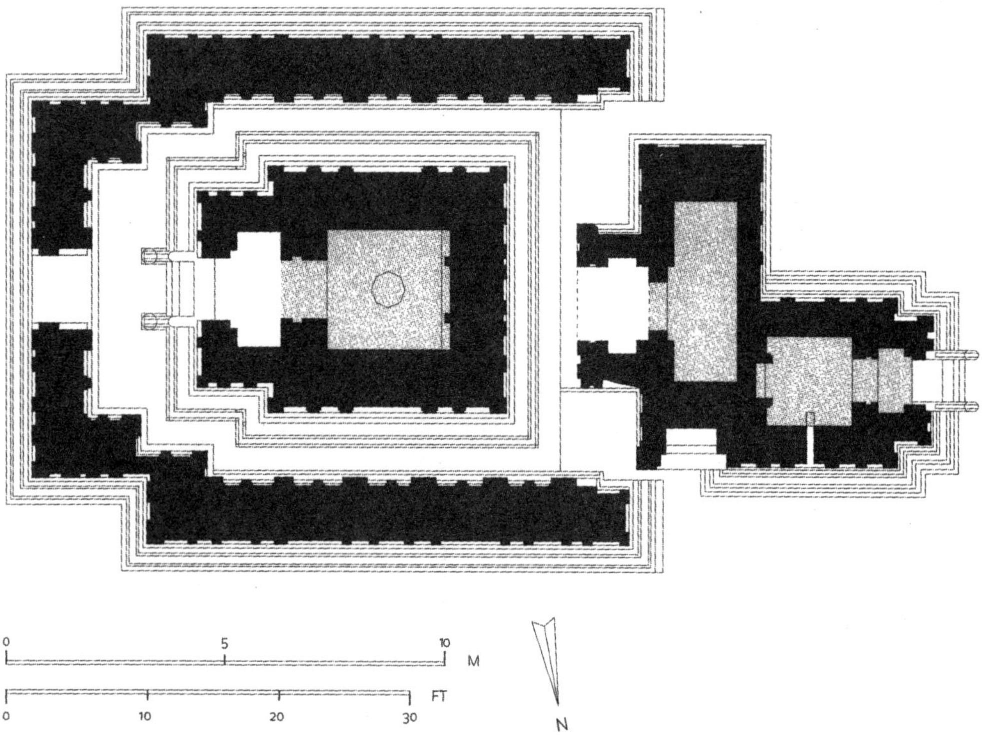

Fig. 75 : Plan of the Shore Temple, Mahābalipuram

not only marked for its rock-cut architecture but also for excellence in the erection of magnificent structural temples. The structural activities are concentrated at their port-town of Mamallapuram (ममल्लपुरम्) (same as Mahābalipuram महाबलिपुरम्) and in their capital city Kāñcīpuram. The experiments on structural temples started during the time of Narasiṁhavarman (नरसिंहवर्मन्) II Rājasiṁha (राजसिंह) (CE 700-28) who caused to build at least five temples.

The earlier structural temples were built of hard igneous rocks like granite (Olakkanneśvara ओलक्कन्नेश्वर temple), leptinite (Shore Temple), and gneiss (Mukundanayanār मुकुन्दनयनार् and the Talagirīśvara तलगिरीश्वर). Later Rājasiṁha resorted to soft sandstone for constructing temples. He used the hard varieties only for slabs and for the top and bottom courses of the *adhiṣṭhāna* (अधिष्ठान).

The so-called "Shore Temple" at Mamallapuram, constructed out of the hard, blackish leptinite rock pieces, comprises three shrines, namely, the Rājasiṁheśvara (राजसिंहेश्वर), the Kṣatriyasiṁheśvara (क्षत्रियसिंहेश्वर) and the Narapatisiṁhapallava Viṣṇugṛha (नरपतिसिंहपल्लव विष्णुगृह) (*Pl.* 76, *fig.* 75). The Rājasiṁheśvara, a three-storeyed *vimāna* type temple, dedicated to Śiva (शिव), has a square plan but the *grīvā* (ग्रीवा) and *śikhara* (शिखर) are eight-sided, hence it is a Drāviḍa (द्राविड) shrine. The topmost *tala* has, however, no *hāra* elements such as *śālā* (शाला),

Pl. 77 : Kailāsanatha temple, Kāñcipuram

kūṭa (कूट) and *pañjara* (पञ्जर) that are supposed to adorn the parapet. The pillars and the pilasters have rearing lions at the base, a characteristic feature of the Rājasiṁha (राजसिंह) style temples.

The Kṣatriyasiṁheśvara temple, facing east, has a four-storeyed *vimāna* with square plan and octagonal *grīvā* and *śikhara* surmounted by a polished basalt finial. This shrine is also dedicated to Śiva. The second and third *tala*s of the shrine have *kūṭa*s and *śālā*s as decoratives of the hara. The topmost *tala* displays images of the *bhūta*s (भूत), i.e. goblins. The corners of the *ādi-tala* (आदि-तल) (the first or the lowermost storey) are adorned with crouching lions.

The Narapatisiṁhapallava Viṣṇugṛha, a *maṇḍapa* (मण्डप) shrine dedicated to Viṣṇu (विष्णु), stands in between the two Śiva temples. It is a *maṇḍapa*-type shrine (i.e. single storeyed hall type) which is devoid of additional storeys.

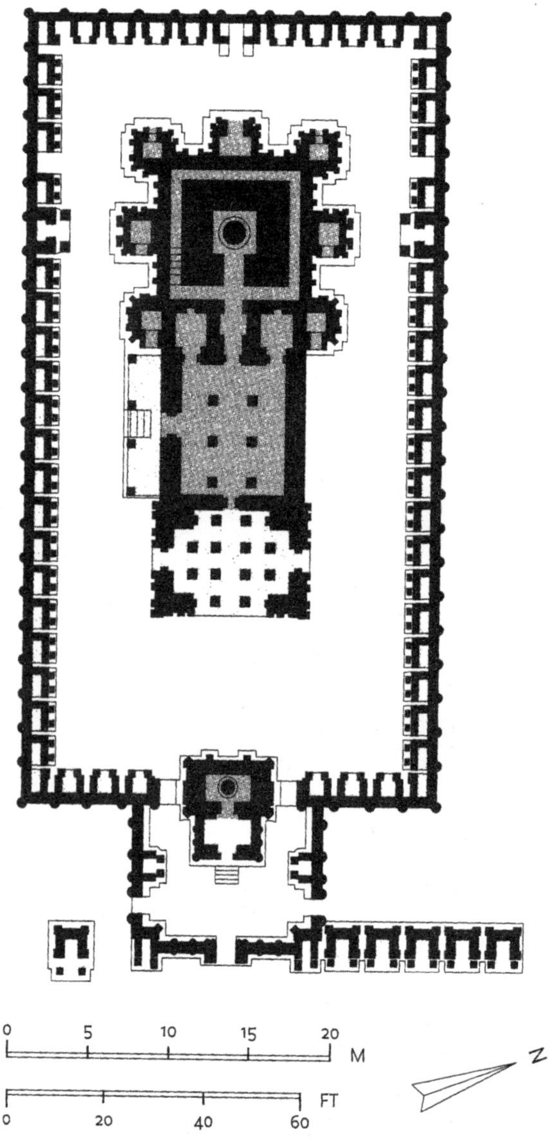

Fig. 76 : Plan of the Kailāsanātha temple, Kāñcīpuram

Kailāsanātha Temple, Kāñcīpuram

This temple, dedicated to Śiva, was built by Rājasiṁha and his son Mahendravarman (महेन्द्रवर्मन्) III in sandstone masonry. The four-storeyed *vimāna* is square in plan with octagonal *grīvā* and *śikhara*. The sanctum is enclosed by another wall providing a circumambulatory passage in between the two walls (*Pl.* 77, *fig.* 76). A Somaskanda (सोमस्कन्द) relief panel adorns the rear wall of the sanctum. The sanctum contains a large fluted *liṅga* (लिङ्ग) fixed on the floor.

The first and third storeys of the *vimāna* have only *kūṭa*s and *śālā*s as parts of the *hāra* decoration. The second *tala* is provided with *pañjara*s while the topmost storey yields Nandīs (नन्दी) at the four corners. The pillars and pilasters depict rearing lions at the base. The entire temple complex is enclosed by a *prākāra* (प्राकार) (outer) wall.

Vaikuṇṭha Perumal Temple, Kāñcīpuram

This temple, dedicated to Viṣṇu (विष्णु), was erected by Nandīvarman (नन्दीवर्मन्) Pallavamalla (पल्लवमल्ल) (CE 731-96). Built of sandstone, it stands on a well-moulded *adhiṣṭhāna* (अधिष्ठान). The square *vimāna* (विमान) rises to four *tala*s (तल) with octagonal *grīvā* (ग्रीवा) and *śikhara* (शिखर). Three walls, one within the other, surround the main shrine forming a pair of covered *pradakṣiṇāpatha*s (प्रदक्षिणापथ) (circumambulatory passages). In this temple, each one of the superimposed storeys contains a cella, each enshrining a Viṣṇu image but in different poses, standing, sitting or reclining. The first three storeys alone include the usual *hāra* (हार) elements such as *śālā*s (शाला), *kūṭa*s (कूट) and *pañjara*s (पञ्जर), the topmost storey had four lions, now replaced by *garuḍa*s (गरुड). The whole complex is enclosed by a *prākāra* (प्राकार) or boundary wall which provides an additional circumambulatory passage to the temple.

The Vaikuṇṭha Perumal (वैकुण्ठ पेरुमल्) temple is considered to be the last architectural achievement of the Pallavas (पल्लव) before the arrival of the

Cāḷukyan (चाळुक्य) King Vikramāditya (विक्रमादित्य) II (733-46) who imitated the temples of Kāñcīpuram (कांचीपुरम्) in his own architectural style. Still, at Paṭṭaḍakal (पट्टडकल) the construction of the Virūpākṣa (विरूपाक्ष) temple was influenced by the architecture of the Kailāsanātha (कैलासनाथ) temple.

10

Pāṇḍya Temples

THE Pāṇḍyas (पाण्ड्य), contemporaries of the Coḷas (चोळ) and the Cheras (छेर), were one of the powerful royal houses in south India. The capital of the Early Pāṇḍyas of the Saṅgam Era (संगम काल) was at Korkai (कोरकइ) but the Later Pāṇḍyas made Madurai (मदुरै) as their capital. The Pāṇḍyas of the Saṅgam Era (*c.* first century BCE to fifth century CE) went into oblivion following the attack of the Kalabhras (कलभ्र). However, it was revived in the sixth century by Kaḍungon (कडुंगोन्). Following the rise of the Coḷas in the fifth century, once again the glory of the Pāṇḍyas faded away. The decline of the Coḷa power towards the end of the twelfth century provided another opportunity for the revival of the Pāṇḍyas. The Pāṇḍya rule reached its zenith during the time of Jaṭāvarman Sundara Pāṇḍyan (जटावर्मन् सुन्दर पाण्ड्य) (CE 1251 – CE 1268). Their power began to decline after 1311 when the Delhi Sultanate attacked the Pāṇḍyan kingdom. However, as petty rulers, their reign continued until the end of the fifteenth century.

Structural Temples

The Pāṇḍyas also built structural temples in hard granite stone. For examples, the Talinātha (तलिनाथ) temple at Tiruppattur (तिरुपत्तुर) (*c.* CE 868) (*Pl.* 78) and the Valīśvara (वलीश्वर) temple at Tiruvalīśvaram (तिरुवलीश्वरम्) are among the earliest granite temples of the Pāṇḍyan architectural style. The *tri-tala vimāna* (त्रि-त्तल विमान) of the Talinātha temple is surmounted by the *kuṭina śikhara* (कुटिन शिखर) which in turn is crowned by the *kalaśa* (कलश) finial. Unlike that of the Pallava (पल्लव) temples, the *śikhara* of the Talinātha shows taller pillars between the cornice and the base. The base of each *tala* (तल) appears to have been supported by the human figures, either on their shoulders or palms. The simple *bhitti* (भित्ति) of the *ādi-tala* (आदि-तल) is divided into projections and recesses.

Like those of the Coḷa temples, the *mūla-prāsāda* (मूल-प्रासाद) of the later Pāṇḍyan (पाण्ड्य) temple was surrounded by the *aṣṭa-parivāra-ālaya* (अष्ट-परिवार-आलय) or eight family shrines. During the early period the image of the Liṅgodbhava-mūrti (लिङ्गोद्भव-मूर्ति) was not represented in the *koṣṭha*s (कोष्ठ) of the *ādi-tala* (आदि-तल), though, it was placed in the niches of the upper stories.

Between fifth and eleventh century, the Pāṇḍya region witnessed an intensive structural activity and many notable temples were constructed during this period. The Pāṇḍyas, following the Pallava (पल्लव) tradition, also followed the *aṣṭāṅga-vimāna* (अष्टांग-विमान) scheme in which three shrines (sanctums) were built one over another to house the deities. For example, the Viṣṇu temple at Mannarkoil (मन्नरकोइल) near Ambāsamudram (अम्बासमुद्रम्); the Saumyanārāyaṇa (सौम्यनारायण) temple at Tirukoṭṭiyur (तिरुकोट्टियुर) and Kudalalagar (कुदललगर्) temple at Madurai (मदुरै) followed the *aṣṭāṅga-vimāna* pattern. In the Pāṇḍya country, the *gaja-pṛṣṭha* (गज-पृष्ठ) or the apsidal temples were very few which indicates that the Pāṇḍyas did not encourage the apsidal plan.

Between CE 1100–1350, the Pāṇḍyas paid more attention to the erection of imposing *gopurams* (गोपुरम्) (literally, cow-gates) to the already existing temples rather than building the temple complexes with imposing *mūla-prāsāda*. The characteristic pyramidal tower of the *gopuram* rests on a single or two-storeyed oblong base. It may rise over 46 m in height. A doorway provides entrance in the centre of its longer side. The lower vertical part, made of solid stone masonry, provides a strong foundation. Lighter materials like brick, timber and plaster usually go into the pyramidal superstructure. The surface decoration of the *gopuram* consists of pillars, pilasters and niches. Like the ground plan, the *śālā-śikhara* (शाला-शिखर) or wagon-vaulted roof is oblong. A row of *stūpīs* (स्तूपी) (finials)

Pl. 78 : Talinātha temple, Pāṇḍya style, Tirupattur, Ramnad district, Tamil Nadu

crowns the whole. For example, the typical Pāṇḍya style can be seen in the Sundara Pāṇḍya *gopuram* (eastern *gopuram*) built around CE 1250 added to the Jambūkeśvara (जम्बूकेश्वर) temple, and the eastern *gopuram* of the Śiva (शिव) temple at Chidambaram (चिदम्बरम्).

The eastern *gopuram* of the Śiva temple at Chidambaram bears an inscription with the name of the Pāṇḍyan ruler Sundara (सुन्दर). The tower rises to a height of forty metres. Some new art elements appear in the surface decoration of the *gopuram* (गोपुरम्). For instance, the junction between the octagonal and square portions of the pillars is differentiated by a snake-band, known as the *nāga-bandham* (नाग-बन्धम्). The *iḍā* (इडा), under the *phalaka* (फलक, abacus), has spiked indentations. *Kuḍu* (कुडु) motifs also take new shape. A miniature *vimāna* (विमान) relief or *kuḍu* surmounts *kumbha-pañjaram* (कुम्भ-पञ्जरम्). The *hāra* (हार) elements, such as *śālās* (शाला) and *kūṭas* (कूट) surmount the *devakoṣṭha* (देवकोष्ठ, niche).

11

Coḷa Temples

THE Coḷas (चोळ), who flourished between fifth and thirteenth centuries ruled a large part of Tamil Nadu. Their empire extended all over Tamil Nadu and also over the peripheral regions of Andhra, Karnataka and Kerala. This period also marked the erection of numerous imposing temples incorporating new architectural members. These temples also adopted various elements of the Pallava (पल्लव) and the Cāḷukya (चाळुक्य) architectural traditions.

According to the peculiarities of the architectural elaborations and the periods of their construction, the Coḷa temples may be divided into three groups:

1. The first phase, datable from the accession of Vijayālaya (विजयालय) to the accession of Rājarāja I (राजराज I, i.e between CE 848–985);
2. The second phase, datable to the period from the accession of Rājarāja I to the accession of Kulottuṅga I (कुलोत्तुंग I) (CE 985–1070); and
3. The third phase, datable from the accession of Kulottuṅga I to the decline and end of the Coḷa empire during the reign of Rājarāja III and Rājendra III (राजेन्द्र III) (CE 1070–1270).

First Phase

Though the early Coḷas followed the Draviḍian architectural tradition, yet the plan and elevation were different from those of the Pallavas. For example, in the Pallava temples the lowermost *tala* (तल) of the *vimāna* (विमान) is projected over the *antarāla* (अन्तराल) whereas in the Coḷa temple such feature is not found. Like that of the Pallava temples, the torus moulding (i.e. the convex moulding which is semicircular in profile) in the *adhiṣṭhāna* (अधिष्ठान) of some of the early Coḷa (चोळ) temples is chamfered, i.e. cut at an oblique angle. However, soon the typical convex moulding superseded the chamfered one. Unlike the Pallava (पल्लव) temples, the *prastara* (प्रस्तर)

Pl. 79. Vijālaya Coḷeśvara temple, Narttamalai

of the Coḷa temples does not show the projecting cornice. Similarly, crouching and rearing lions which had once adorned the pillars of the Pallavas, gradually disappeared from the Coḷa tradition. The *poṭikā* (पोटिका, corbel) on the top of the pillars shows further evolution. The corners of the *poṭikā* are now bevelled to form a tenon-like projection. It is against the *paṭṭa* (पट्ट) or flat band and *taraṅga* (तरंग) or wavy ornamentations of the Pallava *poṭikā*. Also, unlike the Pallava temples, the exterior of the Coḷa temple walls has limited sculptural embellishments.

Some of the temples belonging to the early phase of the Coḷa temples are the Sundareśvara (सुन्दरेश्वर) at Tirukattalai (तिरुकत्तलइ), the Vijayālaya (विजयालय) Coḷeśvaram (चोळेश्वरम्) at Narttāmalai (नर्त्तमलइ) (*Pl.* 79) and the Koraṅganātha (कोरंगनाथ) at Śrīnivāsanallūr (श्रीनिवासनल्लूर). The early Coḷa temples consist of a square *vimāna* (विमान) fronted by the

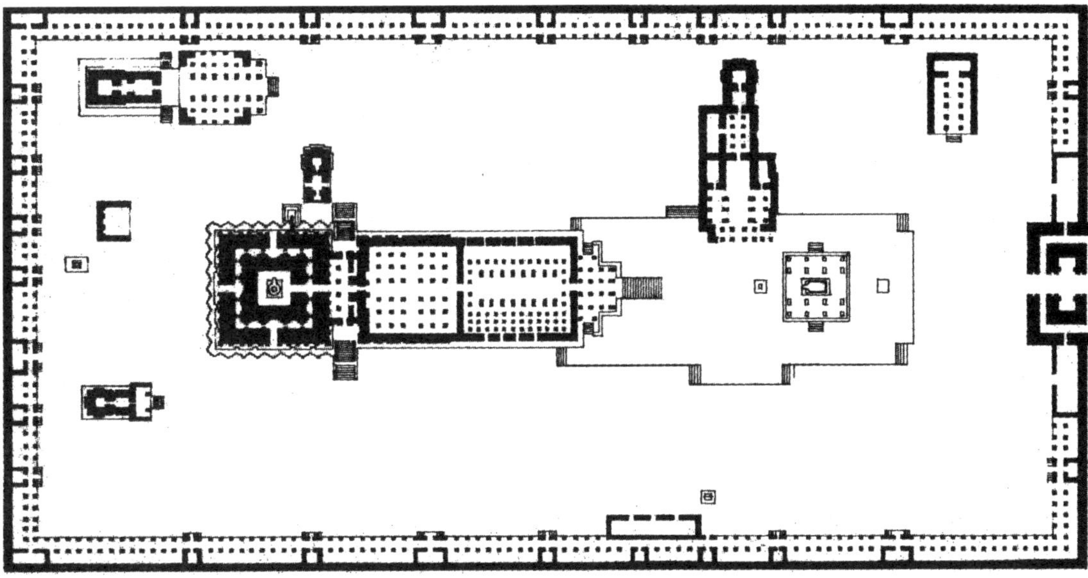

Fig. 77 : Plan of the Rājarājeśvara temple, Tañjavūr

ardha-maṇḍapa (अर्ध-मण्डप). The *vimāna* (विमान) is imposing and it dominates the whole temple complex. The *mūla-prāsāda* (मूल-प्रासाद) or the main temple is surrounded by eight sub-shrines, known as *aṣṭa-parivārālaya* (अष्ट-परिवारालय) or eight family-shrines. These *parivāra* (परिवार) shrines were meant for attendant deities like Gaṇeśa (गणेश), Subrahmaṇya (सुब्रह्मण्य) (= Kārttikeya कार्त्तिकेय), Sūrya (सूर्य), Candra (चन्द्र), Saptamātṛkās (सप्तमातृका), Jyeṣṭha (ज्येष्ठ), Caṇḍikeśvara (चण्डिकेश्वर) and Nandī (नन्दी). The temple complex is encircled by an outer *prākāra* (प्राकार) or boundary wall whose main *gopuram* (गोपुरम्) or gateway-tower stands on the eastern side.

Pl. 80 : Rājarājeśvara/Bṛhadīśvara temple, Tañjavūr

Second Phase

The Coḷa temple architecture reached its zenith during the reign of Rājarāja I (राजराज I) (985-1014) and his son Rājendra I (राजेन्द्र I) (1012-44). They also followed the tradition of their predecessors, though their temples excelled in their complex plan, imposing elevation, and rich sculptural embellishments. Among the famous temples erected during this phase were the Bṛhadīśvara/Rājarājeśvara (बृहदीश्वर/राजराजेश्वर) temple at Tañjāvūr (तंजावूर) by Rājarāja I, and the Bṛhadīśvara at Gaṅgaikoṇḍacoḷapuram (गंगइकोण्डचोळपुरम्) by his son Rājendra I.

The Bṛhadīśvara (बृहदीश्वर) temple at Tañjāvūr (तंजावूर) was constructed out of large blocks of granite stone (*Pl.* 80, *fig.* 77). It stands on a moulded *adhiṣṭhāna* (अधिष्ठान). The temple has the tallest known *vimāna* (विमान), rising to a height of 66 m. (216 ft) through sixteen storeys and the square *adhiṣṭhāna* (अधिष्ठान) which measures 30 sq. m. Each storey carries *hāra* (हार) elements such as *kūṭas* (कूट), *śālās* (शाला) and *pañjaras* (पञ्जर). The topmost storey has *nandī* (नन्दी) at each of the four corners. The *grīvā* (ग्रीवा) and *śikhara* (शिखर) are octagonal. The *vimāna* is crowned by a huge monolithic "cupola" with *stūpī* (स्तूपी) or finial.

Pl. 81 : Bṛhadīśvara temple, Gaṅgaikoṇḍacoḷapuram

In front of the imposing *mūla-prāsāda* (मूल-प्रासाद) is an *antarāla* (अन्तराल) or vestibule with flights of steps or *sopāna* (सोपान) on its northern and southern sides. The *antarāla* is fronted by a large enclosed pillared *mahāmaṇḍapa* (महामण्डप) or main hall. The detached Nandī-*maṇḍapa* (नन्दी-मण्डप) in front of the *mahāmaṇḍapa* is a later addition.

The square *mūla-prāsāda* (मूल-प्रासाद) supporting the majestic superstructure, has two registers separated by a full entablature or cornice mouldings. Pilasters and niches containing images of deities decorate the exterior walls of each storey. In between two pilasters is a new sculptural motif, known as *kumbha-pañjara* (कुम्भ-पञ्जर) (i.e, a *pañjara* pilaster with *kumbha* base), appears in this temple. A two-storeyed *pradakṣiṇāpatha* (प्रदक्षिणापथ) separates the outer wall of the *vimāna* from the inner wall of the *garbha-gṛha* (गर्भ-गृह). The sanctum contains a colossal *liṅga* (लिङ्ग) standing on a large pedestal.

An outer *prākāra* (प्राकार) surrounds the broad open court. It has a *gopuram* (गोपुरम्) at its eastern side. It is in this temple that one notices for the first time two *gopurams* oriented in the same direction.

Other temples of this period are those at Tiruvāji (तिरुवाजि), Melpāḍi (मेलपाडि), Tiruvalañjuli (तिरवलञ्जुलि), Tirumalavāḍī (तिरुमलवाडी), Tiruvaraṅgulam (तिरुवरंगुलम्), Dadapuram (ददपुरम्), etc. In most of these temples the basement is decorated with pilasters. The walls have a greater number of niches.

The *vimāna* of the Bṛhadīśvara temple at Gaṅgaikoṇḍacoḷapuram (गंगइकोण्डचोळपुरम्) with its *pradakṣiṇāpatha antarāla* and *mahāmaṇḍapa* stands on a common *adhiṣṭhāna* (*Pl.* 81). The basement is decorated with relief panels in niches. The *vimāna* (विमान) rises to the height of 50 m to nine storeys. The whole is crowned by a "cupola" over which rests the *stūpikā* (स्तूपिका, finial).

The shrine for the Śakti (शक्ति, female counterpart) of the presiding deity was also erected in the temple complex. However, the earliest examples of consort shrines built simul-taneously with the erection of the *garbha-gṛha* (गर्भ-गृह) for the main male deity are only found from the times of Rājendra (राजेन्द्र) I which is better manifested in the temple of Gaṅgaikoṇḍacoḷa-puram (गंगइकोण्डचोळपुरम्). Such goddess-shrines, known as Tirukkamakoṭṭams (तिरुक्कमकोट्टम्) or Amman Devī, (अम्मन् देवी) shrines, became indispensable part of the temple complex during the later period.

Pl. 82 : Airāvateśvara temple, Darasuram

Third Phase

During this phase the temple complex was more elaborately planned. Besides the *gopuram* (गोपुरम्), additional pillared *maṇḍapas* (मण्डप) were also built within the temple complex, some of them being shaped in the form

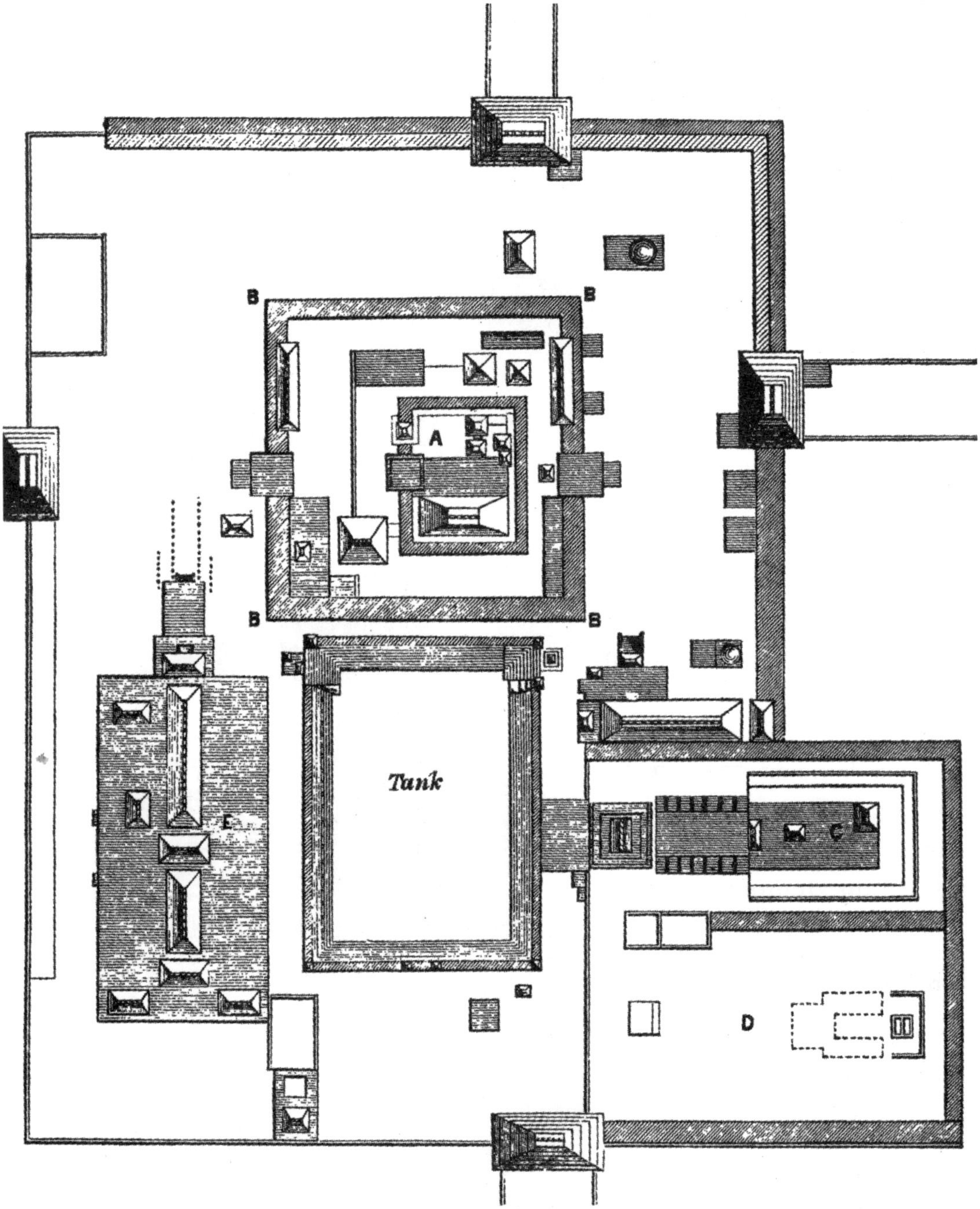

Fig. 78 : Naṭarāja temple, Chidambaram

of a *ratha* (रथ) or wheeled chariot drawn by horses and elephants.

Shrines for Sūrya (सूर्य) were also built during this period. For example, Sūryanār (सूर्यनार) temple at Tirumaṅgalakkuḍī (तिरुमङ्गलक्कुडी) may be dated to the period of Kulottuṅga Coḷa (कुलोत्तुंग चोळ) I (1075-1120) which, according to an inscription, was otherwise known as Kulottuṅga Coḷa Mārtaṇḍa Ālayam (कुलोत्तुंग चोळ मार्तण्ड आलयम्). The *gopuram* of the temple is 15.5 m in height and consists of three storeys. The temple faces west. The presiding deity here is Sūryanārāyaṇa (सूर्यनारायण) in a chariot-like *vimāna*, representing the sun's chariot. At the top of the *śālā* (शाला)-shaped *vimāna* are five cupolas. To the north of the *vimāna* lies the sacred temple tank, known as Sūrya Puṣkaraṇī (सूर्य पुष्करणी). Shrines to the other celestial bodies are located outside the sanctum. The sanctum and the *ardha-maṇḍapam* (अर्द्ध-मण्डप) are built of stones, while the rest of the shrines are brick-structures.

Airāvateśvara (ऐरावतेश्वर) Temple at Dārasuram (दारसुरम्) near Kumbhakoṇam (कुम्भकोणम्) is another imposing temple complex, datable to the period of Rājarāja II (राजराज II) (1146-73) (*Pl.* 82). The temple is described as a "sculptor's dream re-lived in stone." Although the *vimāna* is only about 24 m in height, the front *maṇḍapa* (मण्डप) itself is in the form of a huge chariot drawn by horses. Aesthetically executed paintings, sculptures and relief panels make the temple a veritable storehouse of great works of art and icons. In front of the temple are musical stone pillars that produce different tones (*svaras*, स्वर) when struck. These musical pillars have attracted people all the time.

The Kampahareśvara (कम्पहरेश्वर) temple at Tribhuvanam (त्रिभुवनम्) near Kumbhakoṇam (कुम्भकोणम्) is another masterpiece of the Coḷa (चोळ) architecture. Here also the front *maṇḍapa* is built in the form of a huge chariot. The *vimāna* (विमान) here is larger than that of Dārasuram (दारसुरम्), and is about 36 m in height. Sculptured panels depicting scenes from the *Rāmāyaṇa* (रामायण) adorn this temple. Besides building new temples, the later Coḷas also renovated existing ones and added entrance *gopurams* (गोपुरम्). The evidence for such activities can be seen in the Naṭarāja (नटराज) temple at Chidambaram (चिदम्बरम्) (*fig.* 78) and the Thyāgarājaswāmi (त्यागराजस्वामि) temple at Tiruvarur (त्रिरुवरुर).

12

Hoyasaḷa Temples

THE decline of the Later Western Cāḷukyas (चाळुक्य) in the eleventh century paved the way for the emergence of the Hoyasaḷa (होयसळ) royal house in Mysore (मैसूर) who ruled over Karnataka, parts of Tamil Nadu and western parts of Andhra Pradesh for about two and a half centuries. Their rule is especially known for the unique accomplishments in the field of temple art and architecture. Most of their magnificent temples are spread over Halebiḍ (हलेबिड), Beḷūr (बेळूर), Śṛṅgerī (शृंगेरी) and Somanāthpura (सोमनाथपुर) in Karnataka. The Cennakeśava (चेन्नकेशव) temple, built by the Hoyasaḷa King Viṣṇuvardhana (विष्णुवर्धन) in CE 1117, is the most celebrated of all the temples at Beḷūr (*Pl.* 83, *fig.* 79). Among the Halebiḍ

Pl. 83 : Cennakeśava temple, Belūr

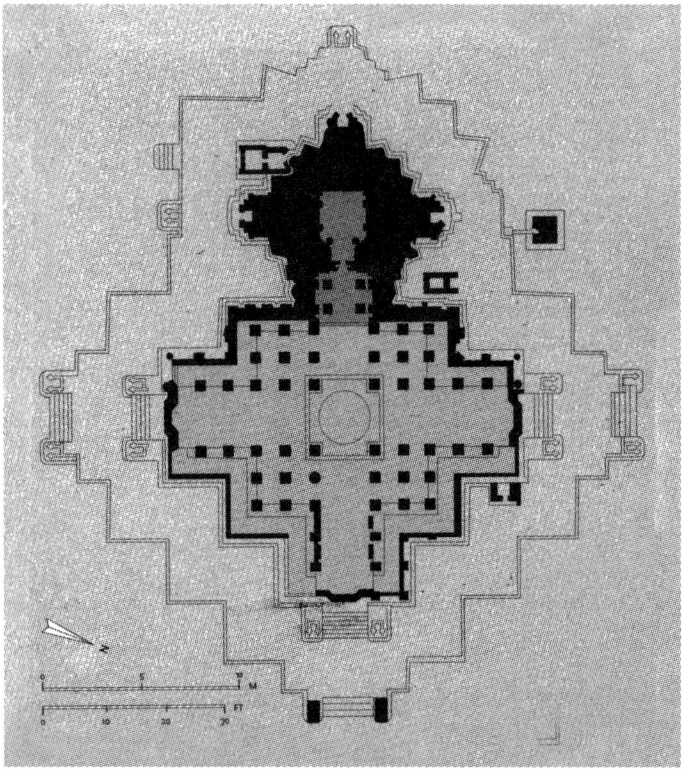

Fig. 79 : Cennakeśava temple, Belūr

temples, the Hoysaḷeśvara (होयसळेश्वर) is the magnificent shrine which is star-shaped (stellate) (*fig.* 80), a lot different in plan and elevation than the other contemporary temples in India which were square or rectangle in plan.

Plan of the Hoyasaḷa Temple

A Hoyasaḷa temple usually stands within an enclosure. The temple complex, however, consists of the usual *garbha-gṛha* (गर्भ-गृह) fronted by an *antarāla* (अन्तराल) and followed by the pillared hypostyle *maṇḍapa* (मण्डप), i.e. *maṇḍapa* with a series of columns, known as *navaraṅga/gūḍha-maṇḍapa* (नवरंग/गूढ-मण्डप). At times a *mukha-maṇḍapa* (मुख-मण्डप) or *sabhā-maṇḍapa* (सभा-मण्डप) was added. All of them, it may be noted, are not necessarily built in a single axis and hence different from, for example, the Western Cāḷukyan planning where all the individual *maṇḍapa*s were in a single axis.

Many of the Hoyasaḷa temples are multi-shrined, i.e. having more than one *mūla-prāsāda* (मूल-प्रासाद), a trend popularized by the Hoyasaḷas. Thus, according to the number of the *mūla-prāsāda*, within a single temple complex, the temples are classified as *ekakūṭa* (एककूट, single), *dvikūṭa* (द्विकूट, double), *trikūṭa* (त्रिकूट, triple), *catuṣkūṭa* (चतुष्कूट, quadruple) and *pañcakūṭa* (पञ्चकूट, quintuple). Most of the Hoyasaḷa temples are *ekakūṭa, dvikūṭa* or *trikūṭa*. For example, in its plan, the Cennakeśava (चेन्नकेशव) temple at Somanāthpura (सोमनाथपुर) is *trikūṭācala* (त्रिकूटाचल) or *trikūṭaśālā* (त्रिकूटशाला), i.e. the *garbha-gṛhas* (गर्भ-गृह) constructed at the three different sides or directions of the central pillared hall (*navaraṅga,* नवरंग) resulting as a whole in the shape of a cross — one shrine with a *garbha-gṛha* at the rear end (western end) and two separate shrines with separate *garbha-gṛhas* at the northern and southern sides of this central shrine, as if flanking it (*Pl.* 84, *fig.* 81).

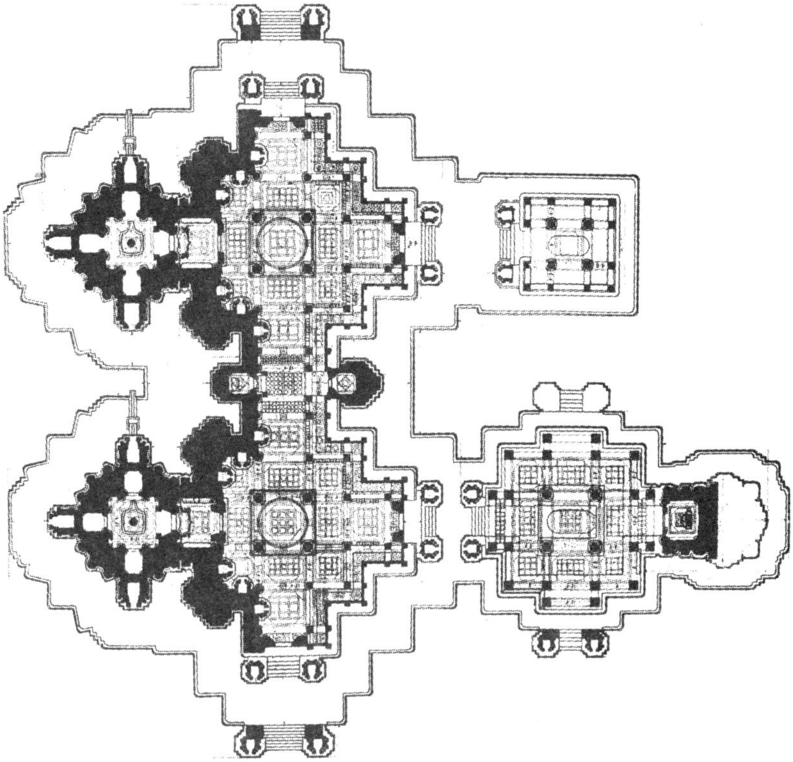

Fig. 80 : Plan of the Hoysaḷeśvara temple, Halebiḍ

In temples with multiple *mūla-prāsāda* (मूल-प्रासाद), all essential parts are duplicated for symmetrical appearance and elegance. For example, Hoyasaḷeśvara (होयसळेश्वर) temple at Halebiḍ (हलेबिड) is a twin temple with highly symmetrical plan except for the two Nandī-pavilions that precede the temples.

Elevation

Unlike the Nāgara (नागर) and the Drāviḍa (द्राविड)

Pl. 84 : Cennakeśava temple, Somanāthapur

orders, the Hoyasaḷa *śikhara* (शिखर) is Vesara (वेसर) in character, i.e. bell-shaped, which is aesthetically blended with the *aṣṭa-bhadra* (अष्ट-भद्र) or star-shaped (polygonal) plan. In this case, the *jagati/upapīṭha* जगति/उपपीठ, *adhiṣṭhāna* (अधिष्ठान) and the *bhitti* (भित्ति) follow the *aṣṭa-bhadra* order. The broad *jagati*, projecting from the *adhiṣṭhāna* of the temple serves as a *pradakṣiṇāpatha* (प्रदक्षिणापथ) providing ample space for circumambulation.

Adhiṣṭhāna

A series of nine mouldings form the *adhiṣṭhāna* of the Hoyasaḷa temples. These mouldings are highly decorated with the friezes of relief sculptures and leafy scrolls. For example, the *adhiṣṭhāna* of the Hoyasaḷeśvara temple depicts a series of superimposed registers of friezes. Here the lowest moulding/band/frieze shows a line of bejewelled elephants in procession. The second moulding depicts a line of lion-like (*vyāla*, व्याल) creatures.

Above it rests a narrow band of foliated scrolls. The next moulding depicts a band of running horses followed by a band of spiralling foliage. The top three registers depict warriors, stylized hippos and *haṁsa*s (हंस, geese-like mythical birds)/(stylized peacocks?) respectively, from bottom upwards. Above this decorative moulded *adhiṣṭhāna* are *kakṣāsana*s (कक्षासन, sloping seat-backs).

Bhitti (Wall)

The *bhitti* (भित्ति) or the temple wall stands on top of the decorated moulded *adhiṣṭhāna*. The *bhitti* has two sections divided by a horizontal band. The lower section depicts Hindu deities and their *gaṇa*s (गण).

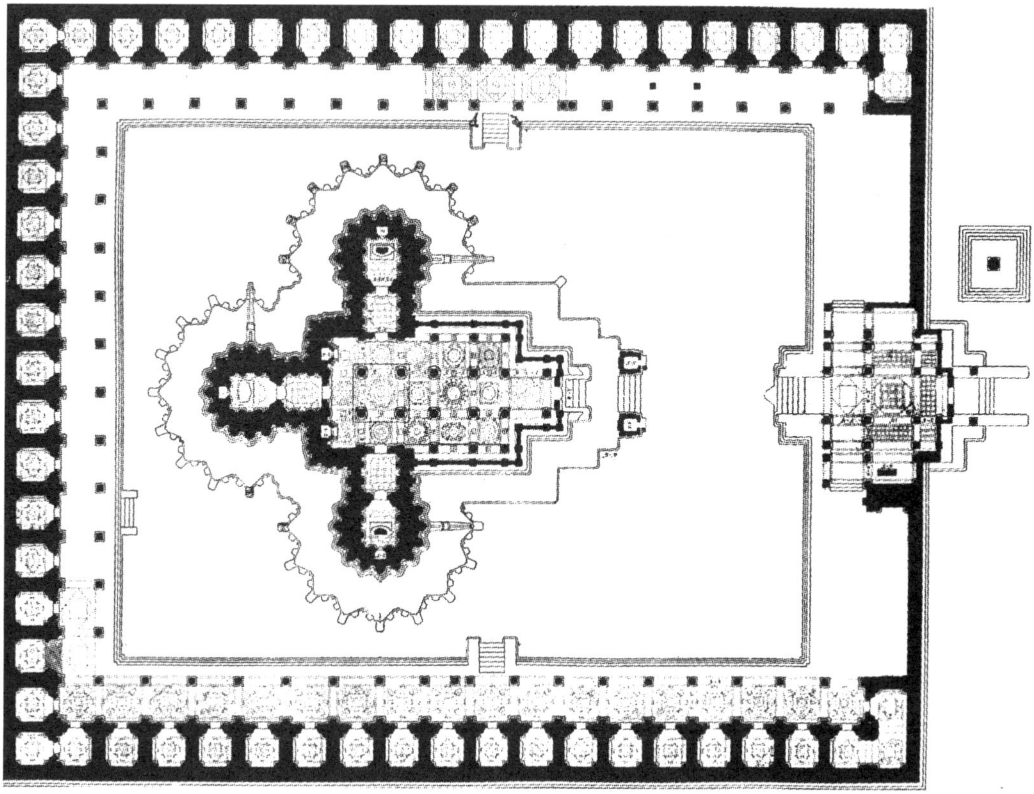

Fig. 81 : Plan of the Cannakeśava temple, Somanāthapur

Pl. 85 : Lathe-turned pillars of the Hoysaḷeśvara temple

The top section is carved with miniature towers or *śikhara*s (शिखर) of Nāgara (नागर) order. On top of the *bhitti* is *chādya/chajjā* (छाद्य/छज्जा, eave) projecting half a metre from the wall. The temples built prior to the thirteenth century possess only one eave. In the later temples there is a second eave running about a metre below the upper eave. Below the lower eaves are the panels of the deities and the divinities. It is a unique feature and shows the desire to innovate and also elaborate the decorative aspect of the temples.

Śikhara

The *śikhara* as usual, starts from top of the *chādya*. It is divided into three or more horizontal sections and more embellished than the *bhitti*. The *śikhara*s of the Hoyasaḷa (होयसळ) temples are among the most developed Vesara (वेसर) forms. The fluted appearance of the Hoyasaḷa *śikhara* beautifully merges with the star-shaped plan of the *vimāna*. The *sukanāsikā* (सुकनासिका), which projects from the *śikhara* of the *mūla-prāsāda* (मूल-प्रासाद), extends over the *antarāla* (अन्तराल) portion. Therefore, the height of the *śikhara* of the *antarāla* is not very imposing.

The main *śikhara* is, however, crowned by a huge thousand-petalled lotus-like member which is capped by a *khapurī* (खपुरी, skull-cap) like stone element. Over it rests the *kalaśa* (कलश) finial in the shape of a beautiful water pot.

Navaraṅga

This is the pillared or hypostyle hall which is a large *maṇḍapa* (मण्डप), comparable with the *gūḍha-maṇḍapa*s (गूढ-मण्डप), with lathe-turned pillars supporting the roof (*Pl.* 85). Similarly, there are fluted or stellate pillars and pilasters in the Hoyasaḷa (होयसळ) temples. The capitals of the lathe turned pillars carry intersecting corbels on which the architraves rest. The brackets of the pillars depict beautiful *madanikā* (मदनिका, damsel) figures. The shaft of the pillar is a monolith with the base left as a plain square block. The lattice work or *jālī*s (जाली, screens) arranged in between short pillars on top of the *kakṣāsanas* (कक्षासन) make it a closed *maṇḍapa* (मण्डप), though allowing the passage of air and light to the interior of the *maṇḍapa*.

The ceilings of the Hoyasaḷa *navaraṅgas* (नवरंग) are specifically known as the "lantern ceilings" because they consist of deep niches or domes constructed by means of stone beams placed diagonally across the corners of the square. However, the ceiling of the Jain Pārśvanātha (पार्श्वनाथ) temple at Halebiḍ (हलेबिड) is a lantern dome formed by stone beams criss-crossing the corners of an octagonal rather than the usual square. These "lantern ceilings" are carved with relief sculptures and floral motifs. For example, the *navaraṅga* of the Amṛteśvara (अमृतेश्वर) temple in Chikmagalūr (चिकमगलूर) district has forty-eight domes with carvings.

Hoyasaḷa Art

The Hoyasaḷa art flourished in the medium of greenish-grey soapstone which is soft when first quarried and, thus, sculptor-friendly. As a result even the most delicate carvings can be done without losing the aesthetic quality. The Hoyasaḷa sculptors made use of this advantage of soapstone while adorning the temples with beautiful relief panels.

The concentric circular or disc-line carved mouldings one over the other over the pillars were carved as it is done in wood-work by mounting the blank stone on a lathe and constantly turned by straps. This is a unique feature of this art.

The other feature that characterizes it is the heavily ornamented icons with minute carvings of jewellery, headgear jewels and *āyudhas* (आयुध); no other school of temple art has this kind of what is sometimes called "over-doing" in which craftsmanship dominates over sophisticated artistic art-creations. This applied particularly to the making of the beads in long tassels decorating the over-sized headgears, *mālā*s (माला) in the neck and on the chest, the girdle ornaments, anklets, etc.

The exterior of the Hoyasaḷa *vimāna* (विमान) is highly ornate and stellate with recesses and aedicules (miniature shrines) whereas the interior of the *mūla-prāsāda* (मूल-प्रासाद) is plain and square. The temple doorway is heavily ornamented with *makara-toraṇa* (मकर-तोरण) depicting a mythical beast. Similarly, the walls, pillars, pilasters and ceilings depict various artistic creations. Themes from Hindu epics like the *Rāmāyaṇa* (रामायण) and the *Mahābhārata* (महाभारत), heavenly maidens commonly known as *śālabhañjikā*s (शालभञ्जिका), *madanikā*s (मदनिका), *devakanyā*s (देवकन्या), etc., mythical beasts like *vyāla*s (व्याल), *kīrtimukha*s (कीर्तिमुख, gargoyles or faces of glory), floral and faunal motifs, ordinary humans, warriors, musicians, dancers, instrumentalists and scenes of daily life became subjects for the Hoyasaḷa temple art. Common themes from the epics depicting Arjuna (अर्जुन) shooting fish, Gaṇeśa (गणेश), Sūrya (सूर्य), Indra (इन्द्र), Mahiṣāsuramardinī (महिषासुरमर्दिनी), Hari-Hara (हरि-हर) and, Brahmā (ब्रह्मा) with Sarasvatī (सरस्वती) are found in most of the temples.

Depiction of the sensual sculptures on the temple walls prevalent during this period in the central India and Orissa also spread to the Hoyasaḷa (होयसळ) country. However, unlike the central Indian and Orissan erotica, the Hoyasaḷa sensual figures generally depicted in the recesses and niches so that they would not immediately come to the fore to embarrass the visitors. However, their placement on the temple-walls was pre-determined by canons and conventions as Devangana Desai has shown in the case of Khajurāho (खजुराहो) temple where recesses in the dark were also utilized for this purpose.

The Hoyasaḷa art, in some examples, was also influenced by the Coḷa tradition due to the proximity of Karnataka with the Tamil country. It is evidenced from the pillar images, known as the *stambha-buṭṭalika*s (स्तम्भ-बुट्टलिक) (*stambha* स्तम्भ = pillar; *buṭṭalika/puṭṭalika* बुट्टलिक/पुट्टलिक = image or sculpture) of the Cennakeśava (चेन्नकेशव) temple at Beḷūr (बेळूर). All the Hoyasaḷa sculptures were carved in every detail from head to toe with unparallel perfection in craftsmanship that gives the Hoyasaḷa art a unique identity among the treasures of Indian art.

13

Temples of Vijayanagara

THE Vijayanagara (विजयनगर) Empire (CE 1336–1565) with its capital at Vijayanagara (modern Hampī, हम्पी) on the Tuṅgabhadrā River (तुंगभद्रा नदी) in the Bellāry (बेल्लारी) district, Karnataka, was the great centre of art and architecture. The Vijayanagara kings not only built many new edifices in hard stones like granite, but, like the Pāṇḍyas (पाण्ड्य), made many additions to the already existing temples. Such additions were mainly in the form of *gopurams* (गोपुरम्, tower-like gateways). The temples of Virūpākṣa (विरूपाक्ष, Pampāpati पम्पापति) (*fig.* 82), the Haẓārarāma (हज़ारराम) and the Viṭṭhalaswāmi (विट्ठलस्वामी) at Hampī (*Pl.* 86, *fig.* 83) are the best examples of the Vijayanagara art and architecture.

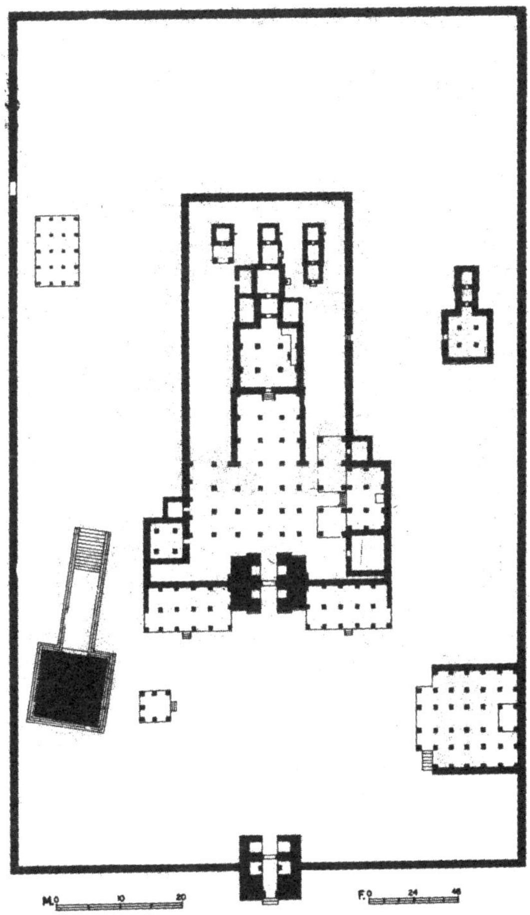

Fig. 82 : Plan of the Virūpākṣa temple, Hampī

The Vijayanagara temple architecture did not confine to the capital city. It spread to Telugu (तेलुगु) region which is better manifested by the temples of Rāyālaseemā (रायालसीमा) area of Andhra Pradesh. For example, the Vijayanagara temples famous for their art and architectural elements in this region are the Lakṣmī-Narasiṁha (लक्ष्मी-

Pl. 86 : Viṭṭhalaswāmi temple, Hampī

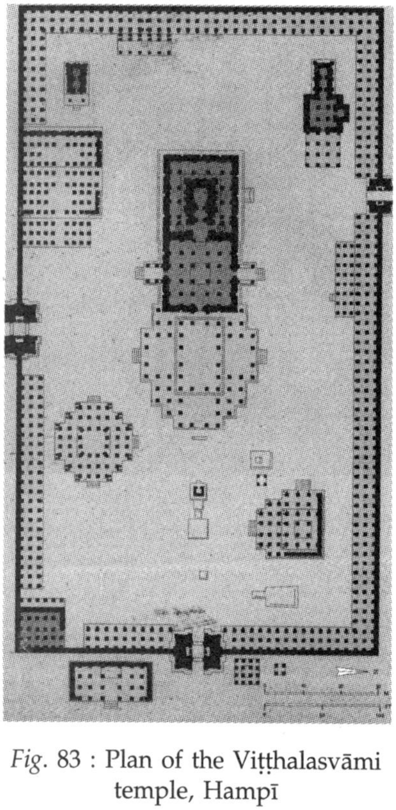

Fig. 83 : Plan of the Viṭṭhalasvāmi temple, Hampī

नरसिंह) temple at Kadiri (कदिरि), the Rāmaliṅgeśvara (रामलिंगेश्वर) and the Veṅkaṭaramaṇa (वेंकटरमण) temples at Tadpatri (तद्पत्रि), the Mādhavarāya (माधवराय) temple at Gorantla (गोरन्ट्ल), the Rāma (राम) temple at Penukoṇḍa (पेनुकोण्ड) (*Pl.* 87) and the Vīrabhadra (वीरभद्र) temple at Lepākṣī (लेपाक्षी), all in Anantapur (अनन्तरपुर) district; the Cennakeśava (चेन्नकेशव), the Santānamalleśvara (सन्तानमल्लेश्वर) and the Umāmaheśvara (उमामहेश्वर) temples at Puṣpagiri (पुष्पगिरि) and the Vīrabhadra temple at Rāyakoṭi (रायकोटि) in the Cuḍḍapāh (कुडडपाह्) district; the Mallikārjuna (मल्लिकार्जुन) and the Kodaṇḍarāma (कोदण्डराम) temples at Candragiri (चन्द्रगिरि), the Cennakeśava temple at Somapalem (सोमपलेम), the Kalyāṇa-Veṅkaṭeśvara (कल्याण-वेंकटेश्वर) temples at Nārāyaṇavanam (नारायणवनम) and Maṅgapuram (मंगपुरम्) in the Chittoor (चित्तूर) district; and the Cennakeśava temple at Markapuram (मर्कपुरम्) and the Mallikārjuna (मल्लिकार्जुन) temple at Śrīśailam (श्रीशैलम्) in the Kurnool (कुरनूल) district. The Buggala Rāmaliṅgeśvara (बुग्गल

रामलिङ्गेश्वर) temple at Tadpatri (तद्पत्रि) depicts the Vijayanagara architecture at its best in this region. The region also yields the evidence of the addition of *maṇḍapas* (मण्डप), *prākāras* (प्राकार) and *gopurams* (गोपुरम्) to the already existing temples. Such additions can be found in the Kālahastīśvara (कालहस्तीश्वर) temple, Kālahasti (कालहस्ति) and the Govindarājaswāmi (गोविन्दराजस्वामि) temple at Tirupati (तिरुपति).

The Vijayanagara rulers incorporated different elements of art and architecture from the various traditions of the Drāviḍa (द्राविड) order of the Pallavas (पल्लव), the Coḷas (चोळ) and the Pāṇḍyas (पाण्ड्य); the Vesara (वेसर) order of the Cāḷukya–Hoyasaḷa (चाळुक्य–होयसळ) tradition and the Indo-Islamic style of the Deccan. The last mentioned could be noticed

Pl. 87 : Śiva temple, Penukoṇḍa

Pl. 88 : West Gopura of Saṅgameśvara temple, Animala

in the structures like the "Lotus Mahal" and the elephant stables. Combining all these elements they built strong fortresses, magnificent palaces and elegant temples.

Their temple complexes consisted of concentric series of rectangular *prākāras* or boundary walls with the *gopurams* at the centre of each side. Their temples consisted of a large number of pillared *maṇḍapas* for various rituals and cultural programmes. Following the tradition of the Coḷas, the temples were also provided with the Amman Devī (अम्मन् देवी) shrine to keep the images of the consort of the enshrined male deity. Another noteworthy feature of the temples is the absence of mortar in their construction.

Gopurams

The Vijayanagara rulers were also inspired by the imposing *gopurams* of the Coḷas and the Pāṇḍyas and erected tall and massive *gopurams*, known as

Pl. 89 : Pillar with Vyali depiction, Vijayanagar

rāya-gopurams (राय-गोपुरम्, lit. King's Gateways) (*Pl.* 88). The *gopurams* are generally seven storeyed, sometimes rising up to eleven storeys as in the Ekāmbaranātha (एकाम्बरनाथ) temple at Kāñcīpuram (कांचीपुरम्). The increase in the height of the *gopurams* and in the number of *prākāras* is yet another feature. The most characteristic *gopurams* of this period are to be found in the temples of Kāñcīpuram, Tiruvannamalai (तिरुवन्नमलइ), Chidambaram (चिदम्बरम्), Kumbhakoṇam (कुम्भकोणम्), Madurai (मदुरै) Śrīraṅgam (श्रीरंगम) and Vellore (वेल्लोर). These are rich with architectural designs like *śālās* (शाला), *karṇa-kūṭas* (कर्ण-कूट) and *alpa-nāsikās* (अल्प-नासिका) rather than rich sculptural embellishments.

Maṇḍapas

The large *maṇḍapas* (मण्डप) of the Vijayanagara period were used for religious rituals and ceremonial observances. The *kalyāṇa-maṇḍapa* (कल्याण-मण्डप), *snapana* (स्नपन) (*abhiṣeka*)-*maṇḍapa* (अभिषेक-मण्डप), *havana-maṇḍapa* (हवन-मण्डप), *alaṅkāra-maṇḍapa* (अलंकार-मण्डप), *saptasvara-maṇḍapa/rāga-maṇḍapa* सप्तस्वर-मण्डप/राग-मण्डप), *raṅga-maṇḍapa* (रंग-मण्डप), etc. are the usual *maṇḍapas* in addition to the *ardha-maṇḍapa* (अर्द्ध-मण्डप), *mukha-maṇḍapa* (मुख-मण्डप) and *mahāmaṇḍapa* (महामण्डप) of earlier times. The *kalyāṇa-maṇḍapa* (wedding-hall) was among the most conspicuous *maṇḍapas* of the period. The so-called "thousand-pillared *maṇḍapa*," a huge hall with many rows of pillars, became another feature of the Vijayanagara temple complex.

The *kapota* (कपोत, cornice) of the *maṇḍapa* also evolved during this period. So far it was thick and curved down. In the Vijayanagara temples, the cornice was fashioned in double-flexed style and it extended forward. The *kumbha-pañjara* (कुम्भ-पञ्जर) and the *kuḍu* (कुडु) motifs became more ornate.

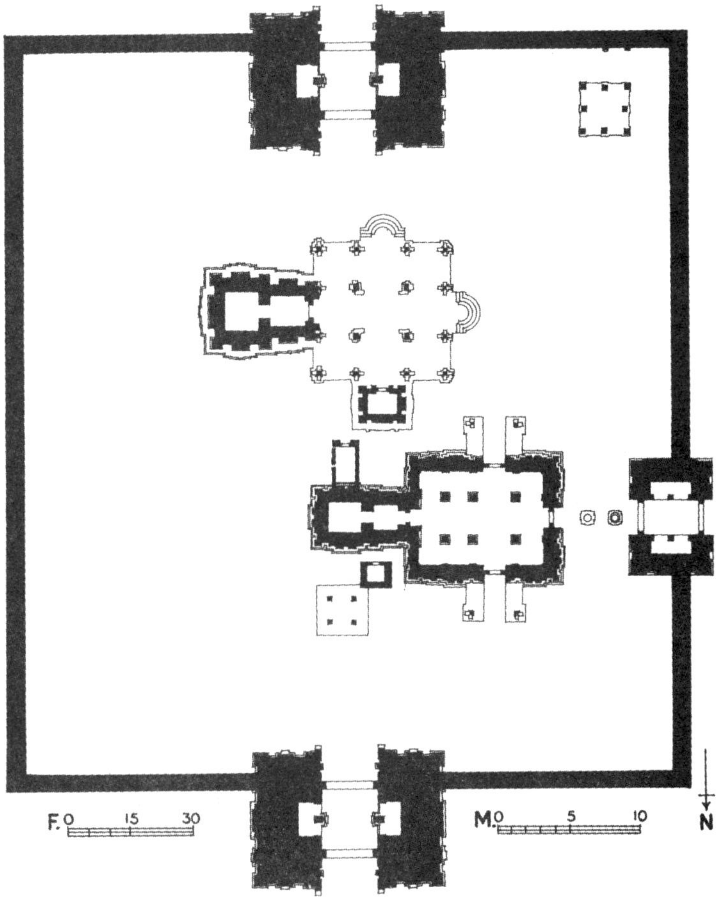

Fig. 84 : Plan of Rāmaliṅgeśvara temple, Tadpatri

Pillars

The Vijayanagara pillars are intricately carved with the characteristic rearing/ crouching *siṁhas* (सिंह, lions) and *vyālis* (व्यालि, lions with elephant trunks) (*Pl.* 89), and also divinities, mortals, mythical beasts/ hippogriffs, and floral and faunal designs. Like those of the Mahendra style (Pallava) pillars, a group of pillars show three sections from bottom upwards, i.e. square *sadūrams* (सदूरम्) at the top and bottom, with a polygonal section, called *kaṭṭu* (कट्टु) decorated with a cross, in the middle. Miniature pillars that are carved out of the same block of stone cluster all around another group of pillars. These miniature pillars sometimes produce seven notes of Indian music (*sapta-svara*, सप्त-स्वर) when they are struck. The *poṭikā* (पोटिका) on the top of the pillars shows further evolution. It has the form of a volute with a hanging lotus bud, known as *puṣpa-poṭikā* (पुष्प-पोटिका).

Viṭṭhalaswāmi Temple, Hampī

The city of Vijayanagara was studded with so many temples that it was called Kovilapura (कोविलपुर), *kovila* (कोविल) means temple. The most splendid temple of Vijayanagara is the Viṭṭhalaswāmi (विट्ठलस्वामि) temple, dedicated to Lord Viṣṇu (विष्णु), near the Tuṅgabhadrā River (तुंगभद्रा). It is considered to be the most ornate of the Vijayanagara temples. In 1513 Kṛṣṇadeva Rāya (कृष्णदेव राय) started its construction, but after the fall of the Vijayanagara Empire in 1563 the temple remained unfinished.

The temple complex is enclosed by a rectangular *prākāra* (प्राकार) with three *gopurams* (गोपुरम्). It consists of the *garbha-gṛha* (गर्भ-गृह), the *mahāmaṇḍapa* (महामण्डप) and the *ardha-maṇḍapa* (अर्द्ध-मण्डप), all aligned in a single axis. The pillars are highly embellished with carvings. Each pillar along with its surrounding miniature pillars, fashioned out of a single large block of granite, becomes itself a work of sculptural art.

The moulded *adhiṣṭhāna* (अधिष्ठान) of the *mahāmaṇḍapa* is carved with friezes of the swan, the horse and the warriors and also the ten forms of Viṣṇu. The *sopāna* (सोपान) or staircase on the east of the *mahāmaṇḍapa* is flanked by elephant balustrade or hand-railing. The centre of the *mahāmaṇḍapa* (महामण्डप) has sixteen pillars decorated with Narasiṁha (नरसिंह) and *vyāli* (व्यालि), forming a rectangular court. The ceiling of the *mahāmaṇḍapa* is also covered with sculptural work.

The *garuḍa-maṇḍapa* (गरुड-मण्डप), in front of the court, assumes the form of a chariot with stone wheels. Its stone wheels, each shaped in the form of a lotus, are capable of revolving. Its earlier form can be seen at Nālandā (नालन्दा) where too we have wheels of lotus form. However, stone chariot here is in turn a static version of the mobile temple chariot.

Rāmaliṅgeśvara Temple, Tadpatri

The temple is situated on the outskirt of Tadpatri (तद्पत्रि) town on the right bank of the River Pennar (पेन्नर) (*fig.* 84). This temple is locally known as the Buggala-Rāmaliṅgeśvara (बुग्गल-रामलिङ्गेश्वर) temple. The temple complex consists of shrines dedicated to Rāmaliṅgeśvara (रामलिङ्गेश्वर), and Rāma (राम) and Pārvatī (पार्वती), the *kalyāṇa-maṇḍapa* (कल्याण-मण्डप) and the outer *prākāra* with *gopurams* in the north, west and south. The north and south *gopurams* are decorated with finely carved sculptures and relief panels. On the inscriptional and stylistic grounds, the temple has been tentatively dated around CE 1450.

The main shrine of the complex dedicated to Rāmaliṅgeśvara (रामलिङ्गेश्वर) follows the axial plan in which the *garbha-gṛha* (गर्भ-गृह), *antarāla* (अन्तराल) and the *mukha-maṇḍapa* (मुख-मण्डप) are built in a single line. The *garbha-gṛha* is flanked by two smaller shrines. There are eight central pillars in the *mukha-maṇḍapa*, arranged in two rows of four each, supporting the roof. The *mukha-maṇḍapa* opens to north and south with porticos. In front of the *mukha-maṇḍapa* were placed the *balipīṭha* (बलिपीठ) and the *dhvajastambha* (ध्वजस्तम्भ) which became an integral part of the south Indian temples.

In its elevation, the *mūla-prāsāda* (मूल-प्रासाद) along with its *antarāla* stands on a high *adhiṣṭhāna* (अधिष्ठान) formed by different mouldings such as *upāna* (उपान), *paṭṭa* (पट्ट, band), *ardha-padma* (अर्द्ध-पद्म), *gala* (गल),

kumuda (कुमुद), *gala* depicting lions and dwarfs, projecting *paṭṭa* with foliage, *gala, ūrdhva-padma* (ऊर्ध्व-पद्म) and *āliṅgapaṭṭikā* (आलिङ्गपट्टिका) from bottom upwards. The back wall of the *garbha-gṛha* is provided with a *gavākṣa* (गवाक्ष)-dormer (blind door) formed by two slender pilasters with surmounting *kuṭina śikhara* (कुटिन शिखर). The wall is also decorated with *kumbha-pañjaras* (कुम्भ-पञ्जर), the typical decorative pilaster style introduced during the Coḷa period.

The *garbha-gṛha* is surmounted by the *śikhara* built of bricks which was plastered all over. It consists of two *talas* (तल) (storeys), each containing the *hāra* (हार) elements such as *kūṭa* (कूट), *pañjara* (पञ्जर) and *śālā* (शाला). The *śikhara* is round and belongs to the Vesara (वेसर) order.

The other shrines dedicated to Rāma (राम) and Pārvatī (पार्वती) form a single unit which shares a common *mukha-maṇḍapa*, which was a rare practice. In this unit only the Pārvatī shrine has the *antarāla*. Sixteen pillars arranged in four rows making a central nave and side aisles support the roof of the *mukha-maṇḍapa*. The south-west corner of the *prākāra* is provided with the *kalyāṇa-maṇḍapa* (कल्याण-मण्डप) which was a highly embellished pillared hall.

Art

The sculptural art of the Vijayanagara period is unique even though they used rough hard granite as the medium of artistic creations. However, unlike the Hoyasaḷa (होयसळ) sculptures, the figures of the Vijayanagara (विजयनगर) temples are somewhat rigid and by and large lack flexibility and animation. The facial expression is less graceful and almost emotionless. Since the craftsmanship became the dominant feature of art, the nose becomes pointed and the cheeks are vertically sculpted. The depiction of draperies, ornaments and other decorative elements of the earlier times continued with great vigour. The *tilaka* (तिलक), the religious mark on the forehead, not found in early periods, makes its appearance in the Vijayanagara figures. It was indeed an innovation.

For the first time in south India, the river goddesses Gaṅgā (गङ्गा) and Yamunā (यमुना) along with their *vāhana*s (वाहन) were represented at the entrances of the *gopuram*s (गोपुरम्) of the temple during this period. The tongue of the *vāhana* takes the shape of a leafy scroll which encircles the figure and rises above with involute circles in which the sculptural reliefs of the ten incarnations of Viṣṇu (विष्णु) were depicted. This was also a great novelty.

The pillar decorations are also noteworthy. The pillars show prominent sculptural works in the form of riders on composite form of lion-and-elephant (*vyāli*, व्यालि). However, most of the relief motifs are diffused as compared to the earlier periods. The highly ornate *kumbha-pañjara* (कुम्भ-पञ्जर) was crowned by the cornice and the *kūṭa* (कूट) shrine. The ornamental capital shows characteristic "lotus bud" pendants.

14

Nāyaka Temples

AFTER the battle of Talikoṭa (तलिकोट) in 1565, Vijayanagara (विजयनगर) lost its integrity and strength which resulted in the emergence of a number of petty chiefdoms under the governors of the erstwhile kingdom, who were known as "Nāyakas नायक." By the first quarter of the seventeenth century the Nāyakas of Gingee (जिंजी), Tañjāvūr (तंजावूर), Vellore (वेल्लोर) and Madurai (मदुरै) asserted their independence, though many of them could not maintain their sovereignty because of internal and external political uncertainty. However, among them, the most successful was Tirumala Nāyaka (तिरुमल-नायक) (CE 1623-59), who made Madurai as his capital and ruled for more than 30 years. His kingdom comprised much of the old Pāṇḍya territories which included Coimbatore (कोयम्बटूर), Tirunelvelī (तिरुनेलवेली), Madurai districts, Aragalur (अरगलूर) in southern Tamil Nadu (तमिलनाडु) and some areas of Travancore (त्रावणकोर) kingdom. His rule is also noted for the efflorescence in art and architecture.

The Drāviḍa (द्राविड) architecture attained its final form under the Nāyakas. Their architectural style, known as the "Madurai Style," is best manifested in the Mīnākṣī (मीनाक्षी) temple of Madurai. Though the temple was originally built by Māravarman Kulaśekhara Pāṇḍya (मारवर्मन् कुलशेखार पाण्ड्य) (1268–1310), its present grandiose form was

Pl. 90 : Main Gopuram of the Jambukeśvara temple, Tiruchirappalli

achieved during the Nāyaka period. They enlarged the temple complex and added many *maṇḍapas* (मण्डप), *pradakṣiṇāpathas* प्रदक्षिणापथ/corridors, *prākāras* (प्राकार) and *gopurams* (गोपुरम्) to the pre-existing temple.

They lavishly incorporated many of the architectural features of their predecessors in their new constructions. For example, the *puṣpa-poṭikā* (पुष्प-पोटिका) and the *yali* (यलि) figures, once adorning the Vijayanagara pillars, continued to be retained in the Nāyaka period also.

Gopurams

Following the Vijayangara (विजयनगर) tradition, the *gopurams* (गोपुरम्) continued to be slender and tall, the typical example being the *gopuram* of the Vaṭapatraśāyī (वटपत्रशायी) Temple at Śrīvilliputtūr (श्रीविल्लीपुत्तूर), which is eleven-storeyed. Further development in the temple *gopuram* can be seen at Madurai. Here, the southern *gopuram* of the Mīnākṣī (मीनाक्षी) temple with its imposing height, stunning concave profile, projecting vertical section with *gavākṣas* (गवाक्ष) through the entire height at the middle of the longer side of the tower is unique in its features. Its innumerable stucco figures, creating rich surface decorations, show one of the most graceful and ornate *gopurams* of the Nāyaka period. Many *maṇḍapas* and *prākāras* (प्राकार) of the temples of Raṅganātha (रंगनाथ, Śrīraṅgam, श्रीरंगम), Jambūkeśvara (जम्बूकेश्वर), (*Pl.* 90, *fig.* 85) Rāmeśvaram (रामेश्वरम्), Tirunelvelī (तिरुनेलवेली) and Chidambaram (चिदम्बरम्)

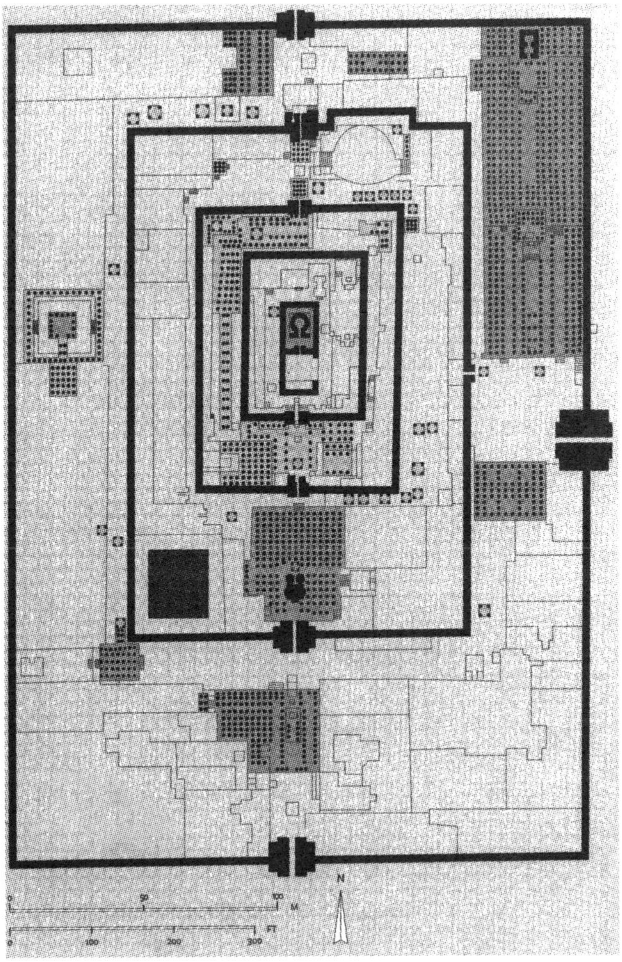

Fig. 85 : Plan of Jambukeśvara temple, Thiruchirappalli, Nāyaka period

yield other notable examples of the Nāyaka temple architecture. For example, Acyutappā Nāyaka (अच्युतप्पा नायक) (1580–1614) covered the *vimāna* (विमान) of the Raṅganātha temple with gold and reconstructed some of the outer *prākāra*s and *gopurams*.

Another beautiful temple originally built by the Nāyakas is the Subrahmaṇya (सुब्रह्मण्य) temple at Tañjāvūr (तंजावूर) (*Pl.* 91). The temple, with its fine *vimāna* and *ardha-maṇḍapa* (अर्द्ध-मण्डप) and *mahāmaṇḍapa* (महामण्डप), stands in the north-west corner of the Bṛhadīśvara (बृहदीश्वर) temple complex

Pl. 91 : Subrahmaṇya temple, Tañjavūr

of Tanjāvūr. It exemplifies the most ornate variety of the Nāyaka temple. The temple, built in fine-textured granite, shows the typical *puṣpa-poṭikā* (पुष्प-पोटिका) and the double-flexed cornice. The *kumbha-pañjaras* (कुम्भ-पञ्जर) and the *deva-koṣṭhas* adorn the temple wall. The *grīvā* (ग्रीवा) and *kuṭina śikhara* (कुटिन शिखर) over the square *vimāna* are hexagonal (six-sided). The mouldings of the *adhiṣṭhāna* (अधिष्ठान) and the pillars are intricately carved.

The galleries or the long corridors of the Nāyaka temples are highly embellished and are flanked by massive columns. For instance, the corridors of the Madurai temple, flanked by monolithic granite pillars, sculpted in the image of *yali*s (यलि), bear on their shoulders the corbelled roof-structure. All the parts of these corridors, including pillars, walls and ceilings are painted in dazzling colours. The corridors of the Rāmeśvaram (रामेश्वरम्) temple are also noteworthy. These corridors also serve as the *pradakṣiṇāpatha*s.

Like the Vijayanagara (विजयनगर) temples, the Nāyaka temple complexes also consisted of different *maṇḍapa*s (मण्डप) like *kalyāṇa-maṇḍapa* (कल्याण-मण्डप) *raṅga-maṇḍapa* (रंग-मण्डप) and *āyiram-kal-maṇḍapam* (आयिरम-कल्-मण्डप, the thousand-pillared hall). In addition to these *maṇḍapa*s, there were many other *maṇḍapa*s like *aṣṭa-śakti maṇḍapam* (अष्ट-शक्ति-मण्डपम्), *ūñjala* (ऊञ्जल, swing) *maṇḍapam, kilikkoodu maṇḍapam,* (किलिकूडु मण्डपम्, parrot-cage), *vasanta maṇḍapam/puthu-maṇḍapam* (वसन्तमण्डपम्/पुथु-मण्डप, etc. in the Mīnākṣī temple. The *kalyāṇa-maṇḍapam* at Vellore and a similar one in the northern *prākāra* of the Raṅganātha temple at Śrīraṅgam are also noteworthy.

What is significant to note is the aesthetic quality of the Nāyaka temples. It has often been said by Western art historians that it is the stage of "degeneration" since although the images are excellent as pieces of craftsmanship, with sharp physical features, yet they completely lack the inner beauty of the Gupta (गुप्त) or Coḷa (चोळ) artistic creations exhibiting spiritual element. However, this kind of value judgement on the basis of comparative studies between chronologically different works of art is unscientific in approach. The fact is that each period tries to differ from the previous one in order to establish its own individuality. To create highly ornate architectural piece, as if it was a work of great art and craft, besides being an architectural marvel, was the motive force of the Nāyakas. We therefore, give a very high rank to the *gopuram*s (गोपुरम्), corridors and *maṇḍapa*s created by the Nāyakas.

15

Temples of Kerala

TEMPLES of Kerala (केरल), variously known as *ambalam* (अम्बलम्), *kṣetram* (क्षेत्रम्), *kōvil* (कोविल्), *tali* (तलि), etc. present a unique indigenous architectural tradition, yet they have assimilated many elements from Drāviḍa (द्राविड) style. The centrally located *śrīkōvil* (श्रीकोविल्, *sanctum sanctorum*) is the main structure of the temple complex. It usually stands in east-west axis. The plan may be square (*fig.* 86), rectangular (*fig.* 87), circular (*fig.* 88), elliptical (*fig.* 89) or apsidal (*fig.* 90).

Pl. 92 : Śiva temple, Vizhinjam, Thiruvananthapuram

The earlier temples were mainly dedicated to prominent Hindu deities like Śiva (शिव), Viṣṇu (विष्णु), Rāma (राम), Paraśurāma (परशुराम), Kṛṣṇa (कृष्ण) and Bhagavatī (भगवती, Goddess). During the later period temples dedicated to Śaṅkara-Nārāyaṇa (Hari-Hara, हरि-हर), Gaṇapati (गणपति, Vināyaka विनायक), Subrahmaṇya (सुब्रह्मण्य) (Muruga or Kārttikeya मुरुग या कार्त्तिकेय) and Sāstha (सास्थ) also became popular.

The architecture of the Kerala temples has been largely influenced by its geographical peculiarities and climatic conditions, particularly,

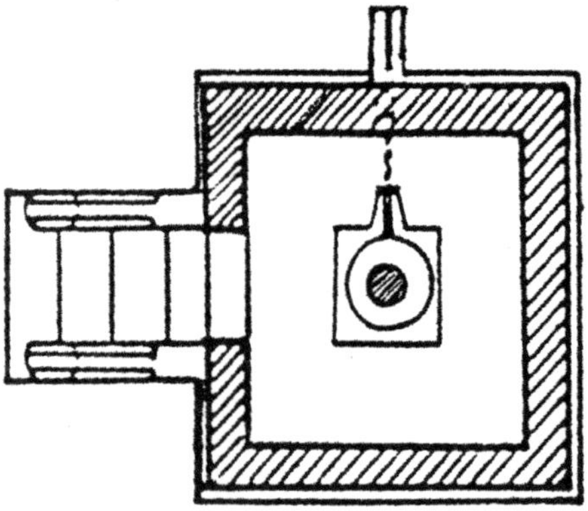

Fig. 86 : Plan of Śrī Śiva temple, Vizhinjam, Thiruvananthapuram

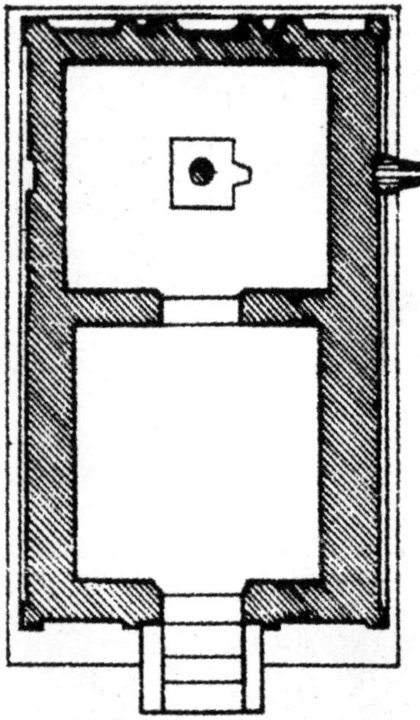

Fig. 87 : Plan of Śrī Brahmā shrine of Paraśurāma temple complex, Thiruvallam, Thiruvananthapuram

torrential rains brought by seasonal monsoons. Because of these reasons the roofs of the Kerala temples are steep and pointed, and thatched with terracotta tiles. During the later period, copper sheets replaced the terracotta roof-tiles and the rulers and wealthy people donated handsomely for such a transformation.

Some of the important treatises, such as the *Tantra Samuccaya* (तन्त्र-समुच्चय) of Nārāyaṇa (नारायण, mid-fifteenth century), *Śilparatna* (शिल्परत्न) of Śrī Kumāra (श्री कुमार, sixteenth century) and *Kriyā Dīpikā* (क्रिया दीपिका in *Putayur bhāṣā* पुतयुर भाषा) of Putayur Vāsudevan (पुतयुर वासुदेवन, 1342) vividly describe the ground plan, elevation, and various elements of the Kerala temples.

The sanctum is fronted by the *namaskāra-maṇḍapam* (नमस्कार-मण्डपम्). There may be a narrow *mukha-maṇḍapa* (मुख-मण्डप) projecting from the *garbha-gṛha* (गर्भ-गृह). The sanctum or *śrīkōvil* (श्रीकोविल्), along with its *namaskāra-maṇḍapam* (नमस्कार-मण्डपम्), is surrounded by a cloistered enclosure, known as *nālambalam* (नालम्बलम्). It has four *dvāra*s (द्वार) (entrances) from four cardinal directions. Around the *śrīkōvil* there are *bali-pīṭha*s (बलि-पीठ) for *aṣṭadikpāla*s (अष्टदिक्पाल) and other deities. To the south of the *śrīkōvil* were placed the *bali-pīṭha*s representing Saptamātṛkās (सप्तमातृका, a group of seven mother goddesses).

The *nālambalam* also houses subsidiary shrines. A kitchen (*thiṭappaḷḷi* थिटप्पल्लि) is located in the south-eastern corner of the *nālambalam*. The main entrance of the *nālambalam* opens into the *agra-maṇḍapam*. If the *agra-maṇḍapam* (अग्र-मण्डप) is absent, the *balikkal-*

maṇḍapam (बलिक्कल्-मण्डपम्) is built in its place. The *balikkal-maṇḍapam* encloses the *valia-balikkal* (वलिय-बलिक्कल्) which resembles the *adhiṣṭhāna* (अधिष्ठान) and the main wall up to the cornice of the Drāviḍa (द्राविड) *vimāna* (विमान). The *dhvaja-stambham* (ध्वज-स्तम्भम्) (flag staff of the temple) is placed in front of the *balikkal-maṇḍapam*. The main entrance to the interior is located here and a straight passage cuts through the *balikkal-maṇḍapam/agra-maṇḍapam* and *nālambalam*.

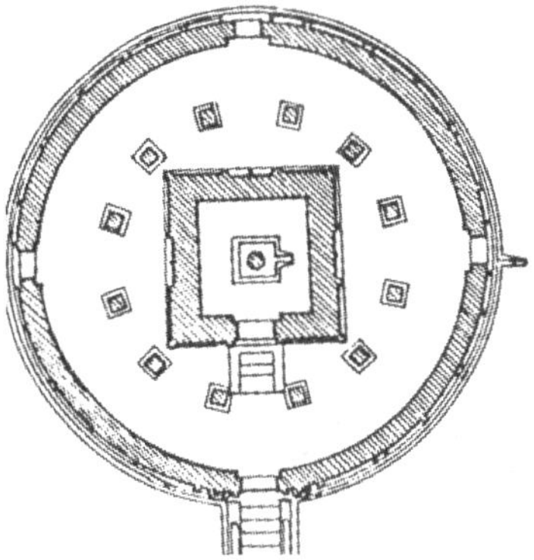

Fig. 88 : Plan of Śrī Subrahmaṇya temple, Mañjeri, Malappuram district

The superstructure of the Kerala temple is generally built of timber, tiles, copper sheets, etc. The *adhiṣṭhāna* of the *vimāna* was built of granite or hard laterite blocks over which rise the wood/brick/laterite walls. Walls and wooden beams supported the superstructure. The gabled-roof, built of wooden planks, beams and rafters, was provided with projecting eaves to protect the temple wall from torrential rains. The roof was covered with terracotta tiles or copper sheets. The circular *garbha-gṛha* (गर्भ-गृह) had conical roof whereas the square or oblong sanctums were topped by pyramidal roof. The roofs were crowned by a *stūpikā* (स्तूपिका, finial) or more than one *stūpikās*.

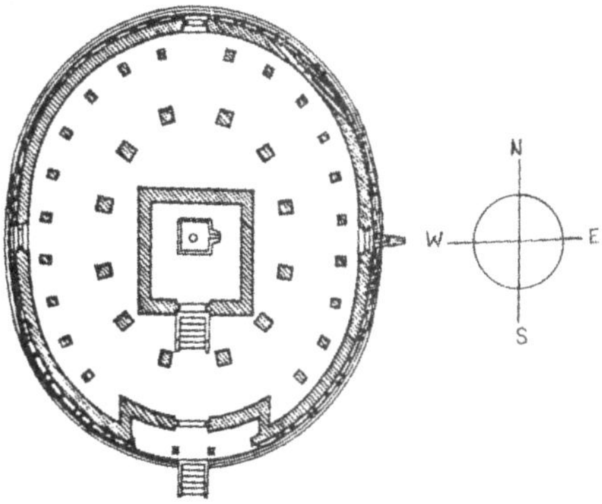

Fig. 89 : Plan of Śrī Mahādeva temple, Vaikom, Koṭṭāyam district

Unlike other parts of India, the inscriptional evidence for the temples of Kerala starts only from the beginning of the ninth century. Broadly speaking, three developmental phases have been noticed in Kerala temple architecture since that time. The Early Phase ranges between CE 800–1000, the Middle Phase between CE 1001–1300, and the Late Phase between CE 1301–1800.

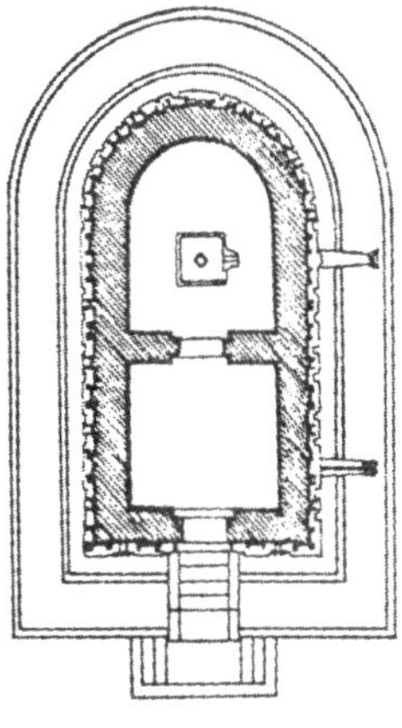

Fig. 90 : Plan of Śrī Śiva temple, Trikkaṇḍiyur, Malappuram district

Pl. 93 : Kattilmadam temple, Chalappuram, Pālaghāṭ district

Early Phase (CE 800–1000)

The Kerala *sthapati*s (स्थपति) were well aware of the basic plan of the Hindu temple, i.e. the square *garbha-gṛha* (गर्भ-गृह) fronted by a small *maṇḍapa* (मण्डप). Such basic plan can be seen in Nāgara (नागर), Drāviḍa (द्राविड) and Kerala style architecture. However, early temples like Śiva (*Pl.* 92) and Bhagavatī भगवती) temples at Viliñjam (विलिञ्जम्) in Thiruvananthapuram (तिरुवनन्तपुरम्) (*c.* eighth century) do not show well-defined *maṇḍapa*s. Kaṇḍiyūr Śiva (कण्डियूर शिव) temple in Alappuzha (अलपपुझा) district (*c.* CE 823), Thiruvañcikulam Śiva (तिरुवञ्चिकुलम शिव) temple in Thrissur (त्रिस्सुर) district (*c.* CE 800), Śiva temple at Netirmaṅgalam (नेतिर्मङ्गलम्) in Pālaghāṭ (पालघाट) district (*c.* fifth century), etc. exhibit *sama-caturasra-vimāna* (सम-चतुरस्र-विमान) fronted by a narrow *maṇḍapa*. Circular and apsidal temples with or without the *mukha-maṇḍapa* are also found in this period.

Both *sandhāra* (सन्धार, with *pradakṣiṇāpatha*, प्रदक्षिणापथ) and *nirandhāra* (निरन्धार, without *pradakṣiṇāpatha*) temples existed in this phase. Many of the temples were of *sarvatobhadra* (सर्वतोभद्र) type in which four *dvāra*s (द्वार, entrances) were attached to the cardinal directions. To avoid monotony, the temple wall had many projections and recess in between. Drāviḍa elements such *śālā* (शाला), *kūṭa* (कूट) and *pañjara* (पञ्जर) can also be seen, though, rarely, between the gabled roof and the wall proper of the *śrīkōvil* (श्रीकोविल्).

Middle Phase (CE 1001–1300)

This period also witnessed the erection of square, circular, apsidal and rectangular shrines. There were both Drāviḍa and the mixture of Drāviḍa and Kerala style temples. For example, the Kattilmadam (कत्तिल्मदम्) temple at Chalapuram (चलपुरम्) in Pālaghāṭ district exhibits a *ṣaḍaṅga-vimāna* (षडङ्ग-विमान, six parts in its elevation) with octagonal *grīvā* (ग्रीवा) and *śikhara* (शिखर) (*Pl.* 93). The *talas* (तल) of the Drāviḍa variety have been decorated with *hāra* (हार) elements such as *kūṭa, śālā,* and *pañjara.*

The *miśra* (मिश्र) or mixed variety, i.e. Drāviḍa-Kerala style, with more indigenous elements, also developed in this period. These temples are mainly *sandhāra* type with one or more than one *pradakṣiṇāpathas*. The mouldings of the *adhiṣṭhāna* became more complex and the *hasti-hasta* (हस्ति-हस्त) banisters of the *sopāna* (सोपान, stairway immediately attached to the sanctum) were decorated with dancing figures and floral motifs. Under the *praṇāla* (प्रणाल, water-chute) of the *garbha-gṛha* was placed a dwarf *bhūta* (भूत) sculpture. Sometimes, this *bhūta* figure supported the end of the *praṇāla.*

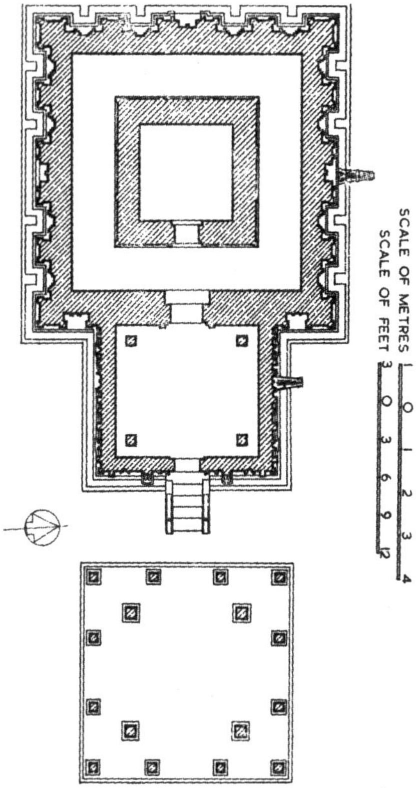

Fig. 91 : Tali temple, Kozhikoḍe

Temples of the *sarvatobhadra* (सर्वतोभद्र) type continued to be built though in some examples the number of original doors varied from two to three. In such cases *ghanadvāras* (घनद्वार, blind doors) were carved at the sides (where the true doors were not given) to make it a *sarvatobhadra*. The consort of the enshrined deity was placed at the back of the *garbha-gṛha*. Many of the temples had *namaskāra-maṇḍapam* (नमस्कार-मण्डपम्) during this phase.

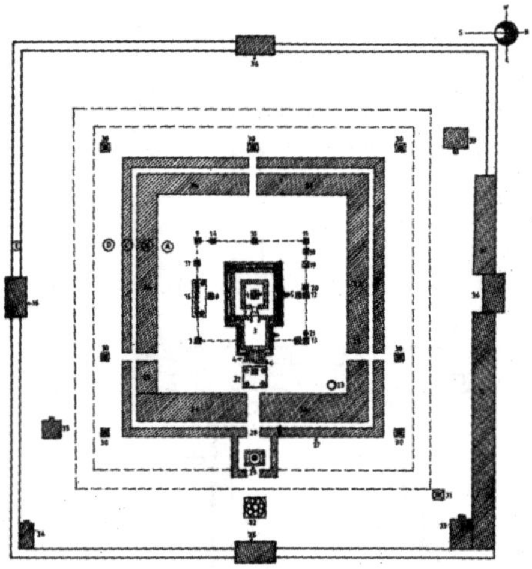

Fig. 92 : Plan of the Pañca-Prākāra scheme of Kerala temple

Late Phase (CE 1301–1800)

During this period, the temple architecture of Kerala attained its perfection by means of enlarging the ground plan, elevation and elaboration of decorative elements. The square, circular, apsidal and rectangular shrines continued to flourish in this period also. The *pradakṣiṇāpatha* became an indispensable part of the sanctum (*fig.* 91). Majority of the temples had more than one *pradakṣiṇāpatha*s.

During this period, *pañca-prākāra* (पञ्च-प्राकार, five concentric enclosures) scheme of Kerala temple architecture reached its zenith (*figs.* 92 & 93). Walls, ceilings, pillars, pillar-brackets and pilasters were intricately carved with various deities, jewel motifs, leafy scrolls, mythical beasts, and floral designs. The wooden ceilings of the various *maṇḍapa*s (मण्डप) were carved with episodes from the epics and the Purāṇas (पुराण). Similarly, the outer wall of the *garbha-gṛha* was beautifully adorned with mural paintings depicting different stories related to various divinities. Entrances were invariably guarded by wooden *dvārapāla*s (द्वारपाल).

Classification of Temples

Kerala temples may be classified as *mahākṣetra* (महाक्षेत्र, great temples with the characteristic features of the *pañca-prākāra* scheme), *valia-kṣetra* (वलियक्षेत्र, big temples), *cheria-kṣetra* (छेरिअ-क्षेत्र, small temples) and *kochu-kṣetra* (कोछु-क्षेत्र, tiny temples) according to their size, plan, and *pūjā*s (पूजा). The *Mudippura*s (मुदिप्पुर) located near the agricultural fields, and the family temples belong to the *kochu-kṣetram* (कोछु-क्षेत्रम्) since they are generally small enough to maintain considerably with a low income.

The Temple Complex

The fully developed Kerala temple complex belongs to the characteristic *pañca-prākāra* (पञ्च-प्राकार) system in which the sanctum proper is surrounded by five *prākāra*s (walls or enclosures) with their associated structures. They were designed in such a fashion that various chambers, open platforms, sub-shrines, granaries and even *pradakṣiṇāpatha*s (प्रदक्षिणा-पथ) can be accommodated within them. These five *prākāra*s are as follows:

1. ***Akathe-balivattam***: (अकथे-बलिवत्तम्) The innermost enclosure.
2. ***Antar-hāra*** (अन्तर्हार) or ***Chuttambalam*** (छुत्तम्बलम्) or ***Nālambalam*** (नालम्बलम्): A cloistered hall surrounding the *śrīkōvil* (श्रीकोविल्).
3. ***Madhya-hāra*** (मध्य-हार) or ***Vilakkumāṭam*** (विलक्कुमाटम्, lit. structure affixed with galaxy of lamps): It is the structure that encircles the *nālambalam*. It is affixed with hundreds of equally-spaced oil lamps.
4. ***Bāhya-hāra*** (बाह्य-हार) or ***Purate*** (पुरते, outer) – ***balivattam*** (बलिवत्तम) or ***Sīvelippura*** (सीवेलिप्पुर): the enclosure between *Vilakkumāṭam* and the outer *prākāra* wall (*maryādā*, मर्यादा).
5. ***Maryādā*** (मर्यादा) or ***Puram-mathil*** (पुरम्-मथिल्): outer-wall, including *gopura* (गोपुर).

AKATHE-BALIVATTAM

The *akathe-balivattam* constitutes the *śrīkōvil*, the *namaskāra-maṇḍapam* (नमस्कार-मण्डपम्), the place for Saptamātṛkās (सप्तमातृका) and the *bali-pīṭha*s (बलि-पीठ). All the above-mentioned units fall within the square *antar-maṇḍala* (अन्तर्मण्डल, inner space) formed by the

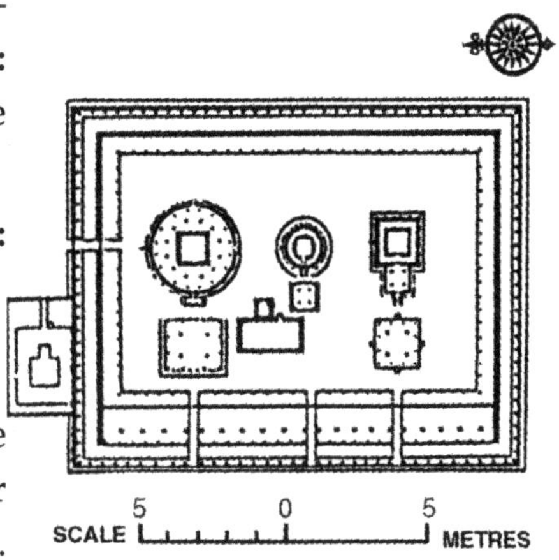

Fig. 93 : Plan of Śrī Vaḍakkunnātha temple complex, Thrissur

*bali-pīṭha*s (small stone blocks carved in the shape of a full-blown lotus). The *bali-pīṭha*s may represent the *aṣṭadikpāla*s (gods ruling the eight directions of the world), Saptamātṛkās and the deities like Gaṇapati (गणपति), Vīrabhadra (वीरभद्र), Sāstha (सास्थ), Ananta (अनन्त) and Durgā (दुर्गा). The *bali-pīṭha*s may be covered with bronze sheets.

Śrīkōvil (श्रीकोविल्) ***or Vimāna*** (विमान): It contains the idol made either of wood or granite or *pañcaloha* (पञ्चलोह, five metals). The plan of the sanctum falls under five categories, namely, square (*sama-catura,* सम-चतुर), rectangular (*dīrgha-catura,* दीर्घ-चतुर), circular (*vṛtta* or *vatta,* वृत्त या वत्त), elliptical (*aṇḍa-vṛtta* or *upa-vṛtta,* अण्ड-वृत्त या उप-वृत्त), and apsidal (*gaja-pṛṣṭha* गज-पृष्ठ, or back of the elephant) of which the first three types are commonly seen in Kerala. If the sanctum is provided with the circumambulatory passage it is known as *sandhāra-prāsāda* (सन्धार-प्रासाद). The *garbha-gṛha* (गर्भ-गृह), in many temples, projects to a narrow *mukha-maṇḍapa* (मुख-मण्डप) which forms an integral part of the sanctum. In front of the *garbha-gṛha* is a *namaskāra-maṇḍapam* (नमस्कार-मण्डपम्) on which the priest makes his customary prostrations.

Elevation of the Śrīkōvil: The shrine proper of the Kerala temple comprises *adhiṣṭhāna* (अधिष्ठान), *vedikā* (वेदिका), *bhitti* (भित्ति), *stambha* (स्तम्भ), *kuḍya-stambha* (कुड्य-स्तम्भ), *uttara* (उत्तर), *śikhara* (शिखर) and *tāzhikakkuṭam* (ताज़िकक्कुटम्, *stūpī* स्तूपी). According to the number of storeys in the *śikhara* the temples are classified into *alpa-prāsāda*s (अल्प-प्रासाद) and the *mahā-prāsāda*s (महा-प्रासाद). The common type of sanctums found in Kerala is *alpa-prāsāda* and may have one to three storeys. *Kuḍu* (कुडु) arches, resembling the *sukanāsikā*s (सुकनासिका), may project from each *tala* (तल) at the cardinal directions. Shrines having more than three *tala*s are called *mahā-prāsāda*s. However, due to functional, aesthetic and climatic reasons, such temples are not seen in Kerala.

Adhiṣṭhāna and Upapīṭha (अधिष्ठान और उपपीठ): The *adhiṣṭhāna* or the basal platform of the temple is formed by a series of mouldings. Each moulding has its own unique name in temple architecture. They are *padma-pādukā* (पद्म-पादुका), *pada* (पद), *jagati* (जगति), *kumuda* (कुम्भ), *kumuda-pada* (कुमुद-पद), *gala* (गल), *kaṇṭha* (कण्ठ), *kampa* (कम्प), *galapati* (गलपति), *uttara* (उत्तर), *valabhī* (वलभी), *paṭṭikā* (पट्टिका), *prathi* (प्रथि), *kapotam* (कपोतम्) and *vājana* (वाजन) from bottom upwards. It is not necessary that the basement of *śrīkōvil*s should have all these mouldings. However, certain essential mouldings like *pādukā*, *jagati*, *kumuda* and *gala* are seen in almost all temples.

Upa-pīṭha (उप-पीठ): is the structure below the *adhiṣṭhāna*. The *upapīṭha* and *adhiṣṭhāna* are generally made up of granite or hard laterite stones.

Vedi or Vedikā (वेदि या वेदिका): *Vedi* or *vedikā* is a series of mouldings which rests over the *adhiṣṭhāna* over which rises the shrine wall. Like the *adhiṣṭhāna*, it also has a number of mouldings, namely, *gala* (गल), *padma* (पद्म), *kampa* (कम्प), and again *gala* (गल). The *adhiṣṭhāna* (अधिष्ठान) and the *vedikā* (वेदिका) may be decorated with various motifs.

***Wall (bhitti,* भित्ति):** The walls are built of granite stones, hard laterite blocks, burnt bricks or wood. If the walls are built of laterite or bricks they were generally plastered with lime mixed with sand. The wall of the *garbha-gṛha* (गर्भ-गृह) may exhibit *ghana-dvāra*s (blind doors), pilasters (*kuḍya stambha*s, कुड्य

स्तम्भ), *kuḍu* arches, niches enshrining relief figures of divinities, pair of pilasters supporting the *prastara* (प्रस्तर) of the *vimāna*, (विमान) etc.

Pillars and Columns: The wooden pillars may be of square, hexagonal, octagonal, hexadecagonal (sixteen-sided) or circular. To enhance the beauty of the pillars *miśra* (मिश्र, mixture) varieties like square top and bottom with octagonal centre were also chiselled. The upper portion of the pillars has many ornamental decorations such as *oma, ghaṭa* (घट), and *poṭikā* (पोटिका). The *uttara* (उत्तर), a long horizontal beam made of stone or wood, rests on the pillars and walls and takes the whole load of the roof.

Praṇāla **(प्रणाल):** The *praṇāla* (water chute), also known as *ōvu* (ओवु) or *gomukha* (गोमुख), is an important part of the *śrīkōvil* (श्रीकोविल्) and it is meant for draining out the *abhiṣeka-tīrtham* (अभिषेक-तीर्थम्, water, milk, ghee, etc. poured over the image of the deity) from the sanctum. They are given different shapes, viz. circular, fluted, square and rectangular. The *praṇāla* appears as if it emerged from the *vyāla-mukha* (व्याल-मुख), or lion's head attached to the bottom of the shrine wall. The other end of the *praṇāla*, in some examples, transforms into a *gomukha* (cow's head). The *praṇāla*s are also decorated with jewel designs, creepers, bands, lotus motifs, etc. In later period a dwarf appears beneath the *praṇāla*.

Roof : The shape of the superstructure varies according to the plan of the *śrīkōvil*. If the sanctum is circular the roof will be in conical shape crowned by a *stūpī* (स्तूपी). In the square temples the roof will be of pyramidal type. The superstructure of the apsidal shrine also follows the same plan, though the roof-top is gabled crowned by a series of *stūpīs* fixed along the long axis with gaps in between.

Sopāna (सोपान): The flight of steps which leads to the *garbha-gṛha* is called *sopāna*. *Sopāna* may be arranged in two ways: (i) flight of steps directly facing the interior of the *garbha-gṛha*, and (ii) those having lateral flight of steps with a landing like those of the Buddhist *stūpas* (स्तूप). The *sopāna* has banisters on either side in the shape of *hasti-hasta* (हस्ति-हस्त, elephant's trunk) or *makara-siṁha* (मकर-सिंह, lion's head with long rolled tongues). During the later period the banisters began to depict divinities, dancing figures, drummers, singers, and faunal and floral motifs.

Namaskāra-maṇḍapam (नमस्कार-मण्डपम्): The smaller *namaskāra- maṇḍapam*, located in front of the *garbha-gṛha* but within the *akathe-balivattam* (अकथे-बलिवत्तम), is a detached hall with four corner pillars supporting the roof. It has the similar *adhiṣṭhāna* (अधिष्ठान) mouldings as those of the *garbha-gṛha*. The *namaskāra-maṇḍapa* has pyramidal superstructure with a *stūpikā* (स्तूपिका, *tazhikakkūṭam* तज़िकक्कूटम्). The ceiling of this *maṇḍapa* is decorated with the images of *navagrahas* (नवग्रह) or *aṣṭa-dikpālas* (अष्ट-दिक्पाल).

In Śiva (शिव) temples the *namaskāra-maṇḍapa* is called the *nandī-maṇḍapam* (नन्दी-मण्डपम्) because of the presence of Nandī (*vāhana,* वाहन of Śiva) and in Viṣṇu temples it is called *garuḍa-maṇḍapam* (गरुड-मण्डपम्) because of the presence of Garuḍa (*vāhana* of Viṣṇu).

ANTAR-HĀRA OR CHUTTAMBALAM OR NĀLAMBALAM

The *prākāra* (प्राकार) or boundary wall unit that immediately encloses the *śrīkōvil* (श्रीकोविल्), or *garbha-gṛha*, from all sides is known as *nālambalam* (नालम्बलम्). Generally, the *nālambalam* has entrances at its four cardinal directions. This structure comprises *valiambalam* (वल्यम्बलम्), *thiṭappaḷḷi* (तिटप्पळ्ळि), *mūlayara* (मूलयर) or *pathāyappura* (पत्तायप्पुरा, *pathāyam* (पत्तायम्) is a wooden storage-box for grains, food articles, etc.), sub-shrines, etc. These structures are an integral part of the *nālamabalam*.

Valiambalam (वलिअम्बलम्): The broad open spaces, that form part of the *nālambalam* and immediately approached from the *balikkal-maṇḍapa* (बलिक्कल्-मण्डप), are called *valiambalam*. The main passage from the *balikkal-maṇḍapa/agra-maṇḍapa* (अग्र-मण्डप) to the *garbha-gṛha* passes through the *valiambalam* (बलिअम्बरलम्). The *valiambalam* is used for conducting *homa*s (होम), recital of Vedic hymns and Purāṇas (पुराण), conducting religious meetings, etc.

Thiṭappaḷḷi (तिटप्पळ्ळि) : It is the kitchen to the sanctum where sacred food (*nivedyam* or *naivedyam* निवेद्यम् या नैवेद्यम्) is prepared for the enshrined deity. This part of the *nālambalam* (नालम्बलम्) is located to the left of the *namaskāra-maṇḍapam* (नमस्कार-मण्डपम्).

Mūlayara (मूलयर): It is the store-house for grains, fruits, utensils and firewood. There might be a *pathāyam* (पत्तायम्, a large wooden box with partitions) to store the grains. It is located in the north of the *nālambalam*.

Kūpa (कूप): A sacred-well (*kūpa*) is necessary for the Kerala temple. Its water is exclusively used for the ablution of the deities and the preparation of the holy food (*nivedyam*). Its position is at the north-east of the *nālambalam*.

MADHYA-HĀRA (मध्य-हार) OR VILAKKUMĀṬAM

The *vilakkumāṭam* (विलक्कुमाटम्), located outside the *nālambalam*, is particular to the Kerala temple. It is a structure with wooden columns and rafters affixed with a galaxy of lamps in many rows and columns. It encircles the *nālambalam*. The lamps of the *vilakkumāṭam* are made of brass or iron. Lamps are to be fixed in equal distance so that they will appear aesthetically very pleasing once they are lit. Only big temples will have separate *vilakkumāṭam*. In small temples multi-tiered brass or stone lamps are fixed on the outer-face of the wall of the *nālambalam*.

BĀHYA-HĀRA OR PURATTHE (OUTER)-BALIVATTAM OR ŚEEVELIPPURA

Bāhya-hāra (बाह्य-हार) covers all outer *bali-pīṭhas* (बलि-पीठ) and structures in between the *vilakkumāṭam* and the outer-wall (*maryādā* मर्यादा) falling in *pañca-prākāra* (पञ्च-प्राकार) scheme and those in between *chuttambalam* and *maryādā* in the context of *catura-prākāra* (चतुर-प्राकार) lay-out. *Bāhya-hāra* comprises the following structural units:

Agra-maṇḍapa (अग्र-मण्डप) ***or Balikkal-maṇḍapa*** (बलिक्कल्-मण्डप) **:** *Agra-maṇḍapa* is a small hall which projects from the *nālambalam* (नालम्बलम्). It houses the *valiabalikkal* (वलियबलिक्कल्) which faces the front door of the *garbha-gṛha* (गर्भ-गृह). The *agra-maṇḍapa* may be provided with seats similar, though in different form, to the *kakṣāsanas* (कक्षासन) of the Nāgara (नागर) style temples.

Valiabalikkal (principal balikkal) **:** It is a dressed stone block which is used for sacrificial offerings. It resembles a Drāviḍa *vimāna* (द्राविड विमान). This aesthetically carved stone block has various mouldings such as *pādukā* (पादुका), *jagati* (जगति), *kumuda* (कुमुद), *kumuda-paṭi* (कुमुद-पटि), *kaṇṭha* (कण्ठ), *gala* (गल), *gala-paṭi* (गल-पटि), *vedikā* (वेदिका), *gala* (गल), *uttara* (उत्तर), *valaru* (वलरु), *kapota* (कपोत), *kapota-paṭṭa* (कपोत-पट्ट) and crowned by an inverted *padma* (पद्म). Each face of the *valiabalikkal* shows a *ghanadvāra* (घनद्वार, blind-door). The *valiabalikkal* may be placed inside the *balikkal-maṇḍapa* or outside the *agra-maṇḍapa*.

Outer Bali-pīṭhas (बलि-पीठ) **:** Immediately outside the *vilakkumāṭam* (विलक्कुमाटम्) are seven smaller stones known as *bali-pīṭhas* arranged at four corners and in front of three subsidiary entrances to the interior. In front of the principal entrance, as noted earlier, was placed the *valiabalikkal* (principal *balikkal*). They represent protective deities of the temple.

Śeevelippura (शीवेलिप्पुर) ***and Pradakṣiṇāpatha*** (प्रदक्षिणापथ)**:** *Śeevelippura* or *śrībalippura* (श्रीबलिप्पुर) is a pillared open-hall with stone-slab paved floor running around the *vilakkumāṭam*. It is known as the *śeevelippura* because *śeeveli* (शीवेलि, the ceremonial procession around the temple done by the priest of the temple carrying the image of the deity) is conducted within this structure. Only a few *mahākṣetras* (महाक्षेत्र) have the "luxury" of the *śeevelippura*. In medium-sized and smaller temples, instead of the *śeevelippura*, they have a paved *pradakṣiṇāpatha* to serve the purpose.

Dhvaja-stambha (ध्वज-स्तम्भ) ***or Koṭimaram*** **:** This tall pillar, in front of the *balikkal-maṇḍapa*, bears on the top the deity's *vāhana* (वाहन) as emblem and one can identify the deity of a temple by seeing it. Śiva temple has Nandī (नन्दी), Viṣṇu (विष्णु) temple has Garuḍa (गरुड),

Durgā (दुर्गा) temple has Lion, Śāstha (शास्त) temple has Horse, Subrahmaṇya (सुब्रह्मण्य) temple has Peacock, Gaṇapati temple has *mūṣika* (मूषिक) and Sarasvatī (सरस्वती) temple has *haṁsa* (हंस) on top of the *dhvaja* (ध्वज). The *aṣṭadikpāla*s (अवृदिक्पाल) adorn the base of the *dhvaja*. It is usually made of wood. The *dhvaja*s of most of the famous and affluent temples of Kerala are covered with copper, *pañcaloha* (पञ्चलोह), silver, bronze or gold.

Ānakkoṭṭil : *Ānakkoṭṭil* (lit. *maṇḍapa* मण्डप of the elephant), a pillared open-*maṇḍapa*, facing *balikkalpura* (बलिक्कल्पुर), is located in front of the *dhvaja*. The main elephant of the temple stands in the *ānakkoṭṭil* during the festivals. This *maṇḍapa* is also used for conducting ceremonies like marriage, *chōrūṇu* (चोरूणु, *chōrūṇu* is the ritual of feeding the child with rice for the first time), *parayeduppu* (परयेटुप्पु, the ceremonial offering of paddy by the devotee to the temple) and *tulābhāram* (तुलाभारम्, the devotee is weighed on a balance against sugar, bananas, butter, or gold and the same is offered to the temple).

Kūthambalam (कूत्तम्बलम्): The *Kūthambalam* (theatre hall) is used to stage the performing arts like *Chākkyār Kūthu* (चाक्कयापर् कूथु), *Kūṭiyāṭṭam* (कूटियाट्टम्), *Oṭṭam thullal* (ओट्टम् तुल्लल्), *Mōhinīyāṭṭam* (मोहिनीआट्टम्), *Kṛṣṇāṭṭam* (कृष्णाट्टम्), *Kathakali* (कथकली), etc. It corresponds to the *raṅga-maṇḍapa/nāṭya-maṇḍapa/nṛtta-maṇḍapa* रंग-मण्डप/नाट्य-मण्डप/नृत्य-मण्डप of the Nāgara (नागर) temples. Unlike those of the Nāgara temples, the *kūthambalam* of the Kerala temple is located on the south-east corner of the temple complex. *Kūthambalam*s are usually in rectangular shape and has three parts, namely, *raṅga-pīḍham*

(रंग-पीढम्, the stage raised from the rest of the floor), *nepadhyam* (नेपद्यम्, green room), and a *prekṣaka-gṛham* (प्रेक्षक-गृहम्, audience hall) for viewers. The *kūthambalams* are profusely decorated with large number of wooden relief panels and sculptures.

MARYĀDĀ OR THE OUTER PRĀKĀRA WALL

The fifth and last *prākāra* (प्राकार) or boundary wall of the temple complex is *maryādā* (मर्यादा) or the outer wall. It comprises *gopura* (गोपुर, the entrance to the temple complex attached to the cardinal directions of the outer *prākāra* wall) (*Pl.* 94), *ūṭṭupura* (ऊट्टुपुर), etc. *Gopuras* are modestly built, though with elegance, which contain a single or tiered-roof and a gateway. The *oottupura* is the dining hall used for *annadāna* (अन्नदान). A large kitchen is attached to the *oottupura*.

Tīrthakkulam (तीर्थक्कुलम्): The *tīrthakkulam* (temple tank, corresponds to the *kuṇḍa* (कुण्ड) of the Gujarat temple) is invariably found in the temples of Kerala. It is meant for purifying one's body before entering into the temple.

Pl. 94 : Gopura of Śrī Vaḍakkunnātha temple complex, Thrissur

Temple Art of Kerala

The Kerala temples were the centres of various forms of arts, including fine arts and performing arts. Stone sculptors, wood-carvers and mural artists contributed enormously to the development of the temple art of Kerala. Stone sculptures, both in high-reliefs and in the round, are found in the niches of the temple walls (*koṣṭha*s, कोष्ठ) and on the pillars and pilasters.

WOOD-CARVINGS

The wood carvings are usually found in *śrīkōvil* (श्रीकोविल्), *namaskāra-maṇḍapam* (नमस्कार-मण्डपम्), *nālambalam* (नालम्बलम्), *kūthambalam* (कूत्तम्बलम्) and *gopura* (गोपुर). They are mainly found in the *śikhara* of the sanctum, ceilings of *namaskāra-maṇḍapa, nālambalam, agra-maṇḍapa* अग्र-मण्डप) and *kūthambalam* and on the pillars and pillar-brackets and pilasters. Ceilings are usually carved with *navagraha*s (नवग्रह) and *aṣṭadikpāla*s (अष्टदिक्पाल). Episodes from the *Rāmāyaṇa* (रामायण) and the *Mahābhārata* (महाभारत) also become the themes for ceiling depictions.

MURAL PAINTINGS

A mural is a painting on a wall, ceiling or other large permanent canvas like the vertical face of the rock. The techniques of mural paintings have been described in the *Viṣṇudharmottara* (विष्णुधार्मोत्तर, fifth century), the *Abhilāṣacintāmaṇi*, (अभिलाषचिन्तामणि, twelfth century) and the *Śilparatna* (शिल्परत्न, sixth century).

Initially, the original wall surface, where the painting had to be done, was plastered. The plaster is prepared from the mixture of powdered rock, clay and cow-dung mixed with chaff or vegetable fibre as *degraissants*. These were mixed in tender-coconut water and vegetable juices. After applying the plaster on the wall it was levelled and polished, when the plaster was still wet. Then, a fine white lime wash was applied as the last coat on the plaster. After that, the wet surface was left to become dry. Painting was, thus, done on the dried plaster. This technique, also used at Ajantā (अजन्ता), is called "Fresco-secco." Pigments were generally made from minerals, vegetables, lime and lamp soot. Ochre-red, ochre-yellow, white, bluish green, pure green and black are the predominant colours that were used in the Kerala murals. Other colours used were golden yellow, brown, yellowish green and greenish blue. White pigment was derived by curing lime, black from lamp-soot, red and yellow from ochre, blue from plants like *nīla amarī* (नील-अमरी, *Indigo ferra*) and green from juice of a plant locally called *eravikkara* (एरविक्कर).

Like wood carvings, murals also adopt the themes from the *Rāmāyaṇa*, the *Mahābhārata* and the Purāṇas. In such thematic depictions a full story was often continuously narrated through panels and friezes. Individual deities with their consorts and children, flora and fauna were also depicted with all their charm and beauty. Considering aesthetic quality, perfection, and above all their sublime beauty amalgamated with serene innocence, Kerala murals are among the finest wall paintings of India.

16

Temples of Jammu and Kashmir

JAMMU AND KASHMIR, the northernmost State of India consists of three divisions — Jammu, Kashmir Valley and Ladakh. It shares a border with Himachal Pradesh to the south, Pakistan to the north and west and the People's Republic of China to the north-east and east. However, the Kashmir Valley lies between the Karākoram (कराकोरम) and the Pīr Pañjāl (पीर-पञ्जाल) mountains of the Himalayan chains. The altitude of the region rises steeply from 305 m to 6910 m above MSL (Mean Sea Level). The presence of high mountains like the Pīr Pañjāl, the Zanskar (जान्सकर) and the Karākoram cause different weather conditions at different places. The summer monsoonal winds from the east bring considerable rainfall in the plains and hills during the summer season while the Mediterranean winds from the west cause heavy snowfall and rainfall in the Valley during the winter. These geographical peculiarities and the climatic conditions deeply influenced and shaped the architecture of Kashmir, both secular and religious.

The history of architecture of Kashmir Valley may be dated back to the introduction of Buddhism in this region. According to Kalhaṇa's (कल्हण) *Rājataraṅgiṇī* (राजतरंगिणी), King Aśoka (अशोक) patronized both Buddhism and Hinduism in Kashmir as also elsewhere. He caused to build two

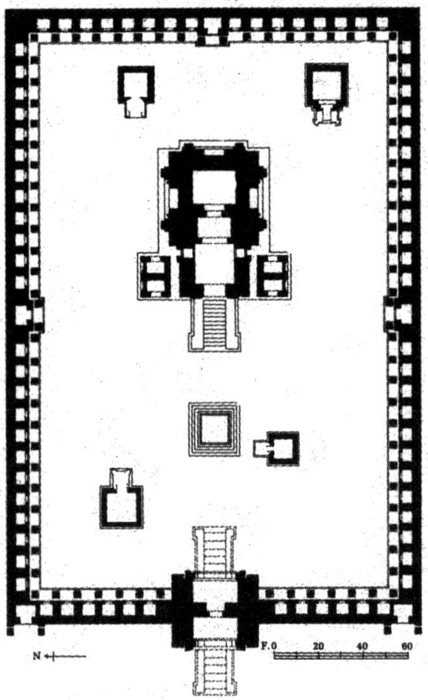

Fig. 94 : Plan of Sun temple, Mārtaṇḍa, Kashmir

Śiva (शिव) temples at Vijayeśvara (विजयेश्वर, Bijbehera बीजवेहेरा) and arranged renovation of several other temples. In Vitastatra (वितस्तत्र, Vethavutur वेथवुतुर) and at Śuṣkaletra (शुष्कलेत्र, Hukhalitar हुखलितर) he built a number of *vihāras* (विहार) and *stūpas* (स्तूप). The Buddhist remains at Harwan, Hoinar and Hutamer have revealed unique tiles, glazed and also unglazed, depicting the fine workmanship in terms of depicting animals, human beings, some with features of foreigners, birds, floral motifs, etc. He is said to have built *stūpas* in Srinagar which contained the relics of Buddha (बुद्ध) which, of course, may not be true.

The next stage of large-scale architectural activities in Kashmir can be found in the times of Kaniṣka (कनिष्क) I of the first century CE. It is said that Kaniṣka built a *stūpa* in Kashmir and deposited in it sheets of red copper engraved with commentary on the *Tripiṭakas* (त्रिपिटक), the earliest groups of Pāli books of the Theravādins. He also erected a *vihāra* (विहार) at Arigoam (अरिगोम्) in honour of Bodhisattva Avalokiteśvara (बोधिसत्त्व अवलोकितेश्वर), a Mahāyānist deity.

After the times of the Kuṣāṇas (कुषाण), around the end of the third century, there was a lull in the field of architectural activities in the valley. It was broken by King Lalitāditya (ललितादित्य) in the first half of the eighth century and not before. He founded a city called Parihāsapura (परिहासपुर). However, by the time of Kalhaṇa (कल्हण, twelfth century), the city was in its total destruction.

Early Historical Temples

Unlike the *Latina* (लटिन), Nāgara (नागर) and the *Kuṭina* (कुटिन) Drāviḍa (द्राविड) styles of temple architecture,

Pl. 95 : Sun temple, Mārtaṇḍa, Kashmir

the temples of Kashmir carry single- or tiered-gabled roof. Such roofs fall in the group of pent-roof and *pagoḍā* (पगोडा) style *śikhara*s (शिखर) that are found in Himachal Pradesh and Nepal. In classic Greek and Roman architecture such gabled roofs were built on the architectural member called *pediment*, a triangular supportive system. Since the *śikhara*s of the earlier temples are missing, it is beyond one's means to establish the true character of the superstructures of the temples of the early historical period. The Greco-Roman tradition, coming ultimately from the Gandhāra (गन्धार) roots, is clearly marked in Kashmir art and architecture, including the fluted pillars and their capitals with acanthus leaf decorations.

Plan and Elevation of the Kashmiri Temples

The temples of Kashmir are either *samacatura* (समचतुर, square) or *dīrkhacatura* (दीर्खचतुर, rectangular) or *aṣṭamukha* (अष्टमुख, octagonal) in plan. There are closed shrines as well as pillared open *maṇḍapa* (मण्डप) raised on a row of pillars called "peristyle," type temples. There was no particular direction to

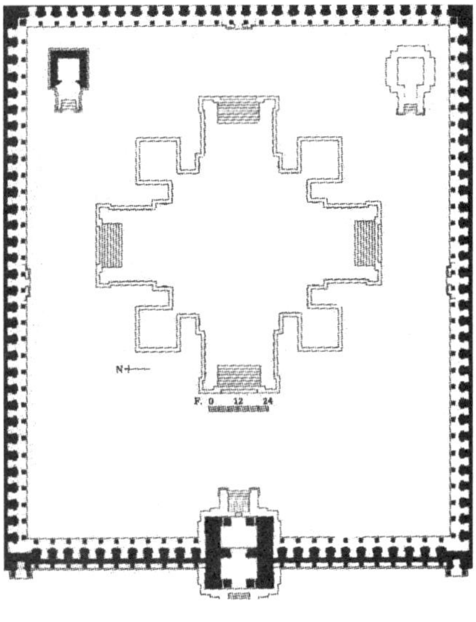

Fig. 95 : Plan of Avantīsvāmi temple, Avantipur

Pl. 96 : Jyeṣṭha temple, Naranāg

Pl. 97 : Viṣṇu temple, Buniar

fix the main entrance to the sanctum. However, the Viṣṇu (विष्णु) temples, as a rule, always faced east. In elevation, the temples had *adhiṣṭhāna* (अधिष्ठान), *bhitti* (भित्ति) and *śikhara* (शिखर). The *śikhara* is crowned by a *kalaśa* (कलश, water-pot).

Amongst the earliest temples of Kashmir is the dilapidated Sun Temple at Mārtaṇḍa (मार्तण्ड, mid-eighth century) believed to be built by King Lalitāditya Muktāpīḍa (ललितादित्य मुक्तापीड) (*Pl.* 95, *fig.* 94). Though the *śikhara* is missing, the temple parts give a fair idea of eighth-century temple architecture of Kashmir. Similar to the Greek temples of Doric order, the Mārtaṇḍa temple has a peristyle (colonnaded courtyard) of about 86 fluted pillars, with the *mūla-prāsāda* (मूल-प्रासाद) in its centre. The temple proper contains *garbha-gṛha* (गर्भ-गृह), *antarāla* (अन्तराल) and closed *maṇḍapa*, approached by a flight of steps. The entrance of the temple is provided with a gabled pediment and the doorway is built into a trefoil (shaped like a trifoliate leaf with three cusps) recess. Such trefoil recesses are typical to the ancient temples of Kashmir. Numerous figures of deities have also been recovered from the shrine. It is because of this architectural and sculptural grandiose that the Mārtaṇḍa temple has been often called "the materialized-spirit of a transcendent vision."

The Avantiswāmi (अवन्तिस्वामि, Viṣṇu) temple, built by Avantivarman (अवन्तिवर्मन्) at Avantipura (अवन्तिपुर) in the latter half of the fifth century is another important temple with Doric influence in fluted pillars and their capitals (*fig.* 95). However, it is more elegant and developed than the Mārtaṇḍa temple. The whole temple complex is surrounded by a pillared cloister. A monolithic pillar in front of the entrance carried a metal figure of Garuḍa (गरुड), the *vāhana* (वाहन) of Lord Viṣṇu.

The pedimented Doric doorway with engaged entrance columns are also found in the temples of Payar (पयर), Narastan (नरस्तान), Naranag (नरनाग), Buniyar (बुनियर) (Bhaniyar भनियार or Bhavaniyar (भवनियर)), Bandi (बन्दी), Patan (पतन) and Pandrethan (पन्द्रेथन), all tentatively dated between eighth and twelfth century CE (*Pls.* 96, 97, 98 & 99). This Mediterranean feature continued up to the twelfth century CE as has been evidenced from Kother (कोथेर) and Mamal (ममल). However, none of the smaller temples as well as later period temples possess characteristic peristyle.

Pl. 98 : Śiva temple, Pandrethan

Another temple of the same time-bracket is the Śaṅkarācārya (शंकराचार्य) temple at Srinagar (श्रीनगर). This east-facing temple stands on a

Pl. 99 : Śiva temple, Payar

solid rock and consists of an octagonal *adhiṣṭhāna* (अधिष्ठान) of 7.1 m high. The temple also possesses gable roof and trefoil recess. A flight of steps leads to the main entrance.

In short, the temples of Kashmir are characterized by a stepped (double) pyramidal roof, the triangular pediment, also known as the gable, with openings on four sides, trefoil niches associated with the entrance, fluted columns of Greek Doric order, cellular peristyle, etc.

Temple Building Materials

Varieties of building materials were used in the construction of Kashmir temples. There were also temples built of only one kind of material from the *adhiṣṭhāna* to the *śikhara*. Limestone, whitish granite, schist and wood were used for construction works. Foundations and the ceilings of the temples were built of a kind of stone locally called *kanait* (कनैत्). Contrary to the evidence from Śāradā (शारदा) inscription of Rāmadeva (रामदेव) there are pieces of evidence from Naranāg (नरनाग) temples that in ancient Kashmir bricks were also used for erecting temples. The stone temples were built in ashlars masonry. Lime mortar was used as binding material as has been amply attested at Wangat (वंगत्). Occasionally, iron dowels were also used to hold together the stone blocks, as has been evidenced in the Mārtaṇḍa (मार्तण्ड) temple.

17

Temples of Himachal Pradesh

The temples of Himachal Pradesh are known variously as *devālaya* (देवालय), *devakula* (देवकुल), *devaghara* (देवघर), *mandira* (मन्दिर) and *devathi* (देवथि), all mean one and the same — "the abode of god." The early temples of Himachal tell us the story of evolution of the Nāgara (नागर) style architecture in this part of the country.

The story starts from the temples of early post-Gupta (गुप्त) period (sixth–eighth century CE). The temples belonging to this phase were miniature shrines. These are found at Kāṅgṛā (कांगड़ा), Kulu (कुलु), Brahmaur (ब्रह्मौर), Cambā (चम्बा), Hāṭkoṭi (हाटकोटि) and Barat (बरत). These temples had square *garbhagṛha* (गर्भ-गृह) that supported incipient *Latina* single facet *śikhara* (शिखर) crowned by a massive *āmalakaśilā* (आमलकशिला). From these early post-Gupta Nāgara shrines evolved the typical Himachal Nāgara (नागर) style temples that can be seen at Dashal (दशल) and Naggar (नग्गर) in Kulu district, Baijnāth (बैजनाथ) near Kāṅgṛā, and Maṇḍī (मण्डी).

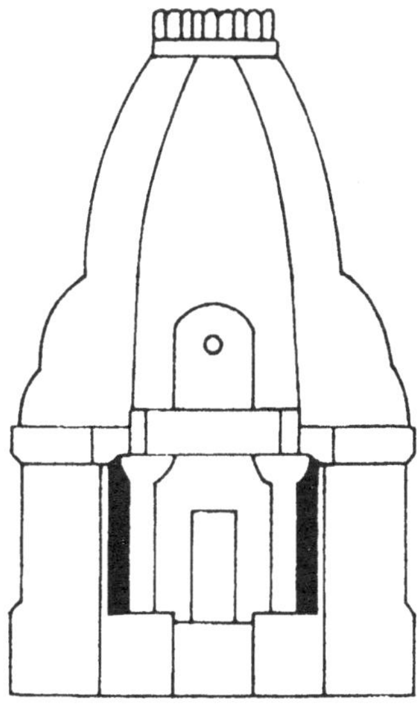

Fig. 96 : Elevation Nāgara temple, Himachal Pradesh

Besides the Nāgara (नागर) temples (*fig.* 96), the ancient temple architects (*sthapatis*, स्थपति) of Himachal are also seen as experts in developing various monsoonal architectural varieties like "pent roof" (*fig.* 97) shrines and *pagoḍā* (पगोडा) (*fig.* 98) temples with sharp and steep tops of the roof so

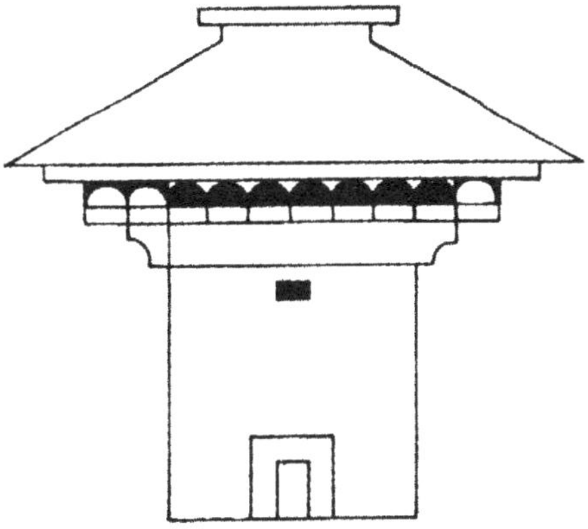

Fig. 97 : Elevation Pent-roofed temple, Himachal Pradesh

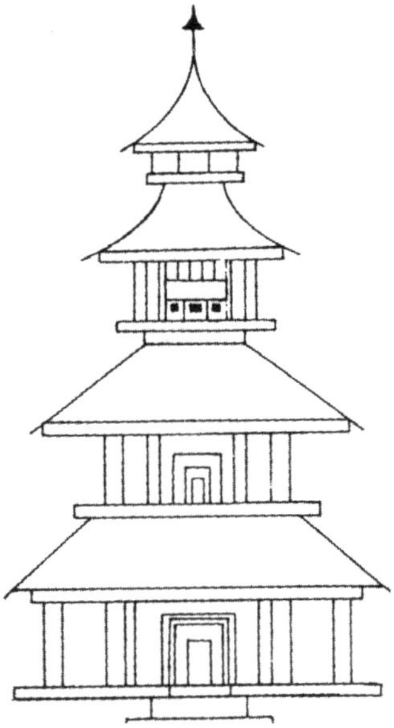

Fig. 98 : Elevation of Pagoḍā temple, Himachal Pradesh

that the waters from the heavy rains as well as snow-water run out quickly and the spire or *śikhara* (शिखर) and the *prāsāda* (प्रासाद) or the main body of the temple are fully saved from the onslaught of the nature. These structures were built in the combination of wood and stones, generally in dry-stone masonry. Due to the paucity of temple inscriptions, the exact dates for the different architectural developments of the Himachal temples are difficult to reconstruct. Whatever dates scholars have suggested, those are based on stylistic grounds.

Nāgara Temples

According to the developmental scheme, developed so far for the Nāgara (नागर) style temples in Himachal Pradesh, there are three phases: Early Phase (CE 700–850), Middle Phase (CE 850–1200) and Late Phase (CE 1200–1400).

EARLY PHASE (CE 700–850)

This phase is represented by the miniature shrines of Barat (बरत), Hāṭkoṭi (हाटकोटि), Nirmand (निर्मन्द), Sawara (सवर), Balag (बलग) (*Pl.* 100), Jagatsukh (जगतसुख) (*Pl.* 101), Ḍhabās (ढबास), Bagheśara (बाघेशर), Suṅgra (सुंग्र) and the bigger temples of Barat and Bajaura (बजौर) as well as the rock-cut shrines of Masrur (मसरुर). The structural temples consist of a small square *garbha-gṛha* (गर्भ-गृह) with a shallow pillared portico or *maṇḍapa* (मण्डप) in front (*fig.* 99). Some of these shrines like those at Barat show shallow pillared porticos attached to the cardinal directions of the *mūla-prāsāda* (मूल-प्रासाद). The *bhitti* (भित्ति) of the temples was built of dressed stones in ashlar masonry without any binding materials. The *śikhara* of these temples were built of narrow strips of stone slabs arranged in diminishing order from bottom upwards. These *śikhara*s show neither true *phaṁsana* (फंसन), i.e. pyramidal nor typical Latina *śikhara* profile. They are the results of attempts to copy the central Indian Nāgara *śikhara* but the attempt could not succeed because of two major reasons — the vast difference in the climatic condition of the two regions and also the non-availability of the central Indian type hard sandstone. The *śikhara* as usual with the Nāgara temples, is crowned by a massive *āmalaka* (आमलक) and, over it, a finial. A simple *śukanāsā* (शुकनासा) projects from the *śikhara* above the doorway. These models of Nāgara temples indicate that the *sthapati*s (स्थपति) of Himachal were handicapped in many ways to deal with the complex form of central Indian Nāgara architecture of the time.

Pl. 100 : Temple no. 1 at Balag, Simla

Most of the temples of this phase do not have any kind of ornamentation on the *adhiṣṭhāna* (अधिष्ठान), *maṇḍovara* (मण्डोवर), *śikhara* (शिखर), *dvāra*s (द्वार),

stambhas (स्तम्भ), *kuḍya-stambhas* (कुड्य-स्तम्भ) or any other architectural member. In some temples, like those at Barat, the *jaṅghā* (जंघा) of the shrines have been carved with simple motifs like leafy scrolls, lotus medallions and arches. The shallow portico in front of the entrance of the sanctum was supported by two pillars, either octagonal or twelve-sided.

By the eighth–ninth century CE the monotony of the plain *śikhara* felt too simple to continue with. The architects wanted it to be a little more elaborate. They did it by providing projections and recesses on the outer face of the *vimāna* (विमान). Moreover, the *śikhara* of the temples was now given more curvilinear profile. For example, the *ratha* (रथ) projections of the Śiva (शिव) temple at Jagatsukh (जगतसुख) in Kulu (कुलु) district made it a *triratha* (त्रिरथ) temple with a *sukanāsā* (सुकनासा) projecting from the *śikhara* over the portico or *mukha-maṇḍapa* (मुख-मण्डप) (*fig.* 100). The central *ratha* projections of the square *vimāna* have *devakoṣṭhas* (देवकोष्ठ) or niches enclosing images of Brahmā, Viṣṇu and Śiva. The pillars supporting the portico are fluted with the square capitals carved with floral motifs.

Pl. 101 : Śiva temple, Jagatsukh, Kulu

During the later period, miniature shrines were also built

near the larger temples as in the case of the Trilokanātha (त्रिलोकनाथ) temple compound in Maṇḍī (मण्डी) and Baijnātha (बैजनाथ) temple in Bilāspur (बिलासपुर). Most of the later temples were on *triratha* plan with *rāha-pagas* (राह-पग) and *koṇaka-pagas* (कोणक-पग), as in central Indian temples. A well-developed *śukanāsikā* (शुकनासिका) projected from the *rāha-paga* of the *śikhara* over the entrance. Some of the temples showing the features of the early phase are Śiva temple at Barat (eighth century), the rock-cut temple complex of Masrur (मसरुर) (*c.* CE 720–800) and the Basesara Mahādeva (बसेसर महादेव) temple of Bajaura (बजौर) (late eighth–early ninth century) (*fig.* 101)

MIDDLE PHASE (CE 850–1200)

The temples of Maṇimaheśa (मणिमहेश) (*Pl.* 102) and Narasiṁha (नरसिंह) of Brahmaur (ब्रह्मौर); the group of temple in the Lakṣmī-Nārāyaṇa (लक्ष्मी-नारायण) complex, Campāvatī (चम्पावती); Vajreśvarī (वज्रेश्वरी) and Harirāī (हरिराई) in Cambā (चम्बा) town; Hāṭkoṭi (हाटकोटि) and Nirath (निरथ) in Shimla belong to the Middle Phase. During this phase the *ratha* (रथ) projections became more elaborate and the temples were built on *pañcaratha* (पञ्चरथ) or the *saptaratha* (सप्तरथ) plan (*fig.* 102). Because of the increasing number of storeys in the temples, the *śikhara* became taller and taller.

The *bhitti* (भित्ति) of the sanctum was elaborately decorated and the *devakoṣṭhas* (देवकोष्ठ) were provided on both sides of the *rāha-paga* (राह-पग). Some of the temples like the one at Nirath (निरथ) had *vedibandha* (वेदिबन्ध) mouldings below the *maṇḍovara* (मण्डोवर, wall)

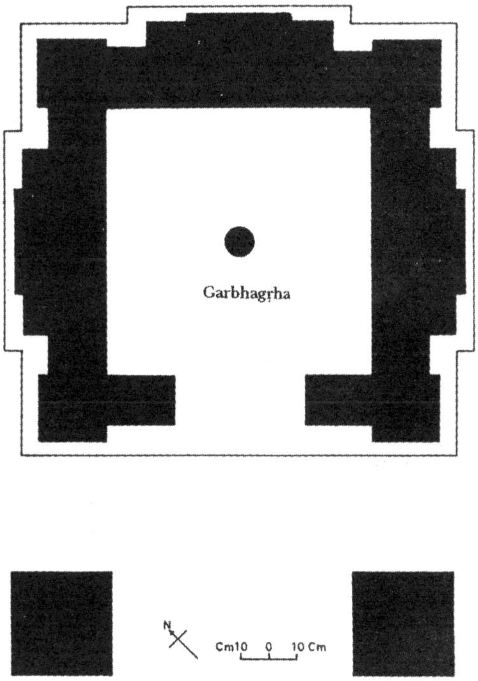

Fig. 99 : Plan of Śiva temple, Jagatsukh, Kulu

Fig. 100 : Śukanāsā projecting from the *śikhara* of the Śiva temple, Jagatsukh, Kulu

whereas the temples of Cambā (चम्बा) and Brahmaur (ब्रह्मौर) had no distinguished *vedibandhas*.

The pillars of the portico, either fluted or plain, were with or without *pūrṇakumbha/ghaṭa-pallava* पूर्णकुम्भ/घट-पल्लव base and capitals. Such fluted pillars can be seen in the temples of Campāvatī (चम्पावती), Nara-siṁha (नरसिंह), Harirāī (हरिराई) and Vajre-śvarī (वज्रेश्वरी). Pilasters on the *maṇḍovara* were also elaborately decorated with jewel motifs and foliated scrolls.

The *śikhara* of the *vimāna* was provided with *karṇa-āmalakas* (कर्ण-आमलक) which divided superstructure into many storeys. However, the *śikharas* are not decorated elaborately; most of them are in fact plain. Sūrya (सूर्य) temple at Nirath (निरथ); the Maṇimaheśa (मणिमहेश) temple, Brahmaur; the Campāvatī temple, Cambā; the Narasiṁha temple, Brahmaur; the temples of Gaurī-Śaṅkara (गौरी-शंकर), Vajreśvarī and Harirāī at Cambā belong to this category. The *śikharas* of the Hāṭkoṭi and Nirath temples are *pañcaratha* (पञ्चरथ) type while those of Harirāī and Maṇimaheśa are *saptaratha* (सप्तरथ) type.

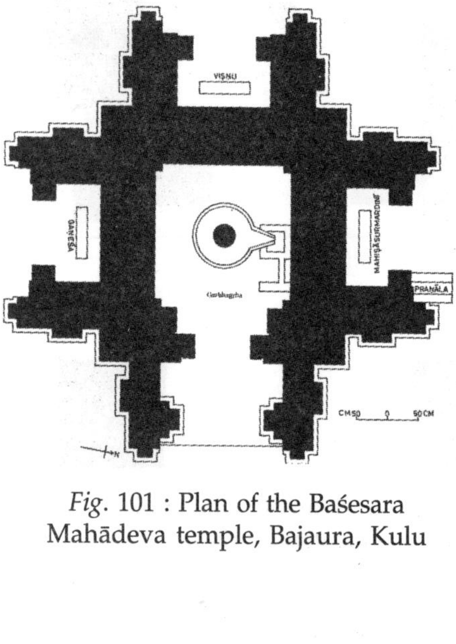

Fig. 101 : Plan of the Baśesara Mahādeva temple, Bajaura, Kulu

The *sthapatis* (स्थपति) of Himachal appear to have tried to introduce *aṅga-śikharas* (अङ्ग-शिखर) of the central Indian temples into their temple architecture. However, in the Himachal temples, the *aṅga-śikharas*/

uraḥśṛṅgas (अङ्ग-शिखर/उर:शृङ्ग) do not develop into full-fledged forms of the central Indian types. It may be noted that their appearance over the doorway caused the disappearance of the *śukanāsikā*s (शुकनासिका). However, *bhadramukha* (भद्रमुख, relief sculpture of an auspicious face) depictions are still seen on the *śikhara*, though now directly placed on the *rāha-paga* above the *uru-śṛṅga* panel.

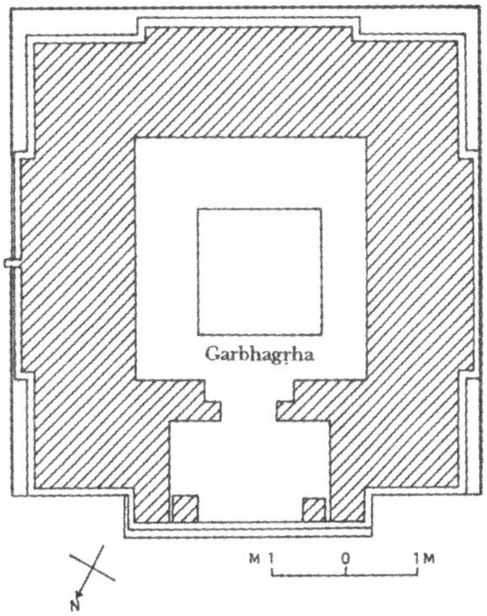

Fig. 102 : Plan of Maṇimaheśa temple, Brahmaur

Another distinguishing feature of the temples of middle phase is the presence of wooden *chatrī* (छत्री) or umbrella-like canopies above the *bisama* (विसम) of the *śikhara* and also over the *āmalaka* (आमलक). The *śukanāsikā* was also covered with sloping roof, resembling a gable-roof. Such protective measures were necessary to keep the temples safe from heavy rains and snowfall. Except the Sūrya temple of Nirath, all other above-mentioned temples of the middle phase possess such wooden canopies. It may be noted that the hard wood of this region is the best material for the canopies which every year face heavy rains; the metal and the stone will neither be more effective nor lighter than this. It is also easily replaceable as well cost-effective. It is also lighter in weight than stone.

Pl. 102 : Maṇimaheśa temple, Brahmaur

LATE PHASE (CE 1200–1400)

This phase is marked by the most developed Nāgara (नागर) style temples in Himachal Pradesh. The Śiva शिव) temples of Dashal (दशल) and Naggar (नग्गर) in Kulu (कुलु) (*Pl.* 103): the Muralīdhara (मुरलीधर)

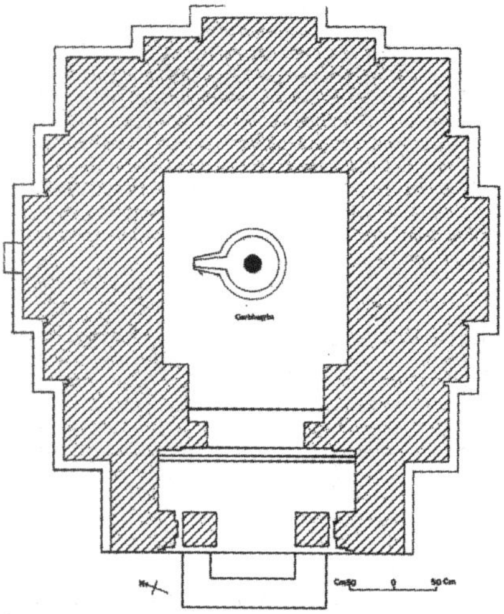

Fig. 103 : Plan of the Śiva temple, Dashal, Kulu

Pl. 103 : Śiva temple, Naggar, Kulu

temple, Thawa (थव) in Kulu and the temples of Baijnātha (बैजनाथ), Siddhanātha (सिद्धनाथ) and Gaṇapati (गणपति) at Baijnātha represent the developed phase of the Nāgara temple-architecture. All of these temples, except the Gaṇapati temple, are *pañcaratha* (पञ्चरथ) on plan while the latter is a *triratha* (त्रिरथ) one (*figs.* 103, 104 & 105). The *maṇḍovara* (मण्डोवर) and the *śikhara* of these temples are more decorated than those of the earlier phases. For example, in the *pañcaratha* Śiva temple at Dashal and the Muralīdhara temple at Thawa, the entire surfaces of the *śikhara*s are embellished with carved arches and jewel motifs. Like the central Indian *śikhara*s, the spire takes its curvature profile right from the *prastara* (प्रस्तर) or cornice. *Karṇa-āmalaka*s (कर्ण-आमलक) adorn the entire height of each corner of the *śikhara*. The *deva-koṣṭha*s (देव-कोष्ठ) adorn the *bāhya-bhitti* (बाह्य-भित्ति or outer wall) of the *vimāna*. The *bhadra* (भद्र) niches adorn the *maṇḍovara* of the *mūla-prāsāda* (मूल-प्रासाद). The sanctum is fronted by a pillared portico. The plain circular pillars have ornamental square base and *ghaṭa-pallava* (घट-पल्लव) capitals.

The thirteenth-century Baijnātha temple is among the most developed temple complexes of the late phase. The square *mūla-prāsāda* is fronted by a *maṇḍapa*, the latter became an integral structure of the sanctum from this period onwards. The sides of the *maṇḍapa* were provided with projecting balconies like those of the central Indian temples. The *maṇḍapa* is surmounted by a pyramidal roof which is crowned by an *āmalakaśilā* (आमलकशिला). The *maṇḍapa* is fronted by a shallow pillared portico, i.e. *mukha-maṇḍapa* (मुख-मण्डप).

This phase is also marked by the development of the *vedibandha* (वेदिबन्ध) mouldings. Now the *vedibandha* has five distinguished horizontal strings or courses, namely, the *khura* (खुर, hoof-shaped), the *kumbha* (कुम्भ, pot-shaped), the *kalaśa* (कलश, water-vessel) the *antara-paṭṭa* (अन्तर-पट्ट, inner-band) and the *kapota* (कपोत, cornice). Except the *khura*, all other mouldings are moderately decorated.

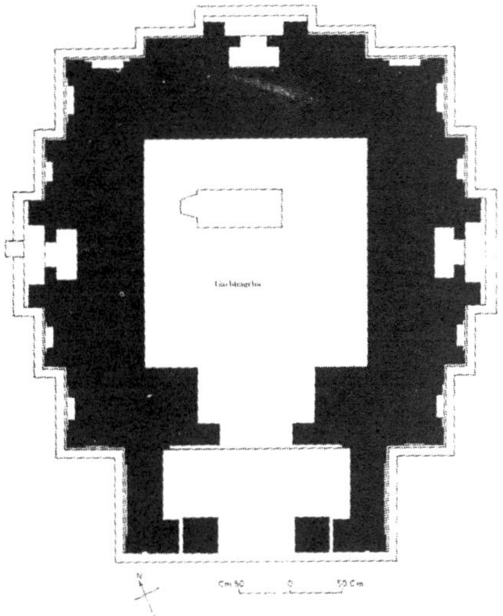

Fig. 104 : Plan of the Śiva temple, Naggar, Kulu

Pent-Roofed Temples

Besides the Nāgara temples, the pent-roofed temples also developed in Himachal. These hut-type temples are typically indigenous in their architectural style. They stand on a low *adhiṣṭhāna* (अधिष्ठान) built of rough-cut stones. The pent-roofed temples are mainly rectangular on plan, though rarely square shrines are also seen. The pillared verandah around the *garbha-gṛha* (गर्भ-गृह) provides the *pradakṣiṇāpatha* (प्रदक्षिणापथ), making the shrine a *sandhāra* (सन्धार) type. The pillars are decorated with *pūrṇa-kumbha/ghaṭa-pallava* पूर्ण-कुम्भ/घट-पल्लव capitals.

The temple wall, up to the level of the cornice, consists of the alternate courses of wooden beams and stones. The spaces in between these alternate courses were filled with dressed stones in dry masonry, i.e. without mortar. This type of architecture is said to be more earthquake proof since the region is prone to tectonic movements.

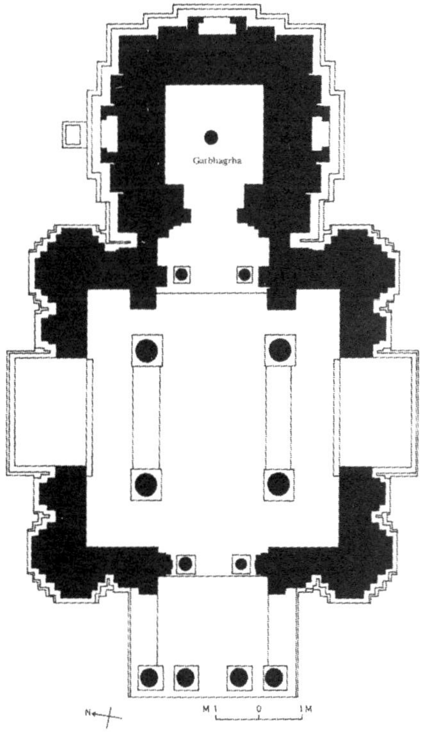

Fig. 105 : Plan of the Vaidyanātha temple, Baijnāth, Kāṅgṛā

The inverted 'V'-shaped pent-roofs have highly projecting eaves. The knife-edged type roof-top is surmounted by a horizontally placed heavy wooden beam, locally known as *kuruda* (कुरुद). A *kalaśa* (कलश)

finial crowns the roof-top. The temple is approached by a single doorway. The doorframes and lintels are richly carved with floral motifs.

Some of the extant pent-roofed temples of Himachal are the Lakṣaṇā Devī (लक्ष्णा देवी) temple, Brahmaur (ब्रह्मौर); the Śakti Devī (शक्ति देवी) temple, Chatrarhi (छत्रर्हि) (*figs.* 106 & 107); the Sandhyā Gāyatrī (सन्ध्या गायत्री) temple, Jagatsukh (जगतसुख) and the Markulā Devī (मर्कुला देवी) temple, Udaipur (उदयपुर). Unfortunately, none of these temples provides any evidence for the date of its construction.

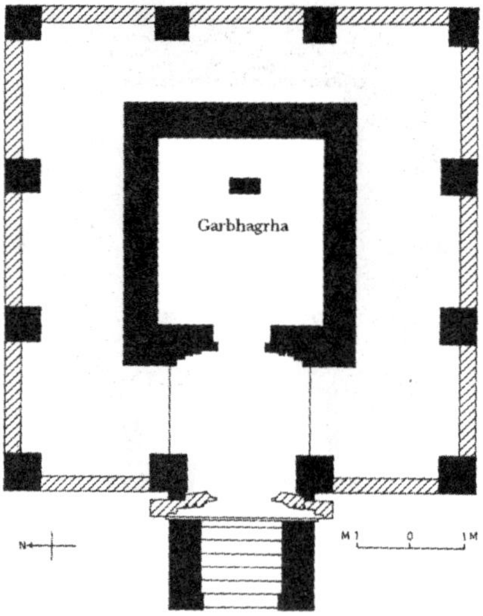

Fig. 106 : Plan of the Śakti Devī temple, Chatraṛhi

Pagoḍā-type Temples

A *pagoḍā* (पगोडा) is multi-storeyed conical structural shrine generally associated with Buddhism. The Hindu *pagoḍā* type temples of Himachal possess all the characteristics of the pent-roofed temples except that the former have a number of diminishing

Fig. 107 : Elevation of Śakti Devī temple, Chatraṛhi

superimposed roofs. The *pagoḍā*s may either stand on low platform built of rough-cut stones or directly on the ground without any basement. Each superimposed tier is provided with a square or rectangular wooden gallery surmounted by a sloping roof. These wooden galleries are intricately carved. The wall of the ground story is built of alternate courses of wood and stone. The decorations on pillars, doors and lintels, verandah and *pradakṣiṇāpatha* (प्रदक्षिणापथ) are similar to those of the pent-roofed temples. However, the walls of the *garbha-gṛha* (गर्भ-गृह) and ceilings are generally without any ornamentation.

The pillars of each storey support wooden beams projecting much beyond the walls and crossing each other at right angles at corners giving support to the projecting eaves. The pillars are square from top to bottom. The capitals are elaborately carved with *pūrṇa-kalaśa* (पूर्ण-कलश) motifs. The eaves are decorated with wooden pendants, called *kharuru* (खारुरु). Some of the important *pagoḍā* temples of Himachal are the Dakhanī Mahādeva (दखनी महादेव) temple, Nirmand (निर्मन्द); the Parāśara Ṛṣi (पराशर ऋषि) temples of Maṇḍī (मण्डी) and Kulu

Fig. 108 : Gaṇeśa temple, Maṇḍī

Fig. 109 : Hiḍimbā temple, Manālī

fig. 110. Tripurasundarī temple, Naggar

(कुलु); the Gaṇeśa (गणेश) temple, Maṇḍī (*fig.* 108); the Hiḍimbā (हिडिम्बा) temple, Manālī (मनाली) (*fig.* 109); the Tripurasundarī (त्रिपुरसुन्दरी) temple, Naggar (नग्गर) (*fig.* 110); the Ādi Brahmā (आदि ब्रह्मा) temple, Khokan (खोकन); the Trijugī Nārāyaṇa (त्रिजुगी नारायण) temple, Dyār (द्यार) and the Manu (मनु) temple, Shenshar (शेनशर).

The temples of Himachal are, therefore, on the one hand, part and parcel of the larger north Indian or Nāgara (नागर) style of temple-architecture, while, on the other, these are marked by some characteristic features which are absolutely regional. The regional characteristics developed because of the regional climatic conditions.

18

Temples of Bengal

THE temples of Bengal are known variously as *mandira* (मन्दिर), *deul* (देउल्), *dehara* (देहर), *devālaya* (देवालय), *devasthāna* (देवस्थान), *devārāma* (देवाराम), etc. Temples of the Gupta (गुप्त) or post-Gupta periods are not found in Bengal. However, excavations at Candraketugaṛh (चन्द्रकेतुगढ़) in the 24 North Parganas have yielded evidence for an imposing Gupta temple. The contemporary architectural styles may be reconstructed from the evidence of miniature replicas and relief sculptures obtained from the site. They share the same characteristic features as the Gupta temples of central India.

Pl. 104 : Ekeśvara Śiva temple, Baṅkurā

Evidence of Pāla (पाल) temple architecture is also far from satisfactory. No

Pl. 105 : Siddheśvara temple, Baṅkurā

extant Pāla temple (seventh–eighth century) is found in Bengal. These were completely destroyed by Muslim invaders from Delhi. None the less, excavations at Nālandā (नालन्दा), Rājagṛha (राजगृह) and Bodh-Gayā (बोध-गया) have yielded remains of doorframes, pillars, and stone sculptures used in early temples constructed both in bricks and stones. Replicas of temples appearing in the sculptures of the period indicate the kind of temple architecture which may have flourished in Bengal during this period.

The Bengal architects used stone, laterite, bricks, wood, terracotta and mud for erecting different types of temples. However, bricks were predominantly used for construction works. Lime and mud mortar were used as binding materials as well as plastering walls and floors. The doorways, lintels, pillars, windows and arches used to be made of wood which were beautifully carved with various panels.

Types of Temples

Various types of temple architecture such as *phaṁsana* (फंसन, pyramidal), Rekhā Nāgara (रेखा नागर, i.e. Nāgara type with *rekhā śikhara* रेखा शिखार), *sarvatobhadra* (सर्वतोभद्र), *ratha*-type, hut-type, etc. developed in Bengal. Square, polygonal and triangular shaped temples are also found in Bengal.

Pl. 106 : Jor-Baṅglā temple, Baṅkurā

PHAṀSANA/BHADRA (PYRAMIDAL TYPE)

In this type of temples the square *mūla-prāsāda* (मूल-प्रासाद) or hall with *garbha-gṛha,* is topped by an imposing multi-tiered pyramidal superstructure (*śikhara*) which diminishes gradually upwards with recess between each storey. The *śikhara* is crowned by an *āmalaka-śilā* (आमलक-शिला) on a circular neck or *grīvā* (ग्रीवा). The Nandī-Maṇḍapa (नन्दी-मण्डप) and the Śiva (शिव) temple at Ekaṭeśvara (एकटेश्वर) in Bāṅkurā (बांकुरा) belong to this category (*Pl.* 104).

REKHĀ NĀGARA PRĀSĀDA

Like the north Indian temples the Rekhā Nāgara temples of Bengal also had a Latina or floral *jāla* (जाल) type *śikhara* with projecting arches known as

Pl. 107 : Temple of Madan Mohan, Baṅkurā

Pl. 108 : Temple of Rādhāśyāma, Viṣnupur, Baṅkurā

sukanāsā (सुकनासा) (nose like that of a parrot). However, here, the *mūla-prāsāda* (मूल-प्रासाद) lacks the presence of frontal *maṇḍapa* (मण्डप). The *śikhara* was crowned by an *āmalaka-śilā* (आमलक-शिला) which supported the *kalaśa* (कलश, finial). The brick temple of Deuliya (देउलिय), Bardhaman (बर्धमान) (ninth century CE) is one of the earliest extant *rekhā* temples of Bengal. Siddheśvara (सिद्धेश्वर) temple of Bāṅkurā (tenth century CE), built in brick, is a curvilinear *śikhara* temple richly adorned with decorations (*Pl.* 105).

SARVATOBHADRA TYPE

It is a square temple with four entrances and ante-

Pl. 109 : Śyāma Rāi Temple, Viṣṇupur, Baṅkurā

chambers on each of the four cardinal sides. For example, from the remains of the sixth–seventh century temple at Pahāṛpur (पहाड़पुर) in Dīnājapur (दीनाजपुर), it may be assumed that four *maṇḍapa*s were attached to the four sides of the square *garbha-gṛha* which provided the temple the shape of a "maltese" cross.

HUT-TYPE

The hut-type temple with sloping curvilinear roof resembling elephant-back (*gaja-pṛṣṭha*, गज-पृष्ठ) is peculiar to Bengal architecture. These temples may have one, two, four or eight jointed slanting roofs with curved eaves. Therefore, *eka-chāla* (एक-छाल, single sloping roof), *do-chāla* (दो-छाल, double sloping roofs), *cau-chāla* चौ-छाल, four), or *aṭa-chāla* (अट-छाल, eight) temples can be found in Bengal.

The temples usually stand on a raised platform, often four to six feet in height. The sanctum is oblong or cubical. The hut-type temples have, generally, a covered verandah in front and, at times, on all sides. The *mūla-prāsāda* (मूल-प्रासाद) is surmounted by spires (*śikhara*). Cārabaṅglā (चारबंगला) temple of Murśidābād (मुर्शिदाबाद) is one of the best examples of this type with elaborate terracotta reliefs all over the façade.

A variety of hut-type temples, known as Jor-Bangla (जोर-बंगला), is built by joining two hut structures (*Pl.* 106). It is surmounted by a small tower with sloping roof. The Jor-Bangla temples are found at Hooghly (हुगली), Bāṅkurā (बांकुरा), Baṛanagar (बड़नगर) and Murśidābād (मुर्शिदाबाद).

The façades of the hut-type temples were decorated with terracotta panels depicting scenes from the *Rāmāyaṇa* (रामायण). Images from the story of Kṛṣṇa (कृष्ण) are seen on the pillars and walls of the Jor-Bangla temple at Bistupur (बिस्तुपुर) in Bāṅkurā district.

RATHA (RATNA/PINNACLED) TYPE

In this type of temples a square or rectangular *mūla-prāsāda* with curved cornice is surmounted by one or more pinnacles or *ratna*s (रत्न). To accommodate the pinnacles on top of the roof, the latter was laid out more or less flat. There are single-towered, five-towered and nine-towered *ratha* (रथ) temples. For example, temples of Madana-Mohana (मदन-मोहन) (1694) (*Pl.* 107), Rādhā-Mādhaba (राधा-माधब) (1737) and Rādhāśyāma (राधाश्याम) (1758) at Viṣṇupura (विष्णुपुर) in Bāṅkurā (*Pl.* 108) belong to single-towered group.

In the five-towered (*pañca-ratna* पञ्च-रत्न) *ratha* (रथ) or temples, the main central tower was surrounded by four miniature towers at the four corners of the shrine roof. Śyāma Rāī (श्याम राय) temple of Viṣṇupura (विष्णुपुर) (1643) (*Pl.* 109) and Rāmeśvara (रामेश्वर) temple of Midnapore (मिदनापुर) (1655-56) belong to this group.

In the nine-towered (*nava-ratna,* नव-रत्न) *ratha*s or temples the miniature shrine, resembling the *mūla-prāsāda* (मूल-प्रासाद), was built on top of the main shrine. At the four corners of the main shrine and the superimposed miniature shrine were placed towers, thus, eight in total. A taller *śikhara* (pinnacle) stood at the centre of these towers forming the shrine a *nava-ratna* (नव-रत्न) type. For instance, the Kantanagar (कन्टनगर) temple, Dinajpur (दीनाजपुर) (1722-23), and Chitpore (चितपुर) temple, Calcutta (1730) belong to this category.

19

Temples of Assam

ASSAM, anciently known as Kāmarūpa (कामरूप), was the seat of many royal powers. One of the earliest references of Kāmarūpa can be seen in the Allahabad pillar inscription of Samudragupta (समुद्रगुप्त) (fourth century). There are quite a few inscriptional references to the erection of temples in the pre-Ahom (i.e. pre-fifteenth century) Assam. The first reference occurs in an inscription of the eastern slope of the Nīlācala (नीलाचल) hill, datable to fifth century CE. It refers to the existence of a cave temple in Kāmākhyā (कामाख्या) hill (Nīlācala hill). However, there is no evidence of any cave temple at the site of the Nīlācala inscription which may have referred to some temple built in the nearby region.

The earliest phase of temple architecture in Assam has been tentatively dated from the sixth century CE when the Varmanas (वर्मन्) ruled Kāmarūpa. They were the contemporaries of the Guptas (गुप्त) in their later phase. Since Assam had cultural contacts with eastern and central India, its art and architecture have also been influenced by these regions. However, except a stray example of the twelfth-century Gupteśvara (गुप्तेश्वर) temple, none of the pre-Ahom temples in Assam is extant. The approximate dates of their construction have been derived from the art and architectural styles, reconstructed from the

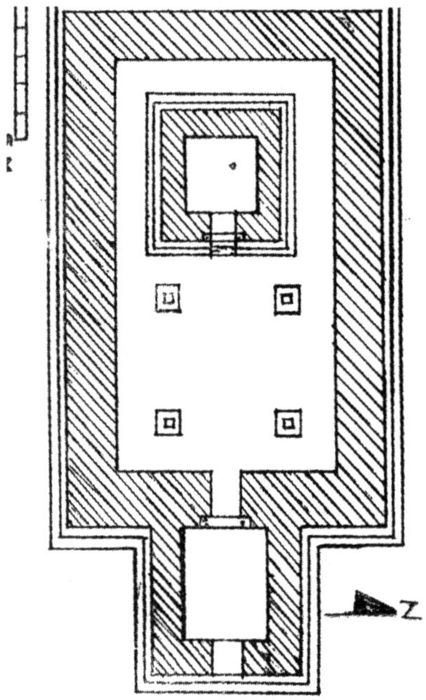

Fig. 111 : Plan of Da-Parbatiyā brick temple, Assam

remnants of the extremely ruined temples.

Pre-Ahom Architecture (the Varmanas and the Śālastambhas)

The earliest known remains of the Nāgara (नागर) style temple from the pre-Ahom Assam is of Da-Parbatiya brick temple with stone gateway and a stone Śivaliṅga (शिवलिङ्ग) (*fig*. 111). It has been tentatively dated to the times of the Varmanas (sixth century) on stylistic ground. The completely ruined *sandhāra* (सन्धार) temple with its axially placed square *garbha-gṛha* (गर्भ-गृह), the pillared *maṇḍapa* (मण्डप) and the *mukha-maṇḍapa* (मुख-मण्डप) exhort the influence of the Gupta temple architecture. The only standing part of the temple is its intricately carved doorway made of sandstone. It consists of doorjambs surmounted by a lintel. The doorway depicts typical late-Gupta artistic creations such as the river goddesses Gaṅgā (गङ्गा) and Yamunā (यमुना) with attendant figures, *lalāṭa-bimba* (ललाट-बिम्ब) showing flying Garuḍa (गरुड) depicted in the centre of the lintel, dwarfs, the *caitya* (चैत्य) motifs, floral scrolls, rosettes, and other designs. However, like the temples of Deogaṛh (देवगढ़) and Bhūmara (भूमर), this temple does not yield evidence for *pūrṇa-kumbha* (पूर्ण-कुम्भ) motif, an artistic contribution of the Guptas.

Following the Varman (वर्मन्) dynasty, Kāmarūpa (कामरूप) was ruled by the Śālastambhas (शालस्तम्भ) (seventh to tenth century CE). They also continued the architectural tradition of their predecessors in the Nāgara (नागर) order. However, the temple remains of Golapāṛā (गोलपाड़ा) district and the remains of Bamunī Pahāṛ (बमुनी पहाड़) and Majgāon (मजगांव)

indicate that the Gupta–Nāgara (गुप्त-नागर) order continued in Assam until the end of the Śālastambha dynasty. Unfortunately, not enough remains of these temples to reconstruct them reasonably well.

Another ruined temple of *c.* tenth century has been identified near Abhyapurī (अभयपुरी) in Golapāṛā district. The temple, dedicated to Gaṇeśa (गणेश), had an east-facing *pañcaratha* (पञ्चरथ) *vimāna* (विमान) and a *dīrghacatura maṇḍapa* (दीर्घचतुर मण्डप), aligned in east-west direction. Like the central Indian and Orissan temples, this temple also stands on a high platform, known as *pīṣṭa* (पिष्ट) or *jagati* (जगति). The floor of the *garbha-gṛha* is paved with stone blocks. A *praṇāla* (प्रणाल, water-chute) was attached to the sanctum. Other remains from the site are doorjambs, a lintel depicting *kīrtimukha* (कीर्तिमुख), Gaṇeśa and Brahmā (ब्रह्मा) images, and floral motifs, *bhūmi-āmalaka*s (भूमि-आमलक), and also the remnants of a *maṇḍapa*. These remains suggest that the temple had a Rekhā–Nāgara (रेखा-नागर) *śikhara* (शिखर). The temple remains of the Śālastambha period have also been found from the Kāmākhyā (कामाख्या) hill in and around Guwahati. They are mostly doorjambs, door sills, lintels, and parts of *śikhara* (शिखर) and *adhiṣṭhāna* (अधिष्ठान). These stone pieces are carved with structural motifs, floral designs and figures of celestial beings.

The ninth–tenth century also witnessed erection of new temples with stellate (star-shaped/polygonal) *mūla-prāsāda* (मूल-प्रासाद) against the Nāgara (नागर) *vimāna* (विमान). For instance, the Maṇikarṇeśvara (मणिकर्णेश्वर) temple in north Guwahati shows the evidence of a stellate plinth of the *garbha-gṛha* (गर्भ-गृह) fronted by a rectangular *mukha-maṇḍapa* (मुख-मण्डप).

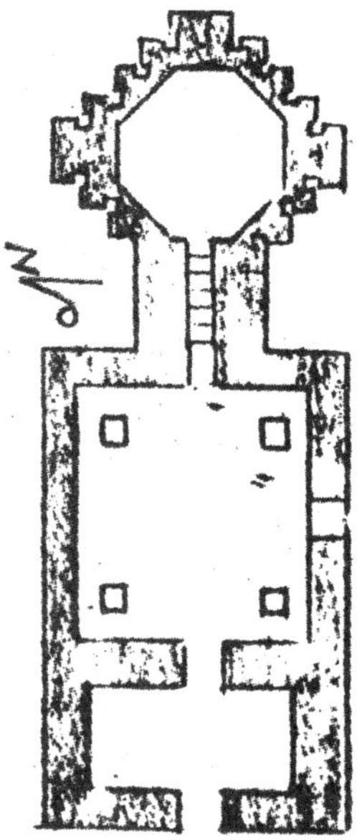

Fig. 112a : Plan of Gupteśvara temple, Singri

The temple remains of Majhgāon (मझगांव) in Tezpur (तेजपुर) gives a clear picture of the architecture of the post-Gupta period. The lintel of the door from the site depicts *pañcaratha* (पञ्चरथ) Nāgara *vimāna* surmounted by the *āmalaka* (आमलक). These reliefs are depicted between floral designs known as *kalpavṛkṣa* (कल्पवृक्ष) motif. Moreover, the temple remains of Bamunī Pahāṛ (बमुनी पहाड़) near Tezpur yield the evidence of *rekhā śikhara* (रेखा शिखर) in the form of *khapurī* (खपुरी), *āmalaka*s (आमलक), *lalāṭa-bimba* (ललाट-बिम्ब), *bhūmi*s (भूमि) and other components. Like the north Indian temples, the main temple at Bamunī Pahāṛ stands on a raised platform. The temple complex here also consisted of *garbha-gṛha* (गर्भ-गृह), *maṇḍapa* (मण्डप) and *ardha-maṇḍapa* (अर्ध-मण्डप).

Fig. 112b : Elevation of Gupteśvara temple, Singri

Pāla Architecture (CE Eleventh–Twelfth Century)

The Pālas (पाल) who succeeded the Śālastambhas (शालस्तम्भ) built many temples in Assam, particularly in and around Guwahati. Unlike the temples of the preceding periods, their temples were smaller in size and were more ornamented with intricate carvings and sculptures. The temple ruins of CE tenth–twelfth century have been reported from Madana-Kāmadeva Pahāṛ (मदन-कामदेव पहाड़), Piṅgaleśvara (पिंगलेश्वर), Chāyāgāon (छायागांव), Baman (बमन), Kenduguri (केन्दुगुरि),

Golāghāṭ (गोलघाट) and Siṅgrī (सिंगरी).

From the remains of the temple of "Madana-Kāmadeva" it may be conceived that the temple was *pañcaratha* (पञ्चरथ) in plan and consisted of *pābhāga* (पाभाग), *jaṅghā* (जंघा), *baraṇḍa* (बरण्ड), and *śikhara* in its elevation. The *aṅga-śikhara*s (अङ्ग-शिखर) found among the ruins are highly decorated. The *rāha-paga*s (राह-पग) of these *aṅga-śikhara*s contain a large *kīrtimukha* (कीर्तिमुख) motif just above the *baraṇḍa*s whereas the *anu-raha* (अनु-रह) and *koṇaka-paga*s (कोणक-पाग) carry *gavākṣa* (गवाक्ष) motifs and floral designs. The remains from the site include ceiling slabs with lotus motifs, *āmalaka*s (आमलक), door-sills, cruciform pillar capitals with bracket figures, architraves with niches encompassing images of deities, and other sculptures. Though the temple is known as of Madana-Kāmadeva (मदन-कामदेव), the image inside the *garbha-gṛha* (गर्भ-गृह) is of seated Umā-Maheśvara (उमा-महेश्वर).

The temples of this period are also provided with moulded *adhiṣṭhāna* (अधिष्ठान). The base of the Piṅgaleśvara (पिंगलेश्वर) temple shows two horizontal mouldings, the lower one depicts a row of elephants while the upper course shows a series of circles containing dancing figures. The ruins also yield the evidence for *aṅga-śikhara*s (अङ्ग-शिखर).

Another important temple, assignable to the later part of the twelfth century is the Gupteśvara (गुप्तेश्वर) temple at Siṅgrī (सिंगरी) in the Darraṅg (दरंग) district (*figs.* 112a & 112b). It gives a complete picture of the temple architecture of Assam towards the end of the Pāla rule. In plan it consists of the Nāgara *vimāna* (नागर विमान), the *antarāla* (अन्तराल), and the *maṇḍapa* (मण्डप) of *do-chāla* (दो-छाल) variety. The entire temple complex is enclosed by a *prākāra* (प्राकार) or boundary wall built of bricks.

The *pañcaratha vimāna* (पञ्चरथ विमान) of the Guptеśvara (गुप्तेश्वर) temple rises to about 11 m and is built of stone. It stands on a moulded *pābhāga* (पाभाग). Like the Orissan temples, the *jaṅghā* (जंघा) is divided horizontally into two sections by a series of mouldings known as *bandhana* (बन्धन). The *baraṇḍa* (बरण्ड) on top of the *jaṅghā* also contains a series of three mouldings. The *śikhara* of the temple tries to imitate central Indian style with four *aṅga-śikhara*s attached to each central *ratha* (रथ) projection of the main *śikhara*. The *vimāna* is also provided with projected *deva-koṣṭha*s (देव-कोष्ठ). The *śikhara* is crowned by a double *āmalaka* (आमलक). However, the *śikhara* has not evolved into a more graceful and elegant central Indian style.

The oblong *antarāla* supports a *do-chāla* roof. It has highly ornate door-frames depicting *dvārapāla*s (द्वारपाल) and human figures. The *lalāṭa-bimba* (ललाट-बिम्ब) contains a sitting Gaṇeśa (गणेश). The square *maṇḍapa* in front of the *antarāla* has also a *do-chāla* roof. The roof of the *maṇḍapa* is supported by four centrally placed pillars which are octagonal in shape.

The decline of the Pāla dynasty towards the end of the twelfth century led to political uncertainty in Assam, the next two centuries witnessed a number of wars between the Ahoms (अहोम्), Kachārīs (कछारी) and Cutiyās (चुतिया). Such a situation continued until fifteenth–sixteenth century when the Ahoms captured the whole of Brahmaputra (ब्रह्मपुत्र) Valley and established their capital at Caraideo under the leadership of Sukapha. Their rule continued until 1826 when the British occupied the region.

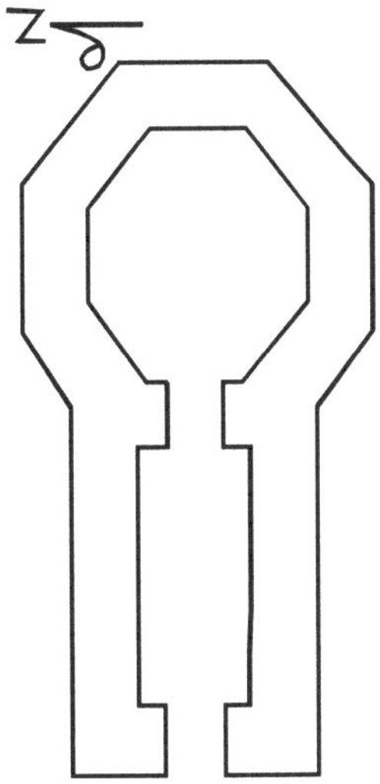

Fig. 113a : Plan of Garakhiya Ḍol, Nazira

Ahom Architecture

Between the third quarter of the fifteenth century and the third quarter of the seventeenth century, the Ahoms built a number of temples in Assam, some of them at Nagheriting (नघेरीतिंग), Garagāon (गरगांव), Biswanāth (बिस्वनाथ), Nazira (नजीर) and Dhalpur (धलपुर). The Garakhiya Dol at Nazira is one of the earliest shrines built by the Ahoms (*figs.* 113a & 113b). The brick-built temple consists of a small octagonal *mūla-prāsāda* (मूल-प्रासाद) fronted by a rectangular *maṇḍapa* (मण्डप). Each wall of the octagonal *jaṅghā* (जंघा) of the *vimāna* (विमान) contains *deva-koṣṭhas* (देव-कोष्ठ) in two rows, each row having four niches. The *maṇḍapa* is completely ruined leaving its plinth. The *garbha-gṛha* (गर्भ-गृह) is surmounted by a conical *śikhara* (शिखर) built of bricks. Similar architectural features can be seen at the temple of Maghnowa (मघनोवा) near Dhalpur in Lakhimpur (लखीमपुर) district. Another interesting aspect of these temples is the presence of some of their architectural features like the octagonal

Fig. 113b : Elevation of Garakhiya Ḍol, Nazira

walls carved with blind window type *deva-koṣṭhas* in rows, and almost domical-shaped superstructure showing the influence of the late medieval Indo-Islamic architecture.

The next phase of the Ahom architecture starts with the accession of Svardeva Singha (स्वरदेव सिंह) in CE 1681. Many of his temples originally dedicated to Tai deity Lankuri (लंकुरी) were later converted into Śiva (शिव) temples. However, only two temples of Svardeva have survived the ravages of time. They are the Thaora Dol in the Sibsagar District and the other is the Śiva temple Umananda near Guwahati.

The Thaora Dol has a square plan with a *cau-chāla* (चौ-छाल) superstructure in the model of Bengal roof. The second temple of Umananda (उमानन्द) gives a better architectural style in brick masonry. The temple is in *pañcaratha* (पञ्चरथ) plan with a Nāgara *śikhara* (नागर शिखर). However, *aṅga-śikharas* (अङ्ग-शिखर) are absent in this temple. It may be noted that instead of the typical spoked *āmalaka* (आमलक), the crowning finial of this temple has three bulbous members in diminishing order.

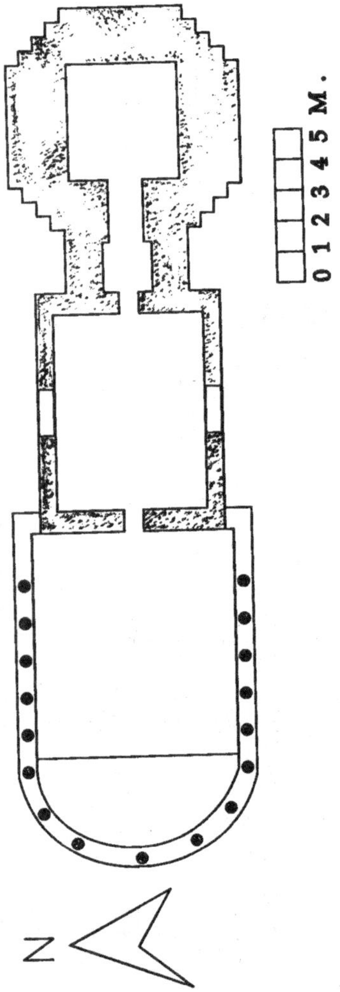

Fig. 114a : Plan of Keśavanārāyaṇa Ḍol, Jaisagar

Further developments in the Ahom (अहोम्) architecture starts with the rule of Svargadeva Rudra Singha (स्वर्गदेव रूद्र सिंह) (CE 1696–1714) who built a number of beautiful Hindu temples on the banks of the Jaisagar (जयसागर) tank. The most notable temple of this time is the Keśavanārāyaṇa Dol (केशवनारायण ढोल), locally known as Jai Dol (जय ढोल) (*figs*. 114a & 114b). It is a fully developed temple complex consisting of a *pañcaratha vimāna* (पञ्चरथ विमान), *antarāla* (अन्तराल) and two *maṇḍapas* (मण्डप), all aligned in east-west axis. The *bāḍa* (बाडा) of the *vimāna* contains *pābhāga* (पाभाग), *jaṅghā* (जंघा) and *baraṇḍa* (बरण्ड). The *pābhāga* contains two plain base mouldings. The *jaṅghā* is divided into a number of horizontal divisions with rosettes and deities in alternate rows. The *śikhara,* it is significant to note, is oval in shape. The stunted *aṅga-śikhara*s (अङ्ग-शिखार) encircle the main *śikhara*. The whole outer surface of the *śikhara* is decorated with net like (*jāla,* जाल) designs embossed with floral motifs. The *śikhara* is crowned by a series of bulbous members in diminishing order. The roofs of the *maṇḍapa* and *antarāla* are *do-chāla* (दो-छाल) type which is suitable for monsoonal regions of the north-east.

Fig. 114b : Elevation of Keśavanārāyaṇa Ḍol, Jaisagar

The final development of the Ahom architecture can be seen in the Nagheriting Śiva Dol near Dergaon in the Sibsagar district, built during the reign of Svargadeva Rājeśwar Singha (स्वर्गदेव राजेश्वर सिंह) (CE 1751-69). This *pañcāyatana* (पञ्चायतन) temple consists of *pañcaratha* Nāgara *vimāna* surrounded by four smaller shrines at its four corners. The main *vimāna* is fronted by a rectangular *do-chāla maṇḍapa* (दो-छाल मण्डप). The sub-shrines are also fronted by smaller *do-chāla maṇḍapa*s.

The Bar Dol at Viśvanātha (विश्वनाथ), on the north bank of the Brahmapurtra (ब्रह्मपुत्र), is another temple

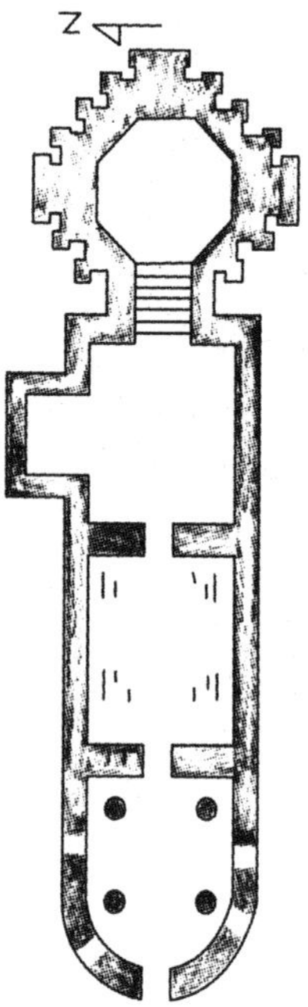

Fig. 115a : Plan of Kāmākhyā temple, Kāmarūpa

built by Rajeswar Singha. The conical superstructure of the *vimāna* is surrounded by a pair of *aṅga-śikhara*s at its each cardinal direction. The arched doorway of the façade is flanked by two *deva-koṣṭha*s (देव-कोष्ठ). The overall appearance of the temple suggests a strong Islamic influence on the architecture.

After the time of Rājeśwara Singha (राजेश्वर सिंह), the decline of Ahom (अहोम्) dynasty started which also affected their architectural activities. The Candra Śekhar (चन्द्र शेखर) temple at Umānanda (उमानन्द) and the Baneśwar (बनेश्वर) temple in Guwahati built by Candra Kānt Singha (चन्द्र कान्त सिंह) (CE 1811-18) depict the pathetic stage of temple architecture towards the end of the Ahom rule.

The Temples of the Koch Dynasty

The Kochas (कोच) were powerful rulers during the sixteenth century whose capital was at Kochbihar (कोचबिहार) in north Bengal. They had influence in upper Assam and built many temples at Goalpāṛā (गोलपाड़ा), Kāmarūpa (कामरूप) and Darraṅg (दरँग).

Fig. 115b : Elevation of Kāmākhya temple, Kāmarūpa

The most famous architectural activity of the Koch dynasty is related to the reconstruction of the

Kāmākhyā (कामाख्या) temple on Nīlācala (नीलाचल) Hill near Guwahati during the time of Koch king Nārāyaṇa (नारायण) (CE 1540-84). The plan of the temple consists of the *garbha-gṛha, antarāla* (अन्तराल), and three *maṇḍapas* (मण्डप), locally known as *calanta* (चलन्त), *pañcaratha* (पञ्चरथ) and *nāṭya-maṇḍapa* (नाट्य-मण्डप). However, the *nāṭya-maṇḍapa* was an addition by the Ahom king Rājeśwar Singha in CE 1759. The *vimāna* (विमान) is a *pañcaratha* (पञ्चरथ) type. It is highly decorated with flowers, foliages, relief panels and sculptures.

Kāmākhyā is the earliest dated monument in its complete form in Assam (*figs.* 115a & 115b). The architecture of the temple is known as "Nīlācala Style" a term coined by R.M. Nath because of its peculiar features. The temple shows more Islamic architectural influence, for example, the domical superstructure is surrounded by isolated *aṅga-śikhara*s (अङ्ग-शिखर), just like the Islamic domes are surrounded by minarets.

The other important temple built by the Kochas is thc Hayagrīva-Mādhava (हयग्रीव-माधव) temple at Hajo (हजो) (CE 1583). The temple is, however, smaller than the Kāmākhyā temple. It consists of *garbha-gṛha, antarāla,* and *maṇḍapa* and the *vimāna* which supports numerous sculptures.

Conclusion

The temples of Brahmaputra Valley, or old Assam, were frequently threatened by torrential rains followed by devastating floods, soil erosion and earthquakes as well as the hatred of invaders. These were the major reasons for the non-survival of most of the temples of Assam.

Though the various rulers of Assam adopted the Nāgara (नागर) model of architecture, none of the ancient temple of the region shows a typical evolved Nāgara style. It is true that there were either Latina or Śekharī (शेखरी) model superstructures that adorned most of the temples. However, these appear to have been poor copies of the Orissan and central Indian architecture prevalent during those days; possibly there was a lack of highly trained architects, quality of stone, money support, etc. Moreover, the *sthapati*s (स्थपति) of post-Pāla (पाल) period were not adroit in stone masonry. It also caused poor performance of their architectural style. The erection of typical *bhūmija śikhara* (भूमिज शिखर) is time-consuming and more complex process as compared to simple domical *śikhara*. It might have been one of the reasons why the *sthapati*s of the region erected dome-like superstructures with or without *ratha* (रथ) projections. Neither *ratha* projections nor the rendition of the *aṅga-śikhara*s (अङ्ग-शिखर) are upto central Indian standards.

However, with all these limitations, the temples of Assam convey a great message that throughout its history, the region tied itself, both culturally and religiously, with the rest of India. The numerous temples dedicated to Śiva (शिव), Viṣṇu (विष्णु), Gaṇeśa (गणेश), Durgā (दुर्गा) and other Brāhmanical deities by the local rulers attest that Assam has never been an isolated region; instead, it always cherished Indian culture and tradition.

Bibliography

Acharya, P.K., 1978, *Encyclopaedia of Hindu Architecture* (2 vols.), Bhopal: J.K. Publishing House.

Agrawal, R.C., 1998, *Kashmir and Its Monumental Glory*, New Delhi: Aryan Books International.

Aryan, Subhashini, 1994, *Himadri Temples* (CE *700–1300*), Shimla: Indian Institute of Advanced Study.

Barrett, Douglas E., 1974, *Early Cola Architecture and Sculpture* (CE *866–1014*), London: Faber.

Brown, Percy, 1965, *Indian Architecture: Buddhist and Hindu Period*, Bombay: D.B. Taraporewala and Sons.

Chandra, Pramod (ed.), 1975, *Studies in Indian Temple Architecture*, Delhi: American Institute of Indian Studies.

Coomaraswamy, Ananda Kentish, 1927, *History of Indian and Indonesian Art*, London: Goldston (reprinted by Kessinger Publishing, 2003).

Cousens, Henry, 1926, *The Cāḷukyan Architecture of the Kanarese Districts*, Delhi: Archaeological Survey of India.(1996 reprint)

Cousens, Henry, 1985, *Mediaeval Temples of the Dakhan*, New Delhi: Cosmo Publications.

Datta, Bimal Kumar, 1975, *Bengal Temples*, New Delhi: Munshiram Manoharlal.

Deheja, Vidya, 1972, *Early Buddhist Rock Temples*, Ithaca, New York: Cornell University Press.

Deva, Krishna, 2000, *The Temples of North India*, New Delhi: National Book Trust.

Encyclopaedia of Indian Temple Architecture, vol. I, part. 1: South India: Lower Dravidadesa, 200 BC – AD 1324, ed. Michael W. Meister, New Delhi: American Institute of Indian Studies, 1983.

Encyclopaedia of Indian Temple Architecture, vol. I, part. 2: South India: Upper Dravidadesa Early Phase (AD 550 – 1075), eds. Michael W. Meister & M.

A. Dhaky, New Delhi: AIIS, 1986.

Encyclopaedia of Indian Temple Architecture, vol. I, part. 4-A: South India: Integrated Styles of South India (c. AD 1289 – 1798), eds. Michael W. Meister & M. A. Dhaky, New Delhi: AIIS, 2001.

Encyclopaedia of Indian Temple Architecture, vol. I, part.3: South India: Upper Dravidadesa: Later Phase (AD 973 – 1326), ed. M.A. Dhaky, New Delhi: AIIS and IGNCA, 1996.

Encyclopaedia of Indian Temple Architecture, vol. II, part. 1: North India: Foundations of North Indian Style, c. 250 BC – AD 1100, eds. Michael W. Meister, M. A. Dhaky & Krishna Deva, (New Delhi: AIIS, 1988).

Encyclopaedia of Indian Temple Architecture, vol. II, part.2: North India: Period of Early Maturity (c. AD 700 – 900), eds. M.A. Dhaky and Michael W. Meister, (New Delhi: American Institute of Indian Studies, 1991).

Encyclopaedia of Indian Temple Architecture, vol. II, part.3: North India: Beginnings of Medieval Idiom (c. AD 900 – 1000), ed. M.A. Dhaky, (New Delhi: American Institute of Indian Studies, 1998).

Fergusson, J.A., 2001 (rpt.), *A History of Indian and Eastern Architecture,* New Delhi: Munshiram Manoharlal.

George Michell, 1975, *An Architectural Description and Analysis of the Early Western Calukyan Temples,* London: Art and Archaeology Research Papers.

Ghosh, Amalananda (ed.), 1974, *Jaina Art and Architecture* (vol. 1), New Delhi: Bharatiya Jnanpeeth.

Grover, Satish, 2003 (2nd edn.), *Buddhist and Hindu Architecture in India,* New Delhi: CBS Publishers.

Gupte, R.S., 1967, *The Art and Architecture of Aihole: A study of early Chalukyan art through temple architecture and sculpture,* Bombay: D. B. Taraporevala Sons & Co.

Jayashanker, S., 1997, *Temples of Kerala,* Directorate of Census Operations, Kerala.

Kak, Subhash 2005, Early Indian Architecture and Art, *Migration & Diffusion – An international journal,* Vol.6/Nr.23, 2005, pp. 6-27.

Kramrisch, Stella, 1996 (rpt.), *The Hindu Temple* (2 vols.), New Delhi: Motilal Banarsidass.

Longhurst, A.H., 1982, *Pallava Architecture* (3 vols.), New Delhi: Cosmo Publications.

Mahalingam, T.V., 1970, *Studies in the South Indian Temple Complex* (Kannada Research Institute Research Lectures, New Series, no. 2), Dharwar: Kannada Research Institute, Karnatak University.

Michael W. Meister, 1988-89, Prasada as Palace: Kutina Origins of the Nagara Temple, *Artibus Asiae*, Vol. 49, No. 3/4, pp. 254-280.

Prasad, B. Rajendra, 1983, *Chalukyan Temples of Andhradesa*, New Delhi: Abhinav Publications.

Ram Raz, 1834, *Essay on the Architecture of the Hindus*, London: John William Parker, for the Royal Asiatic Society, 1834.

Sahai, Surendra, 2006, *Indian Architecture: Hindu, Buddhist and Jain*, Delhi: Eastern Book Corporation.

Sarkar, H., 1978, *An Architectural Survey of Temples of Kerala*, New Delhi: Archaeological Survey of India.

———, 1993 (rpt.), *Studies in Early Buddhist Architecture of India*, Delhi: Munshiram Manoharlal.

Sarma, P.C., 1988, *Architecture of Assam*, Delhi: Agam Kala Prakashan.

Singh, Harihar, 1982, *Jaina Temples of Western India*, Varanasi: Parshvanath Vidyashram Research Institute.

Sinha, A. J., 1996, Architectural Invention in Sacred Structures: The Case of Vesara Temples of Southern India, *The Journal of the Society of Architectural Historians*, vol. 55, no. 4, (Dec., 1996), pp. 382-399, Chicago: Society of Architectural Historians.

Sompura, Prabhashankar, 1960, *Dīpārṇava* (in Gujarātī), Palitana.

Srinivasan, K.R., 1972, *Temples of South India*, Delhi: National Book Trust.

Stierlin, Henri, 2002, *Hindu India: From Khajurāho to the Temple City of Madurai*, Köln: Taschen.

Tadgell, Christopher, 1998, *The History of Architecture in India*, London: Phaidon Press Limited.

Thakur, Laxman S., 1996, *The Architectural Heritage of Himachal Pradesh: Origin and Development of Temple Styles*, New Delhi: Munshiram Manoharlal Publishers.

Tomory, Edith, 2006, *A History of Fine Arts in India and the West*, Chennai: Orient Longman.

Trivedi, R.D., 1990, *Temples of the Pratihāra Period in Central India*, New Delhi: Archaeological Survey of India.

Index